Foundations of World Order

*By Francis Anthony Boyle*

World Politics and International Law (1985)

Defending Civil Resistance under International Law (1987)

The Future of International Law and American Foreign Policy (1989)

The Bosnian People Charge Genocide (1996)

# FOUNDATIONS OF WORLD ORDER

*The Legalist Approach to International Relations (1898-1922)*

*Francis Anthony Boyle*

DUKE UNIVERSITY PRESS   *Durham and London 1999*

© 1999 Duke University Press
All rights reserved
Printed in the United States of America on acid-free paper ∞
Typeset in Trump Mediaeval by Tseng Information Systems, Inc.
Library of Congress Cataloging-in-Publication Data appear
on the last printed page of this book.

# Contents

For Stanley Hoffmann

# Preface

I would like to thank my beautiful wife, Betsy, and my three sons, Brian, David, and James, for their support and understanding throughout the writing of this book and during my many other endeavors around this country and abroad. I would also like to thank my faithful and skilled secretary, Bonnie Anderson, for her first-rate work on this book and on my many other publications over the years. I also want to express my gratitude to my editor at Duke University Press, Reynolds Smith, for his patience and fine editing on the production of this book as well as my previous book with him.

I alone am responsible for the contents of this book. Nevertheless, I wish to acknowledge the profound contribution to my personal intellectual development made by my teachers at the University of Chicago and Harvard. No point would be served here by endeavoring to list them all. Many of their names and publications are mentioned in the Acknowledgments, texts, and footnotes of my previous books. But with respect to this project in particular, I would like to single out three individuals: my international law teacher, the late Richard R. Baxter, under whose supervision this research was commenced; my international organizations teacher, Louis B. Sohn; and my friend the late Leo Gross, whose pioneering efforts in the study of international organizations inspire all scholars working in this field. I would also like to thank my high school history teacher, John Mohan, who first sparked my interest in the imperial era of U.S. foreign policy more than three decades ago.

This book is dedicated to my dissertation supervisor at Harvard, Stanley Hoffmann. My debt to him cannot be expressed in words. What follows are comments I prepared in conjunction with my contribution to a Festschrift in his honor, *International Law and the Use of Force: Beyond Regime Theory*, that was produced by a group of his former students. I have reprinted that essay as an appendix to this book so that the reader will understand what I mean when referring to the post–World War II "regime" of international law and organizations concerning the threat and use of force. I would like to express my gratitude to Westview Press for permission to reprint the essay.

### Hans Morgenthau on Stanley Hoffmann

In a recent contemplative article, Stanley Hoffmann wrote the following about the state of international political theory in the late 1950s:

> I was appalled by the varying forms of crudeness I found in general theories of state behavior or of the international system, and by the methodological fallacies of attempts at blurring the differences between natural and social science. My main targets were Hans Morgenthau and Morton Kaplan. (I later regretted, not the content but the tone of my attack on the former, whom I met frequently in the 1960s. I came to admire his intellectual courage as well as his broad erudition—if not his theorizing.) I concluded that general theory, to be helpful, could be no more than a framework of questions, which could be answered by middle-range theories based on empirical research. Stanley Hoffmann, "A Retrospective," in *Journeys through World Politics: Autobiographical Reflection of Thirty-four Academic Travelers* 263, 270 (James N. Rosenau & William C. Potter, eds., 1989).

Over the years, Stanley Hoffmann has uttered many trenchant and well-justified criticisms of political realism and Hans Morgenthau, but I do not believe that Morgenthau ever held them against him. Rather, Morgenthau greatly respected Hoffmann for the power of his intellect. Neither man had or has any use for sycophants.

In September 1968, I entered the University of Chicago as an undergraduate. There I would commence my study of international relations with the late Hans Morgenthau, who had just published *A New Foreign Policy for the United States.* That same year, Stanley published his classic treatise *Gulliver's Troubles, or The Setting of U.S. Foreign Policy.* Of course, Hoffmann's book was somewhat longer than Morgenthau's. But the latter author had already published the fourth edition of his classic treatise, *Politics among Nations,* in 1966. On these books I cut my teeth as a neophyte student of international relations.

Like Stanley Hoffmann, Morgenthau began his academic career in the field of international law. Thereafter, both scholars moved off to examine more general questions concerning the nature of international relations and the conditions for world order. Nevertheless, the writings and activities of both Morgenthau and Hoffmann, throughout their long and distinguished careers, have always contained a solid core of ethical integrity that is directly attributable in part to their training and origins as international lawyers; in significant part to their broader humanitarian viewpoint based on an "Old World" humanistic education in the classical sense of that term; and in substantial part to the Jewish cultural and religious heritage that they share with so many of my teachers, colleagues, and friends at Harvard, Chicago, Illinois, and elsewhere.

Although I entered the University of Chicago with the intention of later going on to law school in order to become a civil rights lawyer, Morgenthau encouraged me to continue my studies of international relations at the graduate level. Since he would soon be retiring from Chicago in order to move his base of operations permanently to the New School for Social Research (which did not have a law school), I began to consider moving to one of three East Coast universities that would enable me to pursue graduate studies in both law and political science while at the same time staying in close contact with him: Harvard, Yale, or Columbia. Unable to decide among them, I asked Morgenthau for his advice. After taking a good deal of time reviewing the pluses and minuses of the programs in law and political science at these three institutions, Morgenthau concluded: "You should go to Harvard and continue your studies in international relations with Stanley Hoffmann. He is the brightest person in the field today."

The very next day, I sent in my acceptance to the Harvard Law School, and I enrolled there in September 1971. On my arrival at Harvard, I applied for and was accepted to the Ph.D. program in political science at Harvard's Graduate School of Arts and Sciences, Department of Government, the same doctoral program that produced Kissinger, Brzezinski, Huntington, and numerous other realpolitikers. Shortly thereafter, I met with Stanley Hoffmann, informed him of Morgenthau's advice to me, and asked him to serve as my dissertation adviser. Little did Stanley know at the time that this odyssey would take at least another decade.

As I was to discover during those succeeding years, Morgenthau was definitely right: Stanley Hoffmann was and still is the brightest person in the field of international relations today. And yet, even more important, he is also the most principled, ethical, and humanitarian scholar who inhabits the basically Hobbesian world of self-styled international relations experts in the United States of America today. The life of international relations specialists is oftentimes solitary, poor, nasty, brutish, and short, but Stanley conscientiously nourished us all to maturity with his wisdom, wit, kindness, patience, and example. The rest has been up to us. But certainly the best part of our careers was entrusted to his gracious stewardship.

# Introduction

When I was a young man studying international relations at the University of Chicago with the late Hans Morgenthau, I decided one day to ask him what course of study I should pursue if I wanted to become an expert on that subject. Without hesitation, Morgenthau's brief but emphatic reply was: "Study history!" Whether rightly or wrongly, Morgenthau had little use for a good deal of the professional literature articulating so-called theories of international relations, even though he is still generally considered one of the great international political scientists of the post–World War II era. As Hans Morgenthau said in a warning to such theorists in July 1961: "In the world of the intellectual ideas meet with ideas, and anything goes that is presented cleverly and with assurance. In the political world, ideas meet with facts, which make mincemeat of the wrong ideas and throw the ideas into the ashcan of history." For Morgenthau, the truth of international relations could be found only in the details of history. So it was in that direction that I oriented my studies.

I eventually graduated from the University of Chicago with a bachelor's degree in political science because at the time I wanted to acquire a doctorate in international relations—not diplomatic history—in addition to studying international law. Nevertheless, during my last two years at Chicago and thereafter for the next seven years at the Harvard Law School and the Harvard Graduate School of Arts and Sciences, I crammed as many history courses as possible into my schedule. Throughout the process of obtaining all this formal interdisciplinary education, I was continually struck by how little contact there was among historians, political scientists, and professors of law. Both at the time and in retrospect, it seemed to me that the members of all three disciplines could learn an enormous amount from each other about how to better conduct their respective professional tasks.

In particular, it struck me that professional historians and political scientists devoted a great deal of time to an analysis of what could only be called legal documents: treaties and other types of international agreements, their conference proceedings, related diplomatic communiqués, statutes, court opinions, and so on. Therefore, it appeared to me that there would always be some value in having a professional lawyer take a fresh look at such documents in order to see what light could be shed on them and their related events that had not already been generated by historians and political scientists.

As I saw it, a lawyer should be able to develop a more refined interpretation of the precise meaning of legal documents than members of the other two professions. Or at least a lawyer's reading of the documents should be factored into any equation of their true meaning and significance. For example, a lawyer, a political scientist, and a historian will read, analyze, and interpret international agreements in different manners that are determined by their respective professional training. These academic suppositions from my student days have since been confirmed by my subsequent practical experience serving as the legal adviser at two major international peace conferences, where I bore personal responsibility for analyzing, interpreting, drafting, negotiating, and explaining such documents.

Therefore, in this book I reexamine some of the actual historical legal documents related to the conduct of U.S. foreign policy during the first quarter of the twentieth century in order to shed new light on their meaning and thus on the events they concern. By examining these matters from an interdisciplinary perspective I hope to develop a better comprehension of the overall objectives of U.S. foreign policy during that period. Hence, this book does not purport to present a comprehensive diplomatic history of U.S. foreign policy in the early 1900s. Rather, I have chosen to look at U.S. foreign policy during this era from the perspective of international law and organizations. Such matters have been dealt with only tangentially or marginally by professional historians, and almost not at all by political scientists, so there is a serious gap in the historiographical literature dealing with this critical period of American foreign policy.

During the course of this analysis, I will necessarily touch on numerous issues that have already been analyzed quite competently by professional historians. Since I do not intend to go over the same ground again, I will avoid a detailed recounting of the many facts involved. I have assumed that the reader already possesses a basic working knowledge of the major events of world history and U.S. foreign policy during the first quarter of the twentieth century. Nevertheless, it is my hope that this work will provide a perspective on these topics somewhat different from those that have been developed by professional historians and political scientists. It will be my basic thesis that one major component and significant thrust of U.S. foreign policy during the first quarter of the twentieth century was the active promotion of international law and organizations to the rest of the states of the world community.

What follows, then, is a brief history of U.S. foreign policy toward international law and organizations from 1898 to 1922. For reasons that will become clear below, I have decided to describe and summarize this historical experience with the metaphor "laying the foundations for world order." Clearly, the outbreak of the Second World War in 1939 proved that these earlier legalist efforts had not actually created world order. Hence, a follow-up volume that is currently under way will have to deal with the actual creation of world order by a successor generation of American legalists. Yet, although these 1945 American legalists were certainly "present at the creation" of today's world order (viz., Dean Acheson),[1] the turn-of-the-century American legalists definitely laid its foundations.

When the U.S. government set out to construct the post–World War II international political, legal, economic, and institutional world order, it did not write on a tabula rasa. Rather, the American legalist creators of world order in 1945 based their designs on foundations that had been laid by their legalist predecessors from 1898 to 1922. There persists a remarkable degree of continuity and congruence between the world order model of these 1898–1922 legalist founders and the world order model of the 1945 legalist creators.

The legalist creators of world order in 1945 built directly on a "regime" of international law and organizations designed to regulate and reduce the transnational threat and use of force that had been envisioned, proposed, and partially carried out by the U.S. government during its conduct of foreign policy from the immediate aftermath of the Spanish-American War in 1898 until the creation of the League of Nations and the Permanent Court of International Justice as of 1921–22. In its pursuit of these world order policies, the U.S. government was operating under the direct influence and active leadership of the U.S. international law community of that time. These American legalists worked in their official capacities as statesmen, government officials, advisers, diplomats, and members of Congress, as well as teachers, scholars, lawyers, and private citizens.

In 1945 the U.S. government reverted to, relied on, and actually carried out these preexisting plans. Indeed, in one fashion or another, a good deal of the post–World War II regime of international law and organizations to regulate and reduce the transnational threat and use of force had been proposed and created by American international lawyers and the U.S. government between the Spanish-American War and the immediate aftermath of the First World War. To be sure, there were substantial differences, especially concerning the revivification of the defunct League of Nations into the United Nations organization. Nevertheless, the U.S. government's attempt in 1945 to create a new world order was remarkably similar to its attempt to do the same thing between 1898 and 1922. For that reason, then, both historical episodes represent actual case studies of what political scientists call "regime formation" or "regime initiation."[2] In both cases, the U.S. government set out to create a new world order of international law and organizations that would prevent war as well as control and reduce the transnational threat and use of force.[3]

Of course, it could not be said that the U.S. government at the outset of the twentieth century was in any sense of the word a "hegemon" as defined by today's international political scientists. Nevertheless, at that time American international lawyers and, under their influence, the U.S. government set out to construct such a regime for the express purpose of preventing or forestalling a major war among the great powers of Europe that would, they believed, ineluctably draw the United States into its vortex. Their collective fear that the United States would be involved in future wars among the great powers of Europe and Asia unless an international regime was created proved to be tragically correct both in 1917 and again in 1941.

Clearly, American international lawyers of that earlier era—as well as their 1945 successors—thought in such terms. And the fact that the former did not succeed in accomplishing their objectives because of circumstances beyond their control does not mean that their visions were flawed or their efforts defective. To be sure, these early legalists were ahead of their time, both internationally and domestically. But they were certainly not naive, idealistic, or utopian—nor were their legalist successors in 1945. Indeed, the very fact that the creators of 1945 built on the plans and works of the 1898–1922 founders testifies to the wisdom, courage, and perspicuity of the latter.

The early legalist vision of world order was rejected by the U.S. Senate when it repudiated the Treaty of Versailles and U.S. participation in the League of Nations and the Permanent Court of International Justice. It would take a successor generation and yet another brutal world war to convince the Senate as well as the American people that the earlier legalist vision of world order was the appropriate course of conduct for the U.S. government to pursue for the long-term duration of international relations into the indefinite future. The death and devastation wrought on humanity by the Second World War convinced the U.S. Congress, people, and government that if they were to prevent yet another (and perhaps the last) world war, they must not retreat again into the traditional policies of isolationism in peace and neutrality in war that had been generally pursued by the United States since Washington's Farewell Address. In 1945, the mistakes of the 1898–1922 period had been learned, and modifications were made. Nevertheless, the U.S. government basically returned to pursuing the vision of world order that had been articulated by American international lawyers during the first quarter of the twentieth century.

Hence, the creators of 1945 quite consciously and conscientiously proceeded to implement the 1898–1922 founders' plans in order to prevent a war of human extinction. A substantial amount of the international peace, security, justice, and prosperity that a good deal of the world has experienced since then is the direct result of the former's proposed United Nations and its affiliated organizations and institutions. Nevertheless, it is essential to first examine the dreams, schemes, plans, and ventures of the 1898–1922 founders of world order in order to better comprehend the origins, intentions, and plans of the 1945 creators. For their common legalist approach to international relations is responsible for whatever order the world has witnessed from 1945 until today.

## The Gospel According to Political Realism

A cardinal tenet of the "realist," or power politics, school of international political science is that international law and international organizations are irrelevant in conflicts between states over matters of vital national interest;[1] that is, issues of high international politics concerning the very survival of nation-states, the international system, and the human race itself. According to the political realists, considerations of international law do not and should not intrude into such areas. If they do, it should be only to the extent that they serve as a source for the manufacture of ad hoc or ex post facto justifications for decisions taken on the basis of antinomial factors such as Machiavellian power politics and national interest. In the realist view of international relations, international law is devoid of any intrinsic significance within the utilitarian calculus of international political decision making.

According to the realists, international law, morality, ethics, ideology, and even knowledge itself are mere components in the power equation, devoid of noninstrumental significance or prescriptive worth, subject to compulsory service as tools of power when deemed necessary for the vital interests of the state.[2] There are no barriers to the acquisitive nature of the nation-state beyond its own inherent limitations and those constraints imposed on it by the international political milieu. Consequently, the analysis of international relations must concentrate exclusively on the dynamics of power politics and national interest.

The reasons responsible for the realists' negative perception of international law and organizations are more the product of metaphysical speculation than solid empirical research. Realists suppose the nations of the world survive precariously in the Hobbesian state of nature, where the life of states is said to be "solitary, poor, nasty, brutish, and short."[3] In this world there is no law or justice, no conception of right or wrong, no morality, but only a struggle for survival in a state of war by every state and against every state.

According to the realists, the acquisition of power and aggrandizement by one state at the expense of other states in a quest for unattainable absolute national security is the fundamental right, the fundamental law, and the fundamental fact of international politics. Sheer physical survival in a Machiavellian world of power politics, raison d'état, totalitarianism, and nuclear weapons must become the litmus test for the validity of humankind's political, philosophical, moral, and legal presuppositions. International law therefore becomes irrelevant to those matters which count for something in international relations; and it will not become relevant to international politics in the foreseeable or even the distant future.

According to this realist credo, statesmen who disobey the "iron law"[4] of power politics at the behest of international law and organizations invite destruction at the hands of aggressors and thereby facilitate the destruction of third parties, which, in today's interdependent world, cannot realistically hope to remain neutral in a serious conflict between major powers. For historically, whenever statesmen have in good faith interjected determinative considerations of international law and organizations into attempted solutions for the monumental problems of international politics, the probability that violence, war, defeat, death, and destruction would ensue was supposedly increased. Realists' primary case in point is President Woodrow Wilson's approach to international relations after the outbreak of the First World War.

### The Straw Man of Legalism-Moralism

On January 8, 1918, President Wilson delivered an address to a joint session of Congress in which he set forth the war aims and peace terms of the U.S. government for ending the Great War.[5] This is the speech that contains the fabled Fourteen Points, the last of which laid the cornerstone for the League of Nations, the ill-fated predecessor to the United Nations. In that speech and its successors Wilson emphatically decreed the death of Machiavellian power politics and all its essential accoutrements for the postwar world: the balance of power, secret diplomacy, trade barriers, armament races, the denial of national self-determination, etc.

This outmoded and dangerous set of interconnected principles for the conduct of international relations had created such cataclysmic consequences that it had to be replaced completely by an essentially different system based on antithetical operational dynamics: international law and organizations, collective security, open diplomacy, free trade, freedom of the seas, arms reduction and disarmament, and national self-determination. A new era of world history was to dawn with the League of Nations. The "Old World" of barbaric power politics was to be left behind as an evolutionary stage in the human condition to which, like Rousseau's state of nature,[6] humankind would never return.

Unfortunately, the world of power politics returned just two decades later. The political realists laid the blame for the Second World War on the doorstep of Wilson and those Western statesmen who were said to have adopted his "legalist-moralist" approach to the conduct of international relations during the interwar period.[7] According to the realists, these Western leaders had neglected, condemned, and repudiated the techniques of power politics in favor of an anti–power politics approach to international relations when the exact opposite should have been done.

For the Treaty of Versailles,[8] and especially its first part, the Covenant of the League of Nations, were not really the perfect incarnations of truth, justice, peace, and righteousness they were said to be by the leaders of the Allied and Associated Powers. Rather, these were mere instrumentalities of power politics designed by the victorious nations of the First World War to secure and perpetuate the favorable political, economic, and military status quo after the armistices ending the Great War with the maximum possible degree of legal and institutional coercion and control. This treaty was imposed *vi et armis* in contravention of Wilson's express promises given to induce surrender in the Fourteen Points address and subsequent addresses.[9] If the people of the world believed anything else, then they had been sorely deluded by the ideological rhetoric deceptively manipulated by their own leaders to fan the flames of patriotic fervor in order to hasten the war to its successful conclusion.

If the victors of Versailles intended to keep their ill-gotten gains, the realists said, they had to be willing to employ military force against a predictably revanchist Germany whenever the latter attempted to resist the terms of the so-called peace. But the Western democracies lacked the requisite Nietzscheian will to power. Instead of fighting to preserve their hegemony, they preferred to trust in their own illusions. They put their faith into such meaningless pronouncements as Wilson's Fourteen Points, the Kellogg-Briand Pact,[10] and its corollary, the Stimson Doctrine;[11] into the ineffectual organs of the League of Nations and the Permanent Court of International Justice; into vapid and useless legalist-moralist doctrines such as neutrality, disarmament, arbitration, and adjudication; into the codification of international law and the formulation of a definition of aggression. Perhaps most egregiously of all, Western statesmen actually believed in the existence of a beneficent world public opinion that would somehow magically will the world on the path toward peace.

According to the realists, if Western statesmen had been attentive to the historical imperatives of power politics, and not seduced by the chimerical allurements of international law and organizations, the Second World War might never have happened. Or else it would have occurred in the mid-1930s when the devastation might have been far less. They could have fought the war on their own terms and at the time of their own choice, not those of their natural adversaries. The Western democracies had only themselves to blame for the Second World War as it actually transpired.

Furthermore, the political realists argued, faced with a "communist threat" in the aftermath of World War II akin to the fascist threat beforehand, the United States must repudiate its deeply ingrained legalist-moralist approach to international relations in favor of pure Machiavellian power politics in order to survive its confrontation with the Soviet bloc during the so-called cold war. In the political milieu of the cold war, the Western democracies could not repeat the near-fatal mistake they had made after the termination of the First World War—that is, reliance on the fictitious and fatuous strength of international law and organizations to preserve world peace—if they wished to avoid a suicidal Third World War.

This "gospel" according to political realism has exercised a decisive impact on the formulation and conduct of U.S. foreign policy from the outset of the cold war, through its subsequent course of development, and even until today in its aftermath. Indeed, political realism still dominates the U.S. foreign policy decision-making establishment despite the collapse of the Warsaw Pact and the disintegration of the Soviet Union. And there is scant evidence of any major reevaluation of the utility of political realism for the conduct of U.S. foreign policy as it approaches the next millennium.

### International Legal Positivism

In support of their gospel, the political realists constantly invoke George Santayana's hackneyed saying: "Those who cannot remember the past are condemned to repeat it."[12] Those who misinterpret the past are just as likely to repeat it. For, contrary to the underlying assumptions of contemporary international political scientists, the U.S. "legalist" approach to international relations did not begin during or immediately after the outbreak of the First World War, but well before it. This historical oversight has led political scientists to commit the grievous analytical error of confusing and compounding positivist international legal studies with the pursuit of international morality in order to create some phantasmagorical legalist-moralist straw man warranting condemnation for the Machiavellian "sins of princes" alleged above.[13] There has been no monolithic U.S. legalist-moralist approach to world politics during the twentieth century. This is precisely because a modern legalist approach to international relations was purposefully designed and established to function in a manner diametrically opposed to a moralist or moralistic attitude toward foreign affairs.

This self-conscious differentiation of law from morality by turn-of-the-century American international lawyers was explicitly intended to surmount the objections of John Austin, who denied the existence of international law as real "law" and maintained instead that international law represented nothing more significant than the "rules of positive morality."[14] In the late nineteenth and early twentieth centuries, American international lawyers were vigorously engaged in the task of sharply distinguishing a "scientific" or "positivist" approach to the study of international law from its Grotian natural-law heritage and proclivities. They wanted at last to definitively repudiate those elements of their Grotian past which they believed preached international morality under the guise of international law that was piously represented as the incarnation of natural law. As these international legalists saw it, international legal studies had to step irrevocably forward into the twentieth century by developing an actual science of public international law based on a positivist approach that was antithetical to the content and methodology of outmoded natural-law and natural-right theories. Continued reliance on such amorphous concepts by the international legal profession would only provide ammunition for philosophical assault to Austin's omnipresent protégés.

At the outset of the twentieth century, the classic "paradigm"[15] for international legal positivism—which still dominates the profession after almost ninety years[16]—was expounded in the second volume of the *American Journal of International Law* (1908) by the renowned Lassa Oppenheim, Whewell Professor of International Law at the University of Cambridge, the guru of the early U.S. legalists.[17] A "positive" method had to be based on the extant and recognized rules of international law as set forth in the customary practice of states and in the formal conventions concluded between them, instead of on philosophical speculations about some nonexistent law of nature or natural law. The former facts of international life must never be distorted by the latter hypotheses about what international law "ought" to be.

A true international legal positivist must perform seven tasks in order to promote the science of public international law: (1) exposition of existing rules of law, (2) historical research, (3) criticism of existing law, (4) preparation of codifications, (5) maintaining the distinction between old customary law and new conventional law, (6) fostering international arbitration, and (7) popularization of public international law. The American legalists truly believed that domestic public opinion could influence governments in favor of promoting international law and organizations.

This positivist methodology did not preach that international law should never concern itself with the promotion of moral values. Rather, it was premised on the forthrightly admitted assumption that international legal positivism—as opposed to the Grotian natural-law tradition—constituted the superior means to progress toward the Aristotelian "final cause" of international legal studies: preservation of peace among nations to the greatest degree possible under the given historical circumstances. International legal positivism was said to be more conducive to interstate agreement on current and proposed rules of international behavior than was the dogma of Grotian natural-law morality, whose reputed tenets invariably tried to mask perceived national interests and received national prejudices. International legal positivism could therefore help diminish the inevitable friction, and thus ameliorate the unavoidable conflicts between states in their conduct of international relations.

At this time in world history, war, imperial conquest, and the threat and use of force were accepted facts of international life to which the rules of public international law were quite readily accommodated.[18] The purpose of international law was not yet perceived by Americans to be the outlawing of these manifestations of interstate violence, but more simply to reduce their incidence, mitigate their fury, and limit their scope so as to protect neutrals—especially the United States—and thus to prevent the development of a worldwide conflagration. International law was never perceived to be a transcendent end unto itself, but only a means to achieve the ultimate goal of peace in the human condition.[19] The institution of a more just condition in relationships between states would further the maintenance of world peace and thus contribute to the promotion of all human values.

Furthermore, the promotion of international law and organizations was ideally suited to achieving the objectives of a U.S. foreign policy that was predicated on the twin assumptions of maintaining isolationism in peace and preserving neutrality during war vis-à-vis the great powers of Europe and Asia. In this regard, that which was just for the United States and that which was expedient coincided. In an era when the United States was not yet the regime theorist hegemon, a legalist approach to international relations made perfect sense. During the period from 1898 to 1922, the U.S. foreign policy establishment adhered to the proposition that international law and organizations were effective means by which to further the country's national interest. Indeed, the promotion of international law and organizations was defined as a "vital interest" of the United States during this era. In both the literature and the practice of the day, promoting international law and organizations was placed on a par with the Monroe Doctrine in terms of their importance for the formulation and conduct of U.S. foreign policy.

### The Sanction behind International Law

From the perspective of turn-of-the-century international legal positivism, Austin committed a serious methodological error when he mistakenly assumed that international law and municipal law functioned in a similar manner. As the early U.S. legalists saw it, there was a clear-cut distinction between the two systems. The former was essentially one of customary law; the latter was characterized primarily as one of statutory law. Obviously the operational features of each system should be fundamentally different. An analyst cannot profitably evaluate the effectiveness of international law using standards and techniques derived from and applicable to municipal legal systems. This early legal positivist critique can be corroborated by the literature of contemporary international political science examining the so-called level-of-analysis problem: namely, that the functional dynamics of international relations in comparison to domestic affairs are so basically dissimilar that they cannot properly support the delineation of useful comparative analogues.[20]

According to these early international legal positivists, Austin's position that international law was no more than positive international morality also misperceived the essence of the "sanction" behind obedience of municipal law to be coercion and punishment by some absolute Hobbesian sovereign instead of, more appropriately, the effective influence of domestic public opinion. Without considering the power of public opinion, the phenomenon of customary law on either level of analysis—whether international or municipal (such as Anglo-American common law)—cannot be accounted for, except, perhaps, by the fictive maxim that what the sovereign permits he also commands. Since there is no Hobbesian sovereign in international relations, customary international law binds states because they are deemed to have consented to be so bound by the general customs and usage of international intercourse embodied in its rules.

Hence, the ultimate sanction for international law is community public opinion, which, of course, includes fear of war and its converse, pressure for resort to war. This explicit and implicit consent of states to be bound by international law binds their respective citizens as well because international law is incorporated into their domestic legal orders. Citizens are bound by its rules in their mutual relations with each other and foreigners.[21] The efflorescence of a community of such internally and externally law-abiding nations by means of a constantly increasing degree of interaction and interdependence could create a truly global public opinion that will serve as the ultimate sanction for international law.[22]

Explained in somewhat more tangible terms, the real sanction behind international law was said to be the exclusion of a state violating its principles from the benefits accruing from coordinate regulation of its relationships with other states and international agencies with respect to vital concerns of its national interest. The task of the "new diplomacy" incumbent on international lawyers is to establish a framework for cooperation among nations in which substantial advantages can be obtained by joint state action that cannot otherwise be realized by states acting in isolation. This web of international legal ties will become so strong that no state would consider disrupting it by resort to war. And in the unfortunate event that war remains a temporary feature of the international system, many of these legal and institutional patterns of relations can survive and function despite the outbreak of violent hostilities.[23] By the turn of the century, the demands of international intercourse had already required the provision of limited powers of competence and action not subject to the veto of any one state to international administrative organs such as the Universal Postal Union. Although nations are exceedingly reluctant to give such organs more power, it was in this direction that the early legal positivists foresaw international relations proceeding toward the achievement of world peace.[24]

Perhaps at some point in the distant future a world federal state could come into existence organized according to the functional model of the United States of America, whereby the nations of the world would each accept a semisovereign status analogous to that of states in the U.S. Union.[25] Presumably a world federal law would thereafter govern the relations between states. This would require the creation of some form of world government with sufficient legislative, judicial, and executive power to promulgate, adjudicate, and, if necessary, enforce international law against recalcitrant states in a manner that would not precipitate global warfare. Punishment of the culprit would be accepted as legitimate by all other participants since each state would have already consented to be so governed.[26]

## The Principle of Sovereign Consent

In many respects, this turn-of-the-century legalist analysis of international relations constituted a genuine precursor of the contemporary "functional integrationist" school of post–World War II international political science,[27] which in turn served as the theoretical starting point for the "regime theory" school of contemporary international political science toward the end of the twentieth century.[28] Yet, in its attempt to overcome the Hobbesian doctrines that (1) since the will of the sovereign is the source of all law, and (2) where there is no sovereign there can be no law, early twentieth-century international legal positivism succumbed to another variant of the same fiction: the notion of sovereign consent as the sole basis for legitimacy in international relations. At the start of the twentieth century, primary reliance on the principle of sovereign consent as manifested in customary and conventional international law was useful to combat the Austinian denial of international law as real law because, theoretically, sovereign consent was a tangible factor whose presence could presumably be determined by objective criteria, thus avoiding allegations of preaching Grotian natural-law morality under the name of public international law.

Nevertheless, stubborn adherence to sovereign consent for legitimization has created a stark predicament for international legal positivism as the world enters the next millennium. Today the nations of the world are striving to cope with the progressive evolution of a system of international relations that needs to move away from the notion of sovereign consent—precisely because the sanctification of that principle provides an inherent veto power over the creation of new rules to each one of the participants in the international system—and toward its replacement by the principle of consensus founded on reciprocal expectations of state behavior. There is nothing sacrosanct about sovereign consent as the basic legitimizing principle of international law and politics other than by way of analogy to the fact that social contract theorists such as Hobbes, Locke, and Rousseau defined the consent of the citizen to be the essential basis for political legitimacy. But they did this for the express purpose of undercutting the legitimizing role played by the Christian church in Western political philosophy.[29] Yet this analogy raises the level-of-analysis problem from another perspective: Perhaps within the system of municipal affairs the principle of citizen consent still operates in the desired fashion; but within the system of international relations the principle of sovereign consent has proven to be increasingly unworkable.

## Legalism and Realism
The early international legal positivists explicitly embraced the classic Machiavellian dichotomy between the "is" (effectual truth) and the "ought to be" (imaginary truth) of world affairs.[30] They chose to classify international law into the former category and Grotian natural-law morality into the

latter. This categorization of law as an effectual instead of an imaginary truth received active support from Machiavelli himself.[31] To an international legal positivist, the effectiveness of any system of law must depend on the existence of some source of underlying power, whether military, political, economic, or ideological in nature. Thus, for international political scientists to castigate international legal positivists because of their supposed ignorance of, or disregard for, the realities of power demonstrates the former's complete unawareness of the latter's Hobbesian and Machiavellian premises.

This volume will establish that the mainstream attitude of American international lawyers toward the actual and potential role of international law and international organizations in world politics during the crucial period from the Spanish-American War through the establishment of the League of Nations and the Permanent Court of International Justice was not at all naive, idealistic, or utopian; instead it was acutely realistic and relatively sophisticated in its comprehension of the dynamic interrelationship between power and law in international relations. Turn-of-the-century American international lawyers did not shrink from advocating the forceful exercise of U.S. power around the globe, whether as presidents, secretaries of state, secretaries of war, attorneys general, senators, congressmen, ambassadors, diplomats, professors, or lawyers. If anything, as a group they were all too prone to support and encourage the U.S. government in the planning and execution of its imperialistic enterprises in the Western hemisphere by means of elaborating arguments and rationalizations in favor of such policies, which they formulated and justified in terms of the rules of international law and the requirements of maintaining international peace and security.

At the very beginning of this century, Americans in general demonstrated a marked tendency to view international law as whatever the immediate satisfaction of their national self-interests necessitated.[32] In this regard American international lawyers were not essentially different from their intensely nationalistic compatriots. Of course, there was substantial legalist criticism of the 1898 war against Spain itself.[33] But thereafter, apart from a few notable expressions of regret, chagrin, or dissent, American international lawyers as a group mounted no systematic or even significant criticism of the overall conduct of U.S. imperialist foreign policy from the perspective of those supposedly trained in and sensitive to the requirements and needs of a truly international legal order.

## The Legalist Mentality

As a group, American international lawyers and statesmen believed in the inherent superiority of the "white Anglo-Saxon race" or "Teutonic race" of people (i.e., United States, Britain, Germany). As a general rule, most were Anglophiles. The early American legalists also believed in the inherent inferiority of darker-skinned peoples, whether in Latin America, Africa, Asia, or the United States itself.[34] In the legalist opinion, peoples of darker color were not fit for self-government. To be sure, the legalists supported "democracy" as an abstract proposition. But there is no evidence that they paid much attention to or had any respect for the opinions or plight of common, ordinary, everyday American citizens, let alone dark-skinned foreigners. These American legalists were part of the elite, and they were elitists at heart.[35] For the most part, the same is true today.

A majority of the early U.S. legalists—and certainly the most prominent among them—were identified with the Republican party. They had served variously in the administrations of McKinley, Roosevelt, Taft, and Harding. Some had also served in one capacity or another in the Wilson administration. There was a strong ethos of public service embedded in their mindset. After all, America was supposed to be a government of laws, not of "men." As these early legalists saw it, lawyers were the best trained and equipped group of professionals to govern both domestic affairs and international relations in the United States at that time.

Whether Democrats or Republicans, however, all shared a commitment to pursue a legalist approach to international relations. Their collective adherence to the legalist credo was remarkably uniform until the early 1920s, when a serious division would erupt among the legalists over whether or not the United States should join the League of Nations, and if so, on what terms. Even then, almost all of them—Democrats and Republicans, pro-League and anti-League—would favor and support the United States joining the Permanent Court of International Justice. As they saw it, the World Court was "America's Court"; it was said to be America's great gift to the entire world.

To be sure, large-scale co-optation of the skills of American international lawyers during this historical era by all branches of the U.S. government was to be expected because of their critical relevance to the management of the complexities resulting from the conduct of a U.S. foreign policy that was simultaneously striving to reconcile the inexorable demands of a newly launched imperialism with the tenacious pull of the traditional deep-seated isolationism. For example, McKinley chose Elihu Root as his secretary of war, over Root's protestations that he knew nothing about military affairs, because the president wanted a lawyer to be in charge of administering the territories conquered as a result of the 1898 war with Spain.[36] It was thus from within the U.S. governmental foreign policy establishment—and not in opposition to the system—that turn-of-the-century American international lawyers brought their unique perspective on international relations to bear on the policy-formulation process. Indeed, during the interim between the Spanish-American War and the establishment of the League of Nations and the Permanent Court of International Justice, American international lawyers exercised a more profound influence on the formation of U.S. foreign policy than they had as a group at any time since the founding of the Republic. It is to this historical era, therefore, that we must turn in order to delineate the paradigmatic elements of the classic U.S. "legalist" approach to international relations.

### Legalism as a Reaction to the Spanish-American War

The single most formative event in the development of a distinctively legalist approach to international relations in the United States was the 1907 publication of the first volume of the *American Journal of International Law*, under the auspices of the newly founded American Society of International Law, as the first periodical devoted exclusively to international law in the English-speaking world.[37] American scholars and practitioners of international law thereby created a central forum from which to articulate an essentially legalist analysis of international relations that was purposefully intended to be different from the approach taken by political scientists.[38] The birth of both the American Society of International Law and its journal can be attributed to the experience of the United States during its war with Spain in 1898. The exhilarating feeling of the sudden and decisive victory stimulated within all sectors of the country an increased awareness of international affairs and generated a felt need within the U.S. international law community for an organization and a publication in which to express the legal aspects of America's new and far-flung international relations.[39]

Of course, prior to that brief encounter the United States had not subsisted totally within the cocoon of isolationism spun by Washington's Farewell Address and the Monroe Doctrine.[40] The country had engaged in at least two formal international wars with significant hemispheric consequences: the War of 1812 and the Mexican War of 1846. The former's ostensible cause was the need for America to uphold its rights under international law against Great Britain's impressment of Americans and interference with neutral shipping during the course of its war with France.[41] The Mexican-American War was clearly an imperialist enterprise designed to seize most of what is today the southwestern section of the United States to fulfill the country's "manifest destiny" of complete continental expansion.[42] The numerous expeditions against America's indigenous peoples could also be fit neatly within the category of continental imperialist expansion, although some legalists argued that "Indian" occupation was not entitled to any respect, and their subjugation thus did not qualify as an act of imperialism.[43] Yet the net effect of these disputes on their contemporaneous global political environments was relatively insignificant compared with the astounding ramifications for the United States and the world at large ensuing from the Spanish-American War of 1898.

The decrepit Spanish Empire was almost instantaneously dissolved by the war, and the United States assumed its imperial mantle in Cuba, Puerto Rico, Guam, and the Philippines.[44] Acquisition of the former two colonies situated the United States in the heart of the Caribbean, the gateway to the isthmus of Central America. From there it was an almost inevitable imperial step to U.S. intervention in Colombia in order to instigate and secure the independence of Panama for the purpose of facilitating the construction of a canal;[45] to promulgation of the Roosevelt Corollary to the Monroe Doctrine in order to justify U.S. economic receivership for the Dominican Republic;[46] and to repeated military occupations of Cuba pursuant to the Platt Amendment.[47] These developments paved the way for the persistent imperialist interventions into the affairs of Central American and Caribbean countries that has chronically plagued U.S. foreign policy toward the region adjoining the Panama Canal throughout the course of the twentieth century.

On the other side of the world, the decision to take over the Philippines propelled the United States directly into the affairs of the Orient, where the great powers of Europe had already staked out their respective colonial claims,[48] and therefore indirectly into the European balance-of-power system. Efforts to preserve and extend U.S. geopolitical and economic positions in that region of the world, and especially the furtherance of its "open-door" policy in regard to China, ultimately set the stage for the serious and prolonged friction with Japan that eventually culminated in Pearl Harbor four decades later.

In the pre–World War I era of international relations, however, the major philosophical dilemma confronting American international lawyers was the reconciliation of the new U.S. course of world imperialism commenced by the Spanish-American War with the traditional ideals of U.S. foreign policy supposedly based on the inalienable rights of the individual, the self-determination of peoples, the sovereign equality and independence of states, nonintervention, respect for international law, and the peaceful settlement of international disputes. For example, within the U.S. international law community there did exist a minority anti-imperialist sentiment that espoused the "neutralization" of U.S. colonial territories, along the lines of Belgium, in order to remove them from the extant zone of international contention.[49] But the majority legalist viewpoint accepted U.S. imperialism, like war, as an irreversible fact of international life that must be dealt with on its own terms.[50] Nevertheless, even in the mainstream legalist opinion, imperialism could be reconciled with American ideals through recognition of the imperative that the true purpose of U.S. imperial policy—unlike that of Europe—must not be territorial aggrandizement and economic enrichment, but ultimately the achievement of the American dream of freedom, independence, dignity, and equality for all the peoples living within the current U.S. imperial domain and beyond.[51] These milieu objectives could be secured in a manner consistent with America's expansive definition of its national security interests by pursuing a foreign policy that actively promoted international law and international organizations for the rest of the world.

*Legalism as a Rejection of the European Balance-of-Power System*
Near the turn of the century, Americans' analysis of European international politics transpired through the conceptual prism of the "balance of power" —a phenomenon perceived to be the operative determinant of international relations between the states of the Old World. By contrast, the United States still occupied the fortunate position of "splendid isolation" vis-à-vis the machinations of Machiavellian power politics on the continent that it had held throughout the nineteenth century by virtue of the British navy.[52] Admittedly, the European balance-of-power system had achieved worldwide dimensions by including within its grasp the decaying Ottoman Empire,[53] Africa,[54] the Near East, Central Asia,[55] India, Southeast Asia, China, Japan, and the Pacific. As the legalists saw it, only the Monroe Doctrine and the Roosevelt Corollary had prevented Europe from reasserting its stranglehold over Latin America. And despite Europe's presence in the Far East, the U.S. policy of maintaining an "open door" for all to participate in the economic exploitation of China could somehow keep the balance of power for that region in equilibrium.

The rest of the world was duly consigned to the unhappy fate of becoming the arena for intense rivalry and periodic conflict over territory between the major imperial powers of Europe and Japan. In this worldwide struggle for colonies, the rules of international law had little applicability except to the extent that they accorded some semblance of legitimacy and order to the process of imperial subjugation by recognizing the existence of formal legal statuses such as "protectorates" or "condominiums," inter alia, over conquered territory whereby the exclusive or hegemonial position of one or more of the imperial powers could be definitively acquiesced in by its cohorts.[56] Yet, even in respect to this process of colonial conquest, the formation of new international institutions for the peaceful settlement of interstate disputes could play a decisive role in providing useful fora for the amelioration of imperial rivalries among the great powers that were not worth starting a general systemic war over.

Despite strident advocacy in favor of a resolutely interventionist U.S. foreign policy throughout the Western hemisphere in the aftermath of the Spanish-American War, for the most part American international lawyers did not believe that the United States should radically depart from the sage advice of Washington's Farewell Address by actively engaging itself in the European balance-of-power system. As the legalists saw it, the United States had both the luxury and the duty to abstain from choosing sides between the contending alliance systems in Europe because such a choice could easily precipitate America into war over another state's interests. Especially with the disintegration of the Ottoman Empire and the revival of the "Balkan question" by Austria's annexation of Bosnia and Herzegovina in 1908, a monumental struggle between Russia and Austria-Hungary and their respective allies over Serbia seemed to be in the offing.[57] In the event of a general war in Europe, isolationism would ensure that the United States did not jeopardize its newly won possessions in the Far East and its hegemonial position over Latin America, while the international laws of neutrality would permit American merchants to profit handsomely from increased trade with both sets of prospective belligerents.

American international lawyers' acceptance of this generally held prescription for isolationism in peace and neutrality in war did not, however, prompt them to espouse inaction by the U.S. government in the diplomacy of world politics.[58] To the contrary, in the legalists' opinion it was vital for the United States to pursue a foreign policy that actively promoted international law and international organizations to the members of the world community for the express purpose of preventing a general systemic war that could pull in America—just as happened in 1812. This task could be accomplished by a U.S. foreign policy that sought to produce a fundamental transformation in the modus operandi of the European balance-of-power system from the constant threat and use of force to reliance instead on new rules of international law and new institutions for the peaceful settlement of international disputes.[59]

The United States occupied the ideal diplomatic position to spearhead such a war-prevention program on behalf of the world precisely because it had maintained its traditional isolationism from great-power politics that did not directly concern its own interests. America's pristine detachment from the European powers could reduce the respective nationalistic suspicions that inevitably accompany and oftentimes defeat major diplomatic initiatives from their outset. America could most safely and effectively protect both itself and the world at large by preserving its distance and thus its perspective for leadership in the promotion of international law and international organizations. America must not abandon this high moral ground to grasp and wield the dangerous weapons of power politics by becoming a formal member of the European balance-of-power system.

## The Legalist War-Prevention Program for World Politics

Given the inherent limitations created by America's fundamental commitment to observing isolationism in peace and neutrality in war, this pre–World War I U.S. legalist approach to international relations seemed to be as activist and globalist in its orientation as could reasonably be expected under the circumstances. If anything, American international lawyers collectively moved considerably farther and faster down the road of internationalism in advance of most of their isolationist foreign policy establishment colleagues because of their sincere belief in the overarching need for America to seize the initiative in formulating a war-prevention program for the great powers of Europe and Japan on the basis of international law and organizations. As it took shape and matured over a quarter century, the paradigmatic elements of the U.S. legalist approach to international relations during its classical era from the Spanish-American War through the establishment of the League of Nations and the Permanent Court of International Justice came to consist of attaining the following concrete objectives: (1) the creation of a general system for the obligatory arbitration of disputes between states; (2) the establishment of an international court of justice; (3) the codification of important areas of customary international law into positive treaty form; (4) arms reduction, but only after the relaxation of international tensions by means of these and other legalist techniques and institutions; and (5) the institutionalization of the practice of convoking periodic peace conferences for all states in the recognized international community.[60]

In addition, a subsidiary element of the U.S. legalist program was to strengthen the well-established international legal regime of neutrality as well as the humanitarian laws of armed conflict in order to further isolate the bulk of the international community—especially the United States—

from some future war that still might erupt among the great powers of Europe despite the enactment of the above-mentioned preventive legalist devices and institutions. American international lawyers prudently hedged their country's bets on the likelihood of a general systemic war in Europe breaking out. A foreign policy that was solidly based on the promotion of international law and organizations was ideally suited to advance the national security and commercial objectives of a nonaligned great trading power that wanted to prevent the outbreak of a world war for its own self-interest, and, in the alternative, wanted to stay out of any ongoing world war for its own self-interest as well.

Theoretically, these five legalist steps were to be achieved in an approximately sequential fashion, since each stage to some extent depended on fulfillment of the prior goal. But in practice, all were pursued in a roughly contemporaneous manner because of their highly interdependent and mutually supportive nature. Realization of the fifth stage would have represented the first step toward the creation of a rudimentary world legislature, which, when conjoined with an effective world court, would have constituted two-thirds of the branches required for the institution of a world government patterned along the lines of the legislative, judicial, and executive departments of the U.S. federal government.[61] Nevertheless, until after the outbreak of the Great War in 1914, the U.S. international legal community did not devote much time, effort, or resources to founding an executive "league to enforce peace" equipped with an effective international police force and necessarily accompanied by some degree of progressive disarmament by the great powers.[62]

To be sure, such a visionary goal was endorsed by some American international lawyers as a desirable destination for the long-term evolution of international relations.[63] Yet at the time there seemed to exist a general consensus that such a scheme for creating a world government must not be allowed to detract from the immediate realization of the far more practicable agenda outlined above. Moreover, there was no desire or intention on the part of the intensely nationalistic early-twentieth-century American international lawyers to surrender U.S. "sovereignty" to any supranational organization.[64]

### Not a Pipe Dream

Although admittedly far reaching, at the turn of the century the U.S. war-prevention program for world politics that was based on the promotion of international law and organizations seemed to have more than a plausible chance for eventual success because of the relative homogeneity of the system of international relations in the pre–World War I era—at least in comparison with the endemic heterogeneity so characteristic of the post–World War II period.[65] Publicists and statesmen of this earlier epoch actually thought in terms of a real international community of states.[66] Basically, this world community consisted of the countries of Europe, North America, South and Central America, the Ottoman Empire,[67] and Japan.[68] The rest of the world was viewed essentially as an arena for intense colonial competition among the great powers that rendered even more vital the institution of the foregoing legalist mechanisms in order to attenuate and manage the inevitable imperial conflicts.

All of these nations participated in the same system of international political and economic relations and were subject to the same corpus of European public international law. All of the major actors except Japan shared a cultural heritage schooled in the Old Testament, Greece, Rome, medieval Christendom, the Renaissance and Reformation, the European Enlightenment, the Industrial Revolution, the French Revolution and Napoleonic Wars, and the tradition of a "concert" of European powers determining matters of world politics by mutual consent and negotiated agreement throughout the nineteenth century. The U.S. legalist war-prevention program for international relations intended to build on this solid foundation to create an even more stable and secure world order for the twentieth century and humankind's next millennium. It was definitely not a pipe dream, but rather a practical program that could be successfully implemented in the near-term future by means of vigorous U.S. leadership acting to bring forth a reasonable degree of enlightened self-interest on the part of the great powers of Europe and Japan.

During the late nineteenth and early twentieth centuries in the United States, many men of great practical experience in world politics genuinely believed that the institution of an effective system for the obligatory arbitration of international disputes could constitute a viable substitute for recourse to war by states. Of course, there was still the tangible problem of creating a workable "sanction" for international arbitration that was something more than the same world public opinion that buttressed obedience to international law in general. Yet, considerations of national self-interest and security had invariably led to the submission of international disputes to arbitration in the first place, so the record of compliance with arbitral decisions was quite good[1]—and still is today.

In the unlikely event of noncompliance, it was up to neutral third parties to undertake measures of diplomatic, political, or economic retorsion short of war or the use of force against the recalcitrant state that would be sufficient to induce obedience to an arbitral award.[2] The 1898–1914 period of international relations witnessed the zenith of the international arbitration movement in the twentieth century. There proved to be little problem in enforcing arbitral awards because states resorted to arbitration and dutifully complied with awards for reasons of enlightened and rational self-interest.

### Early Precedents

U.S. support for the peaceful arbitration of international disputes went all the way back to the founding of the Republic.[3] The so-called Jay Treaty of 1794 with Great Britain resolved many of the issues that were left over from America's War of Independence.[4] The mixed claims commissions set up under the Jay Treaty served as a precedent for the settlement of the *Alabama* claims with Great Britain that arose from the construction and fitting out of Confederate raiders in British ports during the U.S. Civil War.[5]

The Treaty of Washington signed by the United States and Great Britain on May 8, 1871, established an arbitration tribunal in Geneva that eventually awarded the United States $15.5 million for the direct harm that Confederate raiders had inflicted on federal commerce.[6]

The success of the Geneva tribunal in settling this serious dispute between two great powers, whose prolongation could have degenerated into hostilities, was the momentum propelling the international movement for the obligatory arbitration of international disputes throughout the rest of the nineteenth century and well into the First Hague Peace Conference. The Geneva arbitration also gave birth to the Institute of International Law and the International Law Association.[7] These two nongovernmental international organizations are still active in the promotion of international law and the peaceful settlement of international disputes by professional international lawyers around the world today.

Following the "Spirit of Geneva," the United States and Great Britain signed the Olney-Pauncefote Treaty on January 11, 1897, during the Cleveland administration.[8] This treaty constituted a general arbitration agreement between the two countries that was intended to cover almost all types of controversies that might arise between them. On the retirement of President Cleveland and his secretary of state from office, the new president, William McKinley, expressed his support for the treaty. But the Senate Foreign Relations Committee amended the treaty out of meaningful existence. In particular was the Senate's requirement—which would vex all future U.S. arbitration treaties—that two-thirds of the Senate must give its further advice and consent for the submission of any particular dispute to arbitration under the terms of the treaty.[9] In other words, the general arbitration treaty would not be enough: a special treaty would also be required.

Through the subsequent course of the twentieth century, the U.S. Senate would repeatedly prove to be recalcitrant in espousing this narrow and short-sighted interpretation of its constitutional powers under Article II, section 2, clause 2, of the Constitution. This jealous and selfish attitude would spell defeat for the Olney-Pauncefote Treaty and many other international agreements for the peaceful settlement of international disputes— and for the advancement of international law and organizations in general, up to and including the Treaty of Versailles, the League of Nations Covenant, and the Permanent Court of International Justice. Even today, the Senate still refuses to give its advice and consent to many treaties for the development of international law, the peaceful settlement of international disputes, the creation of international institutions and regimes, as well as the promotion of human rights. Indeed, the few human rights treaties the

Senate has assented to have been basically amended out of meaningful existence.[10]

## The First Hague Peace Conference

The First Hague Peace Conference was convoked on the initiative of Tsar Nicholas II of Russia.[11] The U.S. government decided to accept the Russian tsar's invitation of August 24, 1898, to attend an international peace conference to consider the reduction of armaments and the maintenance of general peace, despite the fact that America was then still technically at war with Spain,[12] on the basis of an explicit Russian assurance that the war would not be discussed at the conference.[13] Article 7 of the Russian foreign minister's circular note of December 30, 1898, setting forth a proposed program for the conference called for the "acceptance in principle" of the usage of good offices, mediation, and "optional arbitration for such cases as lend themselves to it, with a view of preventing armed conflicts between nations."[14]

Despite the recent rejection of the Olney-Pauncefote Treaty of Arbitration with Great Britain by the U.S. Senate,[15] McKinley's secretary of state, John Hay, enthusiastically endorsed the Russian proposition and instructed the U.S. delegation to the First Hague Peace Conference to propose a plan for a permanent international tribunal organized along the lines of the U.S. Supreme Court.[16] According to this plan, each state signatory would have one representative on a permanent tribunal that would always be open for the filing of cases by signatories or other states wishing to have recourse to it.[17] The contracting nations would submit to the tribunal all questions of disagreement between them except those that related to their political independence or territorial integrity.

While at the conference, however, the U.S. delegation concluded that a provision calling for the obligatory arbitration of disputes, even with the noted exemptions, would be unlikely to secure the assent of the other participants. Consequently, they requested and received permission from the State Department to delete the obligatory nature of the proposed tribunal's jurisdiction.[18] As eventually presented to the conference, the U.S. plan for the creation of a permanent international tribunal provided that all differences between signatories could, by common consent, be submitted by interested nations to the judgment of the international tribunal, whose award must then be accepted by the parties.[19]

Despite this change, however, the First Hague Peace Conference preferred instead a British plan calling for the selection of a panel of judges not in session except when actually required for litigation.[20] This British proposal formed the basis for the subsequently adopted plan for the Hague Permanent Court of Arbitration (PCA). Nevertheless, several elements of the U.S. plan found their way into the PCA.[21] Eventually the U.S. scheme for a permanent and standing international tribunal for the peaceful settlement of interstate disputes would be revived and later adopted in principle at the Second Hague Peace Conference.

At the First Hague Peace Conference of 1899, there was no support among the participants for a general multilateral pact calling for the obligatory arbitration of all disputes, let alone politically significant disputes, between states.[22] Germany adamantly opposed a general multilateral pact calling for the obligatory arbitration of even a limited number of categories of disputes possessed of relatively inconsequential political significance.[23] Even the U.S. government insisted on omitting from a Russian list[24] of proposed subjects deemed suitable for obligatory arbitration international conventions relating to rivers, interoceanic canals, and monetary matters.[25]

Germany's unwavering opposition to the principle of obligatory arbitration was based on military considerations.[26] Germany was able to mobilize its troops for warfare in a shorter period than any of its potential adversaries. Hence, Germany's acceptance of obligatory arbitration would give its adversaries more time to mobilize their troops while the arbitration went forward, and thus place Germany at a strategic disadvantage. In retrospect, the German objections to obligatory arbitration that were uttered at the First Hague Peace Conference ominously foreshadowed the outbreak of the First World War in the summer of 1914.[27]

In any event, since the Hague Peace Conference operated on the basis of unanimity in deference to the principle of the sovereign equality of states, Germany's opposition to the principle of obligatory arbitration of disputes proved determinative. Consequently, the First Hague Peace Conference had to content itself with the establishment of the purely voluntary Permanent Court of Arbitration. Along with several other novel procedures and institutions that will be discussed in more detail below, the PCA was established by the First Hague Conference's 1899 Convention for the Pacific Settlement of International Disputes.[28]

## The Permanent Court of Arbitration

The PCA was—and is—not a real "court" of arbitration, but only a list of distinguished jurists appointed by the contracting powers to the convention from which parties to a dispute that could not be settled by means of diplomacy could, if they so desired, choose an arbitrator or panel of arbitrators to settle the dispute in accordance with a fixed set of procedural rules[29] that were established by the convention (art. 20).[30] This list comprised four persons selected by each contracting power for a term of six years (art. 23). In the event the parties could not agree on the composition of the arbitration tribunal, each party was to appoint two arbitrators,[31] who together would choose an umpire (art. 24). If the votes were equal, the choice of the umpire was entrusted to a third power selected by common agreement of the parties. If such an agreement was not reached, each party selected a different power, and the choice of the umpire was made in concert by such powers.[32] This arbitration tribunal then assembled on the date fixed by the parties, ordinarily at The Hague (arts. 24 and 25).

Pursuant to the convention's article 31, resort to the PCA required the parties in dispute to conclude a separate agreement (the *compromis*) in which the subject matter of their difference as well as the extent of the arbitrators' powers would be clearly defined. Article 15 stated that arbitration was to be "on the basis of respect for law." Article 48 authorized an arbitral tribunal to declare its competence in interpreting the *compromis* as well as other treaties invoked in the case "and in applying the principles of international law." The applicable law could also be specified by the parties themselves in the *compromis*.[33]

According to article 16, the contracting powers recognized that in questions of a legal nature, and especially in the interpretation or application of international conventions, arbitration was the most effective and equitable means of settling disputes that diplomacy had failed to settle. By the terms of article 17, the arbitration convention was deemed applicable to questions already in existence or questions that might arise in the future, and to any dispute or only disputes of a certain category; and the PCA was deemed competent to arbitrate all such cases (art. 21). The jurisdiction of the PCA could also be extended to include disputes between noncontracting powers or between contracting and noncontracting powers if they so agreed (art. 26).

Parties to an arbitration bound themselves "to submit loyally" to any arbitral award (art. 18). Conversely, the award itself bound only those parties that had concluded the *compromis* unless a third state formally invoked its right of intervention (recognized by art. 56) when a question of interpreting a convention to which it was a party was involved. The award was to be given by a majority of votes, accompanied by a statement of reasons, and signed by each member of the tribunal (art. 52). The award put an end to the dispute definitively and without appeal unless the parties reserved in the *compromis* the right to demand the revision of the award (arts. 54 and 55). The U.S. delegation insisted on this right of revision at the First Hague Peace Conference, and later successfully defended it at the Second Hague Peace Conference.[34]

## An International Bureau of Good Offices and Mediation

The 1899 Convention for the Pacific Settlement of International Disputes also established the International Bureau at The Hague to serve as the record office for the Permanent Court of Arbitration (art. 22). The bureau was under the direction and control of a Permanent Administrative Council composed of the diplomatic representatives of the contracting powers accredited to The Hague and The Netherlands minister for foreign affairs (art. 28). The expenses of the bureau were to be borne by the contracting powers in the portion fixed for the International Bureau of the Universal Postal Union (art. 29). Each party to an arbitration paid its own expenses and an equal share of those of the tribunal (art. 57).

According to article 27, if a serious dispute threatened to break out between contracting powers, it was the duty of the other contracting powers to remind them that the PCA was open to them, and such reminder could not be treated as an unfriendly act of intervention by the disputants.[35] In specific regard to this provision, however, the U.S. delegation felt it necessary to make a declaration at the First Hague Peace Conference that nothing in the convention shall be construed to require the United States to depart from its traditional policy of nonentanglement in the affairs of another state (i.e., Washington's Farewell Address) or to relinquish its "traditional attitude toward purely American questions" (i.e., the Monroe Doctrine).[36] In other words, even after the conclusion of the convention, the United States government intended to retain its traditional policies of isolationism in peace and neutrality in war vis-à-vis the European balance-of-power system, while at the same time striving to preserve its hegemonial sphere of influence in the Western hemisphere from further European penetration.

In the Second Hague Peace Conference's revision of the 1899 Convention for the Pacific Settlement of International Disputes, the text of article 27 was carried over into the new article 48, whose language was supplemented by a provision that in case of a dispute between two contracting powers, one of them could always send the International Bureau a note containing a declaration that it was ready to submit the dispute to arbitration, and the bureau must at once inform the other power of the declaration.[37] On the subject of article 48 of the 1907 convention, the U.S. delegation to the Second Hague Peace Conference renewed the reservations made in regard to article 27 of the 1899 convention.[38] Nevertheless, this change in article 48 prompted one influential American international lawyer to predict the progressive creation of an International Bureau of Good Offices and Mediation in the not-too-distant future by means of this procedural mechanism.[39]

## The Hay Arbitration Conventions

Despite the defeat of the proposal for a general pact for the obligatory arbitration of some disputes, article 19 of the 1899 convention sought to encourage obligatory arbitration by reserving the right of contracting powers to conclude general or special treaties of obligatory arbitration among themselves. Although article 19 did not seem to possess much significance at the time of its adoption, between the First Hague Peace Conference in 1899 and 1908 some seventy-seven arbitration treaties were concluded by the various countries of the world, and all but twelve provided for some sort of reference to the Permanent Court of Arbitration.[40] Such references were generally subject to reservations concerning certain categories of disputes, typically excluding from arbitration matters involving a state's independence, vital interests, honor, sovereignty, or the rights of noncontracting parties.[41] One treaty between Norway and Sweden differed from the rest in providing for questions over whether disputes that involved the parties' vital interests were to be submitted to the PCA itself.[42]

Pursuant to article 19 of the 1899 convention, between November 1904 and February 1905, Secretary of State John Hay signed a series of arbitration treaties on behalf of the U.S. government with eleven foreign governments, including France, Germany, and Great Britain. These treaties called for the reference of "differences which may arise of a legal nature, or relating to the interpretation of treaties existing between the two Contracting Parties" to the PCA, subject to the usual exemptions from obligatory arbitration.[43] The substantive provisions of the Hay arbitration treaties were modeled on the arbitration treaty concluded between Great Britain and France on October 14, 1903, the first to be negotiated with reference to article 19 of the 1899 convention.[44]

However, common article 2 of the Hay arbitration treaties referred to the *compromis* required by article 31 of the 1899 convention by using the word *agreement*,[45] a term that could have permitted the president and secretary of state to conclude an arbitral *compromis* with the foreign government by the simple exchange of diplomatic notes, without bothering to obtain further advice and consent from the U.S. Senate.[46] Overly jealous of its constitutional prerogatives in the area of international agreements, when the Senate gave its advice and consent to the ratification of ten of the Hay arbitration treaties, it formally amended them by substituting the word *treaty* for *agreement* in common article 2, thus explicitly requiring any arbitral *compromis* to be submitted to the Senate for its further advice and consent.[47]

President Theodore Roosevelt deemed the amended Hay arbitration treaties unacceptable for ratification, considering the Senate amendment to be

tantamount to their rejection.[48] From the perspective of the foreign contracting state, a treaty calling for the obligatory arbitration of disputes possessed little more than symbolic value if the arbitral process could not even
commence unless and until the Senate had given its advice and consent
to the *compromis*. In other words, the Senate amendment had effectively
eviscerated the Hay arbitration treaties by reducing the U.S. obligation of
arbitration to the level of a mere agreement to agree. In addition, Roosevelt considered the Senate amendment to constitute an infringement on
the president's constitutional freedom of action in regard to the negotiation
and conclusion of international agreements relating to arbitration.[49]

### The Second Hague Peace Conference

Despite this major setback for the principle of obligatory arbitration, the
U.S. government's delegation went to the Second Hague Peace Conference
of 1907 prepared to support yet another general treaty for the obligatory
arbitration of disputes modeled along the lines of the unratified Hay arbitration treaties as amended by the Senate.[50] By this time Germany had dropped
its objection to the principle of obligatory arbitration, but now insisted that
the proper approach should be the negotiation of a series of bilateral arbitration treaties between interested states instead of the conclusion of a general multilateral pact.[51] Germany stridently opposed the Anglo-American
project calling for a general pact of obligatory arbitration applicable to differences "of a legal nature and, primarily, those relating to the interpretation
of treaties existing between two or more of the contracting nations," and to
a specified list of subjects without the typical reservations.[52]

Consequently, the Second Hague Peace Conference had to content itself
with the adoption of a unanimous declaration on the subject. This declaration accepted the principle of obligatory arbitration and stated that
differences "relating to the interpretation and application of international
conventional stipulations, are susceptible of being submitted to obligatory
arbitration without any restriction."[53] Thus, in regard to the Permanent
Court of Arbitration, the 1899 Convention for the Peaceful Settlement of
International Disputes was not materially altered by its 1907 revision.[54]

### The Root Arbitration Conventions

The wording of the 1907 declaration on obligatory arbitration was chosen
specifically to enable nations favoring compulsory arbitration to conclude
special treaties on the subject among themselves outside the framework
of the Hague conferences.[55] Pursuant to this recommendation, Secretary of
State Elihu Root promptly negotiated a series of twenty-five general arbitration treaties on behalf of the United States along the model of the unratified

Hay arbitration treaties. However, common article 2 of the Root arbitration treaties explicitly provided: "It is understood that on the part of the United States, such special agreements [i.e., the *compromis*] will be made by the President of the United States by and with the advice and consent of the Senate thereof."[56] Although the addition of this compromise language affirmed the independent role of the president in the negotiation and conclusion of arbitration agreements, it nevertheless represented his capitulation to the Senate on the need for its formal advice and consent to the *compromis*. All of the Root arbitration treaties were ratified by the Senate,[57] and twenty-two eventually entered into force.[58]

During the interim after Roosevelt refused to ratify the amended version of the Hay arbitration treaties, Root had persuaded the president that there was indeed some political and legal merit to be gained for the U.S. government in becoming a party to arbitration treaties of this nature.[59] After all, once ratified, the Root arbitration treaties could hardly be treated as mere phantasms by the U.S. Senate. By giving its advice and consent to an arbitration treaty, the Senate had formally committed itself in advance to some form of arbitral *compromis* concluded thereunder that was acceptable to a foreign contracting party in the event of a dispute.[60] Its pledged word to arbitrate, the power of both domestic and international public opinion in favor of the principles of obligatory arbitration and of the peaceful settlement of international disputes, together with the sincere desire of the U.S. government to fulfill its obligations under an extant international arbitration convention should be sufficient to compel the Senate to give its advice and consent to an arbitral *compromis*.

Moreover, from the perspective of a foreign state, the language of the Root arbitration treaties pertaining to the *compromis* was drafted as an "understanding" instead of a formal amendment or reservation on the part of the United States. A foreign contracting party was thus entitled to construe this understanding as constituting a straightforward enunciation of the requirements of the domestic constitutional procedures of the U.S. government that could not detract from or qualify the latter's obligation to arbitrate in accordance with the fundamental principle of international law decreeing that *pacta sunt servanda*.[61] As far as the foreign state was concerned, obtaining the advice and consent of the Senate to the arbitral *compromis* was a purely internal matter occasioned by the peculiarities of the U.S. Constitution; it was devoid of any international legal significance. The U.S. government was bound to arbitrate disputes thereunder irrespective of any domestic constitutional difficulties that might be created by the Senate's obstinacy over a *compromis*.

Hence, an interpretation of the Root arbitration treaties to constitute international legal nullities was mistaken, for the conventions represented a set of definite agreements to arbitrate, not chimerical agreements to agree. Public international law imposed a perfect equality of fixed obligations in this regard on both of the contracting parties.

### The Abortive Plan for a Compulsory Compromis

One innovative feature of the 1907 Convention for the Pacific Settlement of International Disputes was the inclusion of a provision calling for the compulsory conclusion of a *compromis* by the PCA if the parties in dispute could not agree on the terms of reference, albeit under severely restrictive conditions. Despite its opposition to a general treaty of obligatory arbitration, even Germany favored the compulsory *compromis* in order to overcome the alleged constitutional prerogatives of the U.S. Senate, which, in Germany's opinion, constituted a derogation from the fundamental principle recognizing the sovereign equality of states.[62]

Article 53 of the 1907 convention gave the PCA the competence to settle the *compromis* envisioned by the new article 52 if the parties were agreed to have recourse to it for this purpose. Furthermore, if all attempts to reach an understanding through the diplomatic channel had failed, the PCA was empowered to draw up the *compromis* even if the request was made by only one of the parties in the case of a dispute under an extant general arbitration treaty providing for a *compromis* in all disputes, without explicitly or implicitly excluding the settlement of the *compromis* from the competence of the PCA, excepting if the other party declared that in its opinion the dispute did not belong to the category of disputes that could be submitted to compulsory arbitration, unless the treaty of arbitration conferred on the arbitration tribunal the power of deciding this preliminary question. The same was true in the case of a dispute arising from contract debts claimed of one power by another as due its nationals, for the settlement of which the offer of arbitration had been accepted, unless such acceptance was conditioned on the conclusion of the *compromis* in some other way. Nevertheless, despite this slight advance for the principle of the obligatory arbitration of disputes, the U.S. government's act of ratification for the 1907 convention exercised the option contained in article 53 to exclude the formulation of the *compromis* from the competence of the PCA under all circumstances unless expressly provided otherwise by treaty.[63] No *compromis* was ever drawn up under this article 53 procedure.[64]

### The Golden Age of Modern International Arbitration

Prior to the outbreak of the First World War in 1914, a series of precedential or serious international disputes were submitted to the Permanent Court of

Arbitration at The Hague, including *The Pious Fund Case* (*Mexico v. United States*),[65] *The Venezuelan Preferential Case* (*Germany, Great Britain, and Italy v. Venezuela et al.*),[66] *The Casablanca Case* (*France v. Germany*),[67] *The Grisbadarna Case* (*Norway v. Sweden*),[68] *The North Atlantic Fisheries Case* (*Great Britain v. United States*),[69] *The Orinoco Steamship Company Case* (*United States v. Venezuela*),[70] and *The Savarkar Case* (*France v. Great Britain*).[71] The U.S. government consciously played the role of midwife in bringing the PCA to life by submitting the Pious Fund dispute with Mexico to the PCA as its first case. Between 1902 and 1914, there were fourteen arbitrations before the PCA and about fifty or so more international arbitrations outside its ambit.[72]

From the perspective of maintaining international peace and security, the most significant of the Hague Court's arbitrations were *The Venezuelan Preferential Case* and *The Casablanca Case*. Pressure by President Roosevelt to refer part of the former controversy surrounding the default on its public debts by Venezuela to arbitration before the PCA and the rest of the dispute to mixed commissions contributed to the successful termination of ongoing military hostilities conducted by Germany, Italy, and Great Britain to forcefully collect on their respective nationals' monetary claims against the Venezuelan government.[73] Those actions threatened to draw the United States directly into the conflict in order to protect Venezuela from any anticipatory breach of the Monroe Doctrine.

To be sure, there was significant legalist criticism of the PCA's decision in the *Venezuelan* case because it gave priority to the claims of the states that had resorted to force over the other creditor states.[74] It was argued that this would only encourage creditor states to use force to recover on their public debts from other states. But this criticism could not detract from the key role that reference of the dispute to international arbitration and the PCA played in the Roosevelt administration's solution of the controversy. The long-term problem of more powerful states using force to collect on contract debts owed by less powerful states would be resolved by the 1907 Convention Respecting the Limitation of the Employment of Force for the Recovery of Contract Debts that was sponsored by the U.S. government at the Second Hague Peace Conference.[75]

The Casablanca incident of 1908 was universally considered to have concerned the "honor" of France and Germany—a subject not generally thought appropriate for international arbitration at that time. In this case, French military occupation forces in Morocco seized and detained deserters from the French foreign legion who were under the diplomatic protection of the German consulate there. Given the strong public reactions in both countries,[76] as well as the highly militaristic tenor of that era, nonresolution of this dispute might have resulted in hostilities between the two parties.[77] Such a bilateral conflict could have rapidly escalated into a general systemic war in Europe because of the two parties' respective memberships in competing alliance systems.[78]

Thus, despite its congenital defects, the Permanent Court of Arbitration contributed to the termination of one concerted military operation and to the prevention of at least one war. Consequently, history must judge the PCA an excellent example of the positive role played by international law and organizations in the amelioration of the generally violent conditions of world politics before the First World War.[79] And despite its eclipse by the Permanent Court of International Justice and later the International Court of Justice, the Hague Permanent Court of Arbitration continues to survive and function today.

## Conclusion

It would be fair to argue that the institution of international arbitration constitutes an integral and important component of the overall regime of international law and organizations concerning the threat and use of force in existence today. This subregime of international arbitration provides both a means and a mechanism whereby two contending states can depoliticize a serious dispute by first "legalizing" it (i.e., negotiating the rules for decision in the *compromis*) and then "institutionalizing" it (i.e., submitting it to the arbitration tribunal for decision). Two contending states resorting to the subregime of international arbitration can effectively defuse their respective domestic public opinions over an international dispute by putting the matter "on ice." This recurrent phenomenon has proven the value of international arbitration as a viable subregime for the peaceful settlement of international disputes over and over again throughout the course of the twentieth century.[80]

At the time of the decisions in *The Casablanca Case* and *The North Atlantic Fisheries Case* by the Permanent Court of Arbitration, heated public controversies arose in the United States over the propriety of the "compromise" nature of these arbitral awards.[1] On such grounds, American international lawyers argued that the main shortcoming of international arbitration would be its tendency to assume the form of an essentially political process of negotiation and compromise on the basis of expedience rather than the judicial procedure of impartial adjudication of rights and duties in strict accordance with the rules of law.[2] These American legalists felt that the states of the international community genuinely preferred the clear-cut decision and strict impartiality in determination of their rights and duties that supposedly could be afforded by some international court of justice over all nations instead of the essentially political process of partiality and compromise practiced by an international arbitration tribunal whose members were chosen by the parties in dispute themselves.[3] The international court of justice they envisioned would operate in a manner functionally analogous to the U.S. Supreme Court when deciding questions arising between citizens of the different U.S. states, or between foreign citizens and citizens of the United States, under Article III, section 2, of the U.S. Constitution.[4]

The American legalists analogized the procedure for the Permanent Court of Arbitration to article 9 of the Articles of Confederation of 1781, which created a process of arbitration for the solution of disputes among the American states.[5] The U.S. Constitution superseded the Articles of Confederation in 1789, and replaced this arbitral procedure by extending the federal judicial power to controversies between two or more states and by vesting original jurisdiction in the Supreme Court to adjudicate such controversies.[6] As the legalists saw it, this successful experience in the evolution of dispute settlement techniques for semisovereign political entities provided a useful precedent for the progressive development of international dispute settlement tribunals from arbitration to adjudication.[7]

Likewise analogously, the existence of an international court of justice would permit the development of binding precedential decisions that could guide the future deliberations of the world court and create a stable framework of legal expectations among states conducive to the peaceful settlement of their disputes. Since arbitral awards were ad hoc by nature, they were supposed to possess little precedential significance. Only by means of creating an actual world court could a systematic jurisprudence of international legal decisions for the peaceful settlement of international disputes effectively evolve.

### Arbitration versus Adjudication

In their collective disparagement of international arbitration as an institution inferior to international adjudication, however, American international lawyers manifested scant awareness of the paradox that perhaps one reason responsible for the remarkable success of arbitration as a subregime for the peaceful settlement of international disputes before the First World War was exactly because of, not in spite of, its political dimension. For example, in a dispute between two private parties brought before a municipal court of law, there is usually one clear-cut winner and one clear-cut loser. By contrast, an international panel of arbitration could creatively fashion its award on a purposefully flexible *compromis* so that the two sovereign states in dispute each won something and thus neither lost everything.

During the course of an international conflict, for reasons of both domestic public opinion and international prestige, a government might prefer arbitration over adjudication because a subjective cost-benefit analysis indicates that it is politically better to sustain a high probability of not losing everything and only winning something by means of arbitration than to run a substantially greater risk of losing everything, even though there is also a greater potential to win everything by means of adjudication. According to the literature of contemporary international political science, in the analysis of international conflict as a zero-sum game, rational government decision makers will tend to pursue a strategy that minimizes risks over one that maximizes gains.[8] Hence they might prefer arbitration over adjudication.

Of course, ceteris paribus, the more settled the rules of international law, the more likely the party in a dispute possessing the stronger legal position will be to prefer adjudication over arbitration. So the golden age of international arbitration during the twentieth century quite expectedly occurred in the pre–World War I era of international relations when the European system of public international law was essentially customary instead of conventional, and an actual world court did not yet exist. Conversely, in the aftermath of the Great War, with the establishment of the Permanent Court of International Justice in 1921 and the acceleration of the movement for the progressive codification of international law in the 1920s and early 1930s,[9] international arbitration as a subregime for the peaceful settlement of serious interstate disputes predictably experienced a material decline in comparative significance.

This was precisely the result that was intended by the government of the United States when it sponsored the foundation of an international court of justice at the Second Hague Peace Conference. Thus, it would be gratuitously unfair to criticize the Hague Permanent Court of Arbitration for the eclipse in its own effectiveness as a subregime for the peaceful settlement of international disputes after the First World War. Moreover, it is also important for contemporary government decision makers to bear in mind the continuing practical utility of international arbitration as a subregime for the peaceful settlement of international disputes today—whether by the PCA or otherwise—for the reasons mentioned above.

## The Plan for a Court of Arbitral Justice

Following in the footsteps of the unsuccessful U.S. plan for a world court introduced at the First Hague Peace Conference, the U.S. delegation traveled to the Second Hague Peace Conference having been instructed by Secretary of State Elihu Root to propose the formation of an actual international court of justice that would be judicial in nature and function as opposed to the arbitral proceedings of the Permanent Court of Arbitration, though it was envisioned that the present PCA could, as far as possible, constitute the basis of the court.[10] When it finally emerged from the proceedings of the Second Hague Peace Conference, however, the plan called for the institution of a separate "Court of Arbitral Justice" (CAJ) consisting of an as yet unspecified number of judges appointed in an as yet unspecified manner for a term of twelve years.[11]

According to article 1 of the CAJ Draft Convention, the CAJ was designed not to replace but rather to coexist with the PCA. States would be free to choose between the two institutions. Nevertheless, the implication was quite clear that states would quickly grow to prefer adjudication over arbitration since the CAJ more nearly coincided with their vital national security interests in creating a more effective system for the peaceful settlement of international disputes.

## CAJ Judges

The CAJ judges and alternates were to be appointed by the contracting parties from among persons enjoying the highest moral reputation. They must fulfill, in their respective countries, the conditions required for appointment to high judicial offices or be jurists of well-known competency in matters relative to international law; as far as possible, they were to be selected from among the members of the PCA (art. 2). A CAJ judge could not exercise judicial functions in any case in which he had taken part in rendering a decision of a court of his nation, a court of arbitration, or a commission of inquiry, or if he had figured in the hearing of a case as counsel or attorney for one of the parties (art. 7). No judge could appear as agent or counsel before the CAJ, the PCA, a special tribunal of arbitration, or a commission of inquiry, or act for any of the parties in any capacity during his term of office (art. 7).

Against the objections of the U.S. delegation,[12] a CAJ judge was not prohibited from sitting in a case that involved his state of nationality. However, a member of a CAJ "special delegation" could not exercise his duties when the power that appointed him, or of which he was a national, was one of the parties in dispute (art. 6). Every year the CAJ was to elect a "special delegation" of three judges with the competence to hear arbitration cases coming under article 17 if the parties agreed to apply the summary procedure described in title IV, chapter 4, of the 1907 Convention for the Pacific Settlement of International Disputes (art. 18). This special delegation also had the competence to constitute itself as an international commission of inquiry in accordance with title III of that convention if authorized by common agreement of the parties in dispute.

The CAJ judges were to receive a fixed annual salary, a per diem allotment, and traveling expenses (art. 9), to be paid by the International Bureau of the Permanent Court of Arbitration at The Hague (art. 9), with the contracting powers paying the CAJ's expenses at the request of the PCA's Administrative Council. Judges were forbidden to receive any compensation for performance of their duties from their own government or that of another power (art. 10). The International Bureau was to serve as the record office for the CAJ (art. 13), and the Administrative Council was to perform the same functions toward the CAJ that it did toward the PCA (art. 12).

## Jurisdiction

The CAJ was to assemble in session every year beginning in June and lasting until the end of the year, though provision was made for the calling of an extraordinary session (art. 14). Unlike the Permanent Court of Arbitration, only the contracting powers were given access to the Court of Arbitral Justice (art. 21), since they alone were to bear its general expenses (art. 31). All decisions of the CAJ were to be arrived at by a majority vote of the judges present (art. 27). The judgment of the CAJ had to give the reasons on which it was based and the names of the judges taking part in it, and it had to be signed by the president and the registrar of the court (art. 28). Each party had to pay its own costs and an equal share of the costs of the trial (art. 29).

Title II of the Draft Convention spelled out the jurisdiction and procedure of the Court of Arbitral Justice. Article 17 gave the CAJ jurisdiction in all cases brought before it by virtue of a general or special arbitration agreement. There was no provision similar to the so-called optional clause to the Protocol of Signature Relating to the Statute of the Permanent Court of International Justice (PCIJ) of December 16, 1920, whereby states could accept beforehand, ipso facto and without a special convention, the compulsory jurisdiction of the PCIJ in certain classes of legal disputes between parties in conformity with article 36(2) of the PCIJ Statute.[13] Thus, by comparison, in the absence of a separate agreement, the CAJ was designed to possess no general form of compulsory jurisdiction over legal disputes between parties to its convention.

## A Compulsory Compromis

Like article 53 of the 1907 Convention for the Pacific Settlement of International Disputes concerning the Permanent Court of Arbitration, article 19 of the CAJ Draft Convention provided the aforementioned "special delegation" with the competence to draw up the *compromis* envisioned by article 52 of the 1907 convention if the parties agreed to remit the case to the CAJ. Furthermore, the special delegation was empowered to draw up the *compromis* even when application was made by one of the parties only—after unsuccessfully attempting to secure agreement through diplomatic means—in the case of a dispute under an extant general arbitration treaty providing a *compromis* for every dispute, without explicitly or implicitly excluding the exercise of such competence by the special delegation, provided the other party did not declare that in its opinion the dispute did not belong to the category of questions to be submitted to obligatory arbitration, unless the arbitration treaty conferred on the arbitral tribunal the power to pass on this preliminary question. The same was true in the case of a dispute arising from contractual debts claimed of one power by another as due to persons subject to its jurisdiction, for the settlement of which the proposal of arbitration had been accepted, unless such acceptance was conditioned on the conclusion of the *compromis*. Germany had advocated this procedure for the compulsory conclusion of a *compromis* by the CAJ special delegation as an alternative to the adoption of a general treaty for the obligatory arbitration of disputes at the Second Hague Peace Conference.[14]

## CAJ Law

The CAJ Draft Convention did not contain a provision similar to article 38 of the later PCIJ Statute, which directed the PCIJ to apply three primary sources (conventions, custom, and "general principles of law") and two subsidiary means (judicial decisions, though without entitlement to the principle of *stare decisis* except between the parties in regard to that particular case; and the teachings of publicists) for the determination of the rules of international law in a case.[15] Hence, there was no recognition of the doctrine of *stare decisis* in the CAJ Draft Convention. Nevertheless, the Court of Arbitral Justice was ordered to apply the rules of procedure laid down in the 1907 Convention for the Pacific Settlement of International Disputes, except as otherwise modified by the CAJ Draft Convention (art. 22). This directive would have incorporated article 73 of the 1907 convention authorizing the PCA to declare its competence in interpreting the *compromis*, as well as other papers and documents (e.g., treaties) that might be invoked and in applying "the principles of law." However, article 48 of the 1899 convention, the precursor to article 73, specifically referred to "the principles of *international* law" (emphasis added).

## The CAJ versus the PCA

In the final analysis, despite the initial promotion of the idea by the U.S. government at the Second Hague Peace Conference of creating an actual world court whose judicial nature would be fundamentally different from and superior to the political nature of the PCA, the jurisdiction and procedures of the proposed CAJ were similar to those of the PCA in several material respects. In theory, the primary distinction drawn between the two institutions was the notion that states would choose to submit disputes they believed to be essentially "legal" or "justiciable"[16] in character to the CAJ, while continuing to submit those they perceived to be "political" to the PCA. Yet, if it had ever come to fruition, the CAJ would have emerged as an institution operationally similar to a permanent and standing international tribunal of arbitration.

Of special concern was the fact that CAJ judges would have been appointed directly by the contracting governments—much like an arbitration tribunal. This procedure could have compromised the independence of the judges and thus called into question the impartiality of the tribunal. Even its name—Court of Arbitral Justice—indicated the unavoidably hybrid nature of an international tribunal designed to blend characteristics of both arbitration and adjudication (art. 1).

To be sure, from the perspective of creating a true world court, the Court of Arbitral Justice was a definite advance over the so-called Permanent Court of Arbitration. The CAJ would indeed have constituted an institution along the lines of what Elihu Root had instructed the U.S. delegates to the Second Hague Peace Conference to propose: The CAJ was designed to be a permanent tribunal composed of judges who would function as judicial officers, be paid adequate salaries, have no other occupations, devote full time to the trial of international cases, and operate under a sense of judicial responsibility.[17]

For these reasons, the Draft Convention Relative to the Institution of a Court of Arbitral Justice recommended for adoption by the Second Hague Peace Conference set forth an institutional plan that ultimately represented a crucial intermediate stage in the evolution of international dispute settlement tribunals from the relatively primitive 1899 Permanent Court of Arbitration to the far more sophisticated 1921 Permanent Court of International Justice—the immediate predecessor to the current International Court of Justice. Indeed, in the opinion of James Brown Scott, an American international legal scholar and diplomat who was intimately involved in the preparation of both the 1907 CAJ draft convention and the 1920 PCIJ Statute, the latter "was to most intents and purposes similar to, if not identical with, the draft of 1907."[18]

Thus, in his first speech before the Advisory Committee of Jurists established by the Council of the League of Nations in 1920 to prepare plans for the Permanent Court of International Justice, Elihu Root proposed a resolution that the committee adopt as the basis for its work the acts and resolutions of the Second Hague Peace Conference of 1907.[19] By means of this proposal, Root wanted to establish the continuity between his plan for the 1907 Court of Arbitral Justice and the 1920 PCIJ Statute.[20] In essence, the committee acceded to Root's proposal by continually referring to the 1907 draft convention during the course of its deliberations.[21] Root later commented that the PCIJ Statute "leaves it like the plan for a Court of Arbitral Justice adopted by the Second Hague Conference, but with a settlement of the controversy over the appointment of the judges that was unsolved there, and with a few important additions."[22]

## The Stalemate over the Selection of Judges for a World Court

The primary obstacle to the actual establishment of the Court of Arbitral Justice at the Second Hague Peace Conference proved to be an unbreakable deadlock over the manner for selecting judges to the court. Specifically, the smaller states—and especially the Latin American nations led by Brazil—opposed the selection of CAJ judges from among themselves on a rotational basis while the great powers would each be accorded the right always to have one of their respective appointees sitting on the CAJ.[23] Such an arrangement would have been similar to the system for appointing judges to the proposed International Court of Prize that was also adopted at the Second Hague Peace Conference.[24]

For example, article 6 of a preliminary draft convention for an international court of justice, which was presented by the delegations of Germany, the United States, and Great Britain, provided that judges appointed by Germany, the United States, Austria-Hungary, France, Great Britain, Italy, Japan, and Russia "are always summoned to sit," whereas judges appointed by the other contracting powers would sit on a rotational basis in accordance with a schedule that was supposedly determined by a mixture of the population, industry, and commerce of the appointing states.[25] Since it made sense for the states with the largest naval fleets to insist on the right always to have an appointee sitting as a member of the International Prize Court, a similar arrangement should equally make sense for the great powers of the world concerning the right of continuous presence by one of their respective appointees on any international court of justice. After all, by their voluntary agreement to the institution of an actual world court, the great powers would be restricting their supposed right to threaten and use force to settle their international disputes with the smaller states. The latter would obtain greater protection from the former than otherwise would be the case, while a great power would receive no additional protection from other great powers by means of a world court alone. Therefore, since an international court of justice would primarily benefit the smaller states, they should be willing to compromise on the principle of sovereign equality when it came to the appointment of judges.

Of course, this entire rationale was based on the questionable premise that the great powers actually possessed the legal right to threaten and use force to settle their disputes with smaller states. It is not surprising, therefore, that the foremost opposition to a rotational system for appointing judges to the Court of Arbitral Justice that favored the great powers in this manner came from the Latin American states, where the Calvo and Drago Doctrines had been formulated and generally espoused expressly in order to protect the latter from further imperialist encroachments by the former.[26] The Latin American states, together with other smaller powers, insisted that the principle of the sovereign equality of states be recognized when it came to the appointment of judges to what was intended to become a real international court of justice for the impartial adjudication of disputes among all the members of the international community during peacetime.[27] Ironically, it was the U.S. government under the leadership of Secretary of State Elihu Root that had successfully advocated the admission of the Latin American states to the Second Hague Peace Conference on the basis of equality with the states that had attended the First Peace Conference—over the latter's fear of a U.S.-controlled voting bloc.[28] Now these same U.S. protégés adamantly refused to compromise on the principle of their sovereign equality when it came to the appointment of judges to a world court project that the United States had originally sponsored and labored strenuously to set up.

The net result was that the Second Hague Peace Conference had to content itself with a recommendation that the signatory powers adopt the annexed Draft Convention Relative to the Institution of a Court of Arbitral Justice "as soon as an agreement shall have been reached upon the selection of judges and the constitution of the court."[29] This language was purposefully chosen in the hope that a large number of nations would be willing to ignore Latin America's objections to the judicial appointment procedure and constitute the Court of Arbitral Justice among themselves through normal diplomatic channels in the immediate aftermath of the Second Hague Peace Conference.[30] This would permit definitive results on the foundation of some international court of justice to occur well before the convocation of the Third Peace Conference, which in 1907 was tentatively scheduled to begin in 1915.[31]

### Keeping the World Court Plan Alive

Pursuant to this recommendation, the U.S. government, under Root's interim successor as secretary of state, Robert Bacon, sought to finesse the judicial appointment dispute by suggesting to the great powers present at the London Naval Conference of 1908 (Germany, United States, Austria-Hungary, Spain, France, Great Britain, Italy, Japan, The Netherlands, and Russia) that the proposed International Prize Court (IPC) should be invested with the jurisdiction and procedures of the Court of Arbitral Justice, and that the 1907 CAJ Draft Convention be utilized by the IPC when so acting for consenting states.[32] This could be accomplished by adopting an article additional to a draft protocol concerning the International Prize Court that was then under consideration at the London Naval Conference. This article would permit any signatory of the Prize Court Convention to provide in its act of ratification that the IPC shall be competent to accept jurisdiction over and decide any case arising between signatories of the proposed article that was submitted to the IPC for arbitration in accordance with the procedures of the CAJ Draft Convention of 1907.

A purposive interconnection between these two institutions for the peaceful settlement of international disputes during war and peace, respectively, was testified to by article 16 of the CAJ Draft Convention, which provided that judges and deputy judges of the CAJ could also exercise the functions of judges and deputy judges of the IPC.[33] The U.S. government pointed out that it is always easier to expand the jurisdiction of an existing institution than to call into being a new one.[34] Nevertheless, the delegates to the London Naval Conference determined that the U.S. proposal exceeded the scope of their powers, and no action on this matter was taken there.[35]

### The Four-Power Conference in Paris

The United States continued to pursue the establishment of a world court through normal diplomatic channels.[36] This initiative eventually culminated in a meeting of representatives from the United States, Great Britain, Germany, and France at Paris in March 1910 to consider the actual creation of a Court of Arbitral Justice among states willing to accept the rotational system for appointment of judges to the International Prize Court as the basis for appointments to the CAJ, instead of the simple expedient of vesting the IPC with the powers and procedures of the CAJ previously proposed by the United States.[37] The Paris conference produced a four-power draft convention for contracting states to put into effect the CAJ Draft Convention recommended for adoption by the Second Hague Peace Conference.[38] In this fashion the Court of Arbitral Justice itself could have been created by a limited number of states.

According to the four-power plan, the CAJ would be composed of fifteen judges, with nine constituting a quorum. Judges and substitute judges would be appointed by the contracting powers in accordance with the system of rotation established by article 15 of the International Prize Court Convention and the annexed table. This system would have given the eight great naval powers (Germany, United States, Austria-Hungary, France, Great Britain, Italy, Japan, and Russia) the right to always have an appointee sitting on the CAJ, whereas the appointees of the other contracting powers would rotate on the basis of their relative maritime interests. Provision was also made for a noncontracting power to bring an action before the CAJ and its special delegation on the former's assumption of an appropriate share of expenses due to the action as determined by the court or its special delegation. The four-power draft convention was to come into effect as soon as eighteen powers could ratify it and could furnish nine judges and nine substitute judges capable of actually sitting on the court. This four-power draft convention was further amended by the parties at The Hague in July 1910.[39]

### The Scott Initiative

The representatives of the four powers who wrote the 1910 draft convention believed that their scheme depended on the prior successful institution of the International Prize Court, even though the document did not expressly state this condition.[40] The refusal of Great Britain to ratify the Declaration of London and, consequently, the International Prize Court Convention as well, spelled defeat for the four-power plan to institute a Court of Arbitral Justice. Still undaunted, however, Philander C. Knox, secretary of state to President Taft, requested James Brown Scott—technical delegate of the United States to the Second Hague Peace Conference, former solicitor for the Department of State, U.S. representative to the 1910 Paris Conference, and managing editor of the *American Journal of International Law*—to undertake a mission to Europe to initiate negotiations concerning the formation of a Court of Arbitral Justice that was to be independent of the stalled International Prize Court Convention. On November 25, 1912, Knox approved and signed a memorandum and an identical circular note drafted by Scott to that effect, but they were not issued and the scheme never got off the ground.[41]

With the advent of the Wilson administration, Scott addressed a personal letter, dated January 12, 1914, to the minister of foreign affairs of The Netherlands suggesting that the Dutch government initiate negotiations through diplomatic channels for an agreement among Germany, the United States, Austria-Hungary, France, Great Britain, Italy, Japan, and Russia to create a Court of Arbitral Justice among themselves and with a provision for its use by noncontracting parties. Scott included with his letter a proposed draft convention along these lines, a supporting memorandum he had drafted, the earlier memorandum and circular note to that effect drafted by him and approved by Knox, and other supporting documentation.[42] By then, however, the time was fast approaching for preparations for the proposed Third Hague Peace Conference to begin, and Scott's personal efforts concerning the international court were almost immediately overtaken by a formal diplomatic initiative by the U.S. government to plan for the convocation of this next conference.[43] All further progress in either direction was interrupted by the outbreak of the general war in Europe during the summer of 1914.

### The Creation of the Permanent Court of International Justice

The pre–World War I labors by the U.S. government to establish an international court of justice eventually bore fruit in article 14 of the Covenant of the League of Nations. President Woodrow Wilson's first draft of the League Covenant did not contain any provision for an international court of justice.[44] But the European allies—especially the British—persuaded Wilson to accept a provision for the establishment of the Permanent Court of International Justice in article 14 of the Covenant.[45] Also, providing some degree of continuity with the work of the Second Hague Peace Conference, James Brown Scott, then legal adviser to the American Commission to Negotiate Peace at Paris, had urged the inclusion in the League Covenant of a provision calling for the establishment of a Permanent Court of International Justice.[46]

Article 14 expressly provided the following:

> The Council shall formulate and submit to the Members of the League for adoption plans for the establishment of a Permanent Court of International Justice. The Court shall be competent to hear and determine any dispute of an international character which the parties thereto submit to it. The Court may also give an advisory opinion upon any dispute or question referred to it by the Council or by the Assembly.

Notice first that article 14 did not actually create the Permanent Court of International Justice. That would come later. Also, the permissive language "which the parties thereto submit to it" would arguably seem to preclude the Court from having compulsory jurisdiction over states. Finally, granting power to the Court to give an advisory opinion at the request of League organs would provide serious ammunition to those American politicians who opposed the Permanent Court of International Justice as nothing more than the "League's court" as opposed to a real "world court."[47]

### The Selection of PCIJ Judges

Pursuant to Covenant article 14, in February 1920 the Council of the League of Nations voted to form the Advisory Committee of Jurists to prepare plans for the Permanent Court of International Justice and to report to the Council.[48] The main problem facing the Advisory Committee was the outstanding issue of the selection of judges to a world court in a manner that did not compromise on the principle of the sovereign equality of states. The long-standing deadlock over this matter was broken by the suggestion of Elihu Root, the U.S. representative on the panel, who proposed that PCIJ judges should be selected by the concurrent action of the League Council and the League Assembly, coupled with a procedure for the creation of a joint committee composed of representatives from both bodies to resolve any disagreements.[49] Root got his idea for this two-step procedure from

James Brown Scott, who derived it from his analysis of the system for the representation of large and small states in the U.S. Senate and the House of Representatives, where legislation must be approved independently by both bodies, and a conference committee resolves any differences.[50]

Article 3 of the Statute of the Permanent Court of International Justice provided that the PCIJ shall consist of fifteen members: eleven judges and four deputy judges. According to article 4, the judges of the PCIJ shall be selected by the Assembly and by the Council from a list of persons nominated by the national groups in the Permanent Court of Arbitration, with provision made for members of the League not represented in the PCA. No national group could nominate more than four persons, not more than two of whom shall be of their own nationality (art. 5). In no case could the number of candidates nominated be more than double the number of seats to be filled.

The Secretary-General of the League would prepare a list in alphabetical order of all the persons thus nominated and submit it to the Assembly and to the Council (art. 7). The Assembly and the Council would then proceed, independently, to select the judges first, then the deputy judges (art. 8). Candidates who obtained an absolute majority of votes in the Assembly and the Council would be considered elected (art. 10).

If, after the first meeting held for the purpose of the election, one or more seats remained unfilled, a second, and if necessary a third, meeting would take place (art. 11). If, after the third meeting, one or more seats still remained unfilled, a joint conference consisting of six members, three appointed by the Assembly and three by the Council, would be formed at the request of either the Assembly or the Council, for the purpose of choosing one name for each seat still vacant; the names would then be submitted to the Assembly and the Council for their respective acceptance (art. 12). If the joint conference was satisfied that it would not succeed in procuring an election, those members of the PCIJ who had already been appointed would proceed to fill the vacant seats by selecting from those candidates who had obtained votes either in the Assembly or in the Council.

Although admittedly cumbersome, the Root-Scott arrangement not only broke the controversy over the manner of the selection of PCIJ judges but also ensured that these judges would not be appointed directly by their governments. This clearly was an advance over both the Permanent Court of Arbitration (in which the states in dispute picked their own "judges") and the Court of Arbitral Justice (in which the states parties to the CAJ Convention would have appointed the judges). On its face alone, the PCIJ election procedure was designed to establish the independence of the World Court judges from their respective states of nationality. Based on my own experience litigating before the International Court of Justice, however, it is fair to say that World Court judges have rarely been immune from the viewpoints of the governments of which they are citizens.

## The Great Power Veto

Article 9 of the PCIJ Statute charged the state electors in the Assembly and the Council to ensure not only that all the persons appointed as members of the court should possess the qualifications required but that the whole body should represent the main forms of civilization and the principal legal systems of the world. Yet, the Root-Scott arrangement gave a veto power over the selection of judges to both the great powers represented on the Council and the smaller powers represented in the Assembly. Textually this procedure did not derogate from the principle of the sovereign equality of states since it did not explicitly guarantee each great power the right always to have a national sitting on the PCIJ. Functionally, however, the voting arrangement could effectively ensure this outcome because article 4(1) of the Covenant of the League of Nations provided that the Council was always to consist of representatives of the Principal Allied and Associated Powers (i.e., United Kingdom, France, Italy, Japan, and the United States), together with representatives of four other members of the League selected by the Assembly.

Admittedly, this procedure indirectly accorded preferential treatment to the wishes of the great powers in the election of PCIJ judges. But in a defense of his proposal against this objection before the Advisory Committee of Jurists at The Hague, Elihu Root persuasively argued that this slight compromise with the principle of the sovereign equality of states was a fair price for the smaller powers to pay in return for the protection against the great powers that would be afforded to them by an international court of justice.[51] Similar arguments had already been successfully advanced to justify permanent representation by the great powers on the League of Nations Council. The experience of the First World War had obviously exerted a chastening influence on the tendency of minor powers to impede the great powers from creating international institutions for the elimination, reduction, and regulation of international conflict in the name of upholding the principle of the sovereign equality of states.

## Origins of the Optional Clause

The other major topic dealt with by the Advisory Committee of Jurists was the question of whether or not the PCIJ should exercise any type of compulsory jurisdiction over states. Root persuaded a majority of the Committee of Jurists that the Court should have compulsory jurisdiction.[52] According to his proposal, the court was to have compulsory jurisdiction—without any additional special convention—to hear cases between member states of a legal nature concerning (1) the interpretation of a treaty; (2) any question of international law; (3) the existence of any fact which, if established, would constitute a breach of an international obligation; (4) the nature or extent of reparation to be made for the breach of an international obligation; and (5) the interpretation of a sentence passed by the Court.[53] Also, any dispute as to whether or not a case came within any of these specified categories was to be settled by the decision of the Court itself.[54] In regard to these five categories of disputes deemed fit to be subject to compulsory judicial settlement, all but the last category had been taken from and followed the language of article 13(2) of the League of Nations Covenant.[55]

In the late fall of 1920, both the Council and the Assembly of the League of Nations rejected the proposal by the Advisory Committee of Jurists to endow the PCIJ with compulsory jurisdiction concerning the five above-mentioned categories of disputes.[56] Opposition came from the great power members of the League Council under the leadership of Great Britain.[57] It has been this author's professional experience that great powers prefer to resolve their disputes by means of diplomacy because they can better bring to bear their preponderant power by that means rather than in court, where such power differentials can be reduced but not altogether eliminated. In fairness, however, during the debates at that time it was also pointed out that the permissive language of article 14 of the Covenant contemplated that the Court would not have any type of obligatory jurisdiction. If approved by the League Council, the Committee's proposal would have effectively amended the Covenant, which gave states the option of submitting their disputes to the Council, to arbitration, or to judicial settlement pursuant to articles 12, 13, 14, and 15. Ultimately, this legal argument prevailed.[58]

In this respect, therefore, the Statute of the Permanent Court of International Justice would follow the scheme of the 1907 Draft Convention Relative to the Institution of a Court of Arbitral Justice recommended for adoption by the Second Hague Peace Conference, which omitted any provision calling for the obligatory adjudication of disputes.[59] Thus, article 36 of the PCIJ Statute provided that the jurisdiction of the Court comprised all cases the parties referred to it and all matters specially provided for in treaties and conventions in force.

The smaller states in the League Assembly objected to the deletion of compulsory jurisdiction for the World Court. In their opinion, without compulsory jurisdiction, the Court would be not much more than an international arbitration tribunal.[60] But the smaller powers saw the handwriting on the wall and went along with the great powers' wishes on this matter.

As a compromise, however, the Brazilian delegate proposed that alternative texts be offered.[61] That way, states that wanted to accept the compulsory jurisdiction of the World Court in specified categories of legal disputes could do so and still have the ability to make reservations limiting their acceptance of the Court's compulsory jurisdiction.[62] This voluntary acceptance of the Court's compulsory jurisdiction was included as an addition to article 36 of the PCIJ Statute and became known as the "optional clause."[63]

Thus, in its entirety, article 36 of the PCIJ Statute read as follows:

> The jurisdiction of the Court comprises all cases which the parties refer to it and all matters specially provided for in treaties and conventions in force.
>
> The Members of the League of Nations and the States mentioned in the Annex to the Covenant may, either when signing or ratifying the Protocol to which the present Statute is adjoined, or at a later moment, declare that they recognize as compulsory *ipso facto* and without special agreement, in relation to any other Member or State accepting the same obligation, the jurisdiction of the Court in all or any of the classes of legal disputes concerning:
>
> (a) the interpretation of a treaty;
>
> (b) any question of international law;
>
> (c) the existence of any fact which, if established, would constitute a breach of an international obligation;
>
> (d) the nature or extent of the reparation to be made for the breach of an international obligation.
>
> The declaration referred to above may be made unconditionally or on condition of reciprocity on the part of several or certain Members or States, or for a certain time.
>
> In the event of a dispute as to whether the Court has jurisdiction, the matter shall be settled by the decision of the Court.[64]

Toward the end of 1921, eighteen states had made such declarations under the optional clause; but as of that time, the declarants did not include any of the great powers.[65]

After the Second World War, the optional clause procedure was carried forward into article 36(2) of the Statute of the International Court of Justice (ICJ), which became an integral part of the United Nations Charter. In the drafting of the ICJ Statute, both the United States and the Soviet Union opposed endowing the World Court with any type of compulsory jurisdiction and preferred instead to maintain the system of voluntary submission of disputes to the World Court under the optional clause procedure.[66] Once again, it would be the great powers that would preclude the rest of the world from moving toward a system establishing the compulsory adjudication of legal disputes. These shortsighted and self-interested reasons against compulsory jurisdiction by the great powers in 1945 were still much the same as they had been in 1920.

## U.S. Rejection of the Permanent Court of International Justice

The Statute of the Permanent Court of International Justice was unanimously approved by the Assembly of the League of Nations on December 13, 1920; the Protocol to establish the PCIJ went into effect on August 20, 1921; and the Court was formally opened at The Hague on February 15, 1922.[67] Judges were elected from all five of the great powers. Their ranks included John Bassett Moore from the United States, even though his government had neither joined the League of Nations nor ratified the Protocol of Signature for the PCIJ Statute.[68] Moore's election to the Court was possible because the nominating bodies were the national groupings of the Permanent Court of Arbitration at The Hague, to which the United States belonged, and each national group had to recommend four names, of whom only two could be its own nationals.[69] Elihu Root had declined the offer of a PCIJ judgeship because of age.[70]

Of course, the U.S. government never joined the League of Nations and never became a party to the PCIJ Statute because of strident opposition to both organizations consistently mounted by isolationist members of the U.S. Senate. Even the technical separation of the Court from the League by the device of adopting a Protocol of Signature for the PCIJ Statute that permitted non–League members to ratify the latter without joining the League was insufficient to induce the U.S. Senate to give its advice and consent to the Protocol on terms that could ever prove acceptable to its contracting parties.[71] Indeed, the PCIJ Statute had been drafted for the express purpose of enabling the United States to participate in the world court even if it did not join the League.[72] But to no avail.

Opponents of the League of Nations argued that the PCIJ was not a "world court" but rather the "League's court." Also, both proponents of and opponents to the League saw America's participation in the Court as paving the way for its eventual entry into the League. The Court was viewed by many as the "backdoor" to the League.

In regard to the League of Nations itself, many members of the U.S. international legal community favored U.S. participation because they perceived the League to be the ultimate culmination of the pre–World War I legalist war-prevention program for world politics that they had pioneered from the time of the First Hague Peace Conference. On the other hand, a strong minority of American international lawyers opposed U.S. membership in the League on the ground that article 10 of the Covenant guaranteed the existence of an essentially unjust European status quo in favor of France against Germany.[73] But the overwhelming majority of the U.S. international legal community was united in its enthusiastic support for U.S. participation in the PCIJ even if the nation did not join the League.[74] Moore, for example, accepted the PCIJ judgeship even though he opposed U.S. membership in the League.[75] Of course, a few American legalists vigorously opposed both the League and the Court.[76]

## PCIJ versus ICJ

The membership of the United States in the World Court and in some "league to enforce the peace" would occur only after, and as a direct result of, the tragic experience of the Second World War. At the San Francisco Conference of 1945, the drafters of the United Nations Charter decided to establish the International Court of Justice as one of the six "principal organs" of the United Nations under article 7. And the Statute of the International Court of Justice became an "integral part" of the United Nations Charter under article 92. Hence, member states of the United Nations would automatically become parties to the ICJ Statute, thus indissolubly linking the two institutions. It would not be possible for a state to join the United Nations without also joining the ICJ system. Indeed, article 92 of the Charter designated the International Court of Justice as the "principal judicial organ" of the United Nations.

By comparison, the PCIJ Statute was not an integral part of the League Covenant. A state could join the League without joining the Court, and vice versa. To be sure, however, the jurisdiction of the World Court would remain as voluntary under article 36 of the ICJ Statute as it was under article 36 of the PCIJ Statute.

The Statute of the International Court of Justice is similar to the Revised Statute of the Permanent Court of International Justice of 1929, which went into effect in 1936.[77] The ICJ Statute also established some degree of formal continuity between the two institutions. Article 37 thereof provides that whenever a treaty or convention in force provides for reference of a matter to a tribunal to have been instituted by the League of Nations, or to the Permanent Court of International Justice, the matter shall, as between the parties to the ICJ Statute, be referred to the International Court of Justice. Likewise, ICJ Statute article 36 (5) provides that the above-mentioned Declarations made under the optional clause of article 36 of the Statute of the Permanent Court of International Justice that are still in force shall be deemed acceptances of the compulsory jurisdiction of the International Court of Justice for the period which they still have to run in accordance with their terms as between parties to the ICJ Statute.

Indeed, today the International Court of Justice routinely refers to and relies on decisions taken by the Permanent Court of International Justice for their precedential significance. Nevertheless, for obvious political reasons, the United Nations Organization as a whole was never deemed to be the formal successor-in-law to the failed League of Nations. In 1946 the League Assembly simply dissolved itself and the Permanent Court of International Justice, and transferred its archives and property to the United Nations Organization.[78]

## Conclusion

From 1898 to 1922, American international lawyers perspicuously envisioned the need for, and championed the cause of, building institutions for the avoidance and management of international conflicts and disputes. It was certainly not their fault that the habitually cantankerous U.S. Senate refused to implement the constituent elements of the U.S. international law community's war-prevention program for world politics that were embodied in the Covenant of the League of Nations and the Protocol of Signature for the Statute of the Permanent Court of International Justice. Had the Senate cooperated in these efforts, the Second World War might not have occurred. In any event, the lineal successors to these two early U.S. legalist institutions—the United Nations and the International Court of Justice—have been substantially responsible for maintaining order, peace, justice, security, and prosperity in the world since 1945.

The third element of the turn-of-the-century U.S. legalist approach to international relations was the codification of customary international law. No point would be served here by attempting to detail the efforts to codify customary international law on a day-by-day, subject-by-subject basis at the First and Second Hague Peace Conferences; that task has been thoroughly documented elsewhere.[1] Rather, this chapter will select for analysis one particular area of customary international law (i.e., the laws of war at sea) for extended discussion because of the interconnection between their attempted codification and the establishment of an international institution (i.e., the International Prize Court). Instead of focusing on the rather dry subject of how international law is actually codified on a daily basis,[2] we will examine this process by reference to the efforts by the world community to create an international institution for the administration and regulation of this body of codified law. In other words, this chapter will analyze an early attempt by the world community to actually construct an international "regime" for this functional area of international relations.

Later, in chapter 8, I will analyze the codification of the customary international laws of neutrality during land and sea warfare at the Second Hague Peace Conference in 1907. I will then explore the attempts by the United States government to apply and enforce these rules on neutrality and maritime warfare after the outbreak of the First World War while America remained neutral. Chapter 8 will conclude with the argument that the U.S. government eventually entered into the First World War precisely in order to uphold these customary international laws of neutrality as well as of sea warfare that had been codified into positive treaty form.

*The Codification of Rules for Land Warfare*
When discussing the codification of customary international law, brief reference must be made to the monumental efforts by both the First and the Second Hague Peace Conferences to codify the international laws applicable to land warfare found in Hague Convention Number 2 with Respect to the Laws and Customs of War on Land of 1899 and its successor, Hague Convention Number 4 Respecting the Laws and Customs of War on Land of 1907, together with their annexed Regulations.[3] These so-called Hague Regulations constituted the bulk of the international legal rules on land warfare that were applicable during the First and the Second World Wars.

These Hague codifications of the laws of war on land traced their origins back directly to the Instructions for the Government of Armies of the United States in the Field prepared by Dr. Francis Lieber, a professor at Columbia College in New York during the American Civil War, that were promulgated by President Lincoln on April 24, 1863, as General Orders Number 100.[4] The so-called Lieber Code represented the first codification of the customary laws of war. The Lieber Code was the basis for the work on the laws of war at the Brussels Conference in 1874, which in turn was the basis for the Conventions on Land Warfare of 1899 and 1907 of the two Hague Peace Conferences.[5]

The 1899 Hague Convention on Land Warfare was ratified and adhered to by all the belligerents in the First World War, which were thus strictly bound to obey its rules.[6] Technically speaking, however, the Hague Peace Convention's 1907 revision did not formally apply to any of the belligerents during the First World War because several were not contracting parties to this treaty, which expressly provided in article 2 that all belligerents must likewise be parties to the convention—the so-called general participation clause.[7] Nevertheless, most of the provisions of the 1907 convention were found in the 1899 convention, which was binding. Furthermore, most of the provisions of the 1907 convention were deemed to be declaratory of customary international law and thus binding in any event.[8] As such, the Hague rules on land warfare were generally adhered to by the belligerents during the course of the First World War.

Of course, the gross deficiencies of the Hague rules on land warfare—especially for the protection of civilian populations—were tragically demonstrated for the entire world to see during the Second World War as well as before the international military tribunals at Nuremberg and Tokyo. As a result of this terrible experience, the world community of states would agree to supplement the Hague Regulations by means of adopting the Four Geneva Conventions in 1949[9] and, later, for somewhat similar reasons, their two Additional Protocols in 1977.[10] These interconnected treaties, which codify the customary international laws of warfare as well as of international humanitarian law, constitute a distinct subregime that is "nested" within the overall regime of international law and organizations concerning the threat and use of force that is still in existence today.

Finally, for the sake of completeness, and technically speaking, none of the other conventions concluded at the Second Hague Peace Conference that dealt with various components of the rules for the conduct of sea warfare formally applied as such to the belligerents during the First World War because these treaties contained general participation clauses that expressly precluded their applicability unless all belligerents were parties to the respective convention, which was not the case for any of these treaties: Number 6 on the Status of Enemy Merchant Ships at the Outbreak of Hostilities, Number 7 on the Conversion of Merchant Vessels into War-Ships, Number 8 on the Laying of Automatic Submarine Contact Mines, Number 9 Concerning Naval Bombardments, Number 10 for the Adaptation to Naval Warfare of the Principles of the Geneva Convention, Number 11 on Certain Restrictions upon the Right of Capture in Naval Warfare, and Number 13 on the Rights and Duties of Neutral Powers in Naval Warfare.[11] Nevertheless, many of the rules set forth in these conventions were deemed to constitute customary international law. As such, the First World War belligerents were bound to adhere to these rules.

In any event, the comprehensive subregime of conventions and rules for the conduct of both land and sea warfare created by the First and the Second Hague Peace Conferences constituted a seminal source for perceptions of legality and illegality, right and wrong, and good and evil on the part of governmental decision makers throughout the First World War, and especially within neutral powers such as the United States. Their perceptions in turn conditioned their responses to the Great War as it developed over time and in intensity. As established below, it was Germany's wanton and gross disregard of this subregime that would finally propel the United States into the war on the side of the Triple Entente, for the expressed purpose of upholding and vindicating the rule of international law. This proved to be the ultimate and definitive "sanction" for international law in general and its subregime on land and sea warfare in particular.

## Codification and the World Court
At the turn of the century, American lawyers generally believed that any viable scheme for the creation of some international court of justice required the contemporaneous codification of international law, because

states would be less willing to submit their disputes to judicial resolution so long as the European system of public international law remained primarily one of customary law instead of conventional law.[12] In this regard, the codification of customary international law was also necessitated by the fact that a majority of judges on any international court would undoubtedly be trained in the Continental tradition, which varied significantly from the Anglo-American heritage in numerous important respects. This unavoidable arrangement created a significant risk that the minority of judges from Anglo-American common-law countries might be consistently outvoted in court decisions attempting to settle disputed principles of customary international law.

Without preexisting codifications for the various subjects of customary international law, the anticipated principle of majority rule on any international court might predetermine the inevitable demise of the distinctively Anglo-American practices. This in turn could produce a subtle transformation in the international political, economic, and military status quo to the substantial benefit of Continental states at the direct expense of the United States and Great Britain. The progressive codification of customary international law was therefore deemed essential in order to mitigate the consequences of such an imbalance in the composition of an international court, and thus to encourage the evolution of institutions for the peaceful settlement of international disputes from the relatively primitive level of arbitration to the supposedly more advanced and effective stage of adjudication.

## The International Prize Court

Some of the theoretical and practical problems concerning the codification of customary international law, its crucial importance for the promotion of international adjudication, its relationship to the creation of an international institution, and the establishment of an international "regime" are illustrated by the unfortunate history of the aborted International Prize Court. This project was launched at the Second Hague Peace Conference by Great Britain and Germany with the active support of the U.S. government.[13] Indeed, at the time, one of the principal achievements of the Second Hague Peace Conference was deemed to have been its adoption of Convention Number 12 Relative to the Creation of an International Prize Court (IPC).[14]

The IPC would adjudicate appeals from decisions by national prize courts of belligerent captors of neutral and enemy property involving application of the intricate and, in places, unsettled and hotly disputed rules of international law applicable to maritime warfare. The Prize Court was intended to eliminate a chief cause for serious friction between neutrals and belligerents that might impel the former to enter the war in order to prosecute their rights against the latter—just as the United States had done against Great Britain in the War of 1812. The IPC was designed to limit the scope of an ongoing war through the techniques, principles, and institutions of international law.

Alternatively, with the failure of the U.S. proposal at the Second Hague Peace Conference for the creation of an actual world court (i.e., the Court of Arbitral Justice), the United States viewed a successfully established Prize Court as an intermediate means for the formation of an international court of justice. As was noted above, this could be accomplished through the simple expedient of subsequently vesting an extant International Prize Court with the jurisdiction and procedures of the proposed Court of Arbitral Justice in order to empower the IPC to adjudicate disputes between consenting states arising during peacetime. In either event, realization of the plan for the International Prize Court would have constituted the first step toward the creation of an international court of justice, and thus in the progressive evolution of international dispute-settlement techniques from the supposedly flawed "political" stage of arbitration to the presumably superior "legal" stage of adjudication.[15]

## IPC Organization

The Prize Court was intended to be a permanent standing tribunal consisting of fifteen judges appointed by the contracting powers for a term of six years, with judges appointed by the eight great naval powers (Germany, United States, Austria-Hungary, Great Britain, France, Italy, Japan, and Russia) "always summoned to sit" on the court, and the other seven positions rotating among judges appointed by the remaining signatories according to their maritime interests, although during wartime each belligerent would be represented by an appointee (arts. 14, 15, and 16). Pursuant to article 3 of the convention, judgments of national prize courts could be brought before the IPC when they affected the property of a neutral state or individual, or affected an enemy ship captured in the territorial waters of a neutral state when not made the subject of a diplomatic claim by the latter, or affected enemy property when a claim alleged the seizure to be in violation of a treaty between the belligerents or an enactment by a belligerent captor. The appeal against the national prize court's judgment could be based on the ground that it was erroneous either in fact or in law.

When the International Prize Court had jurisdiction under article 3, the national courts could not deal with a case in more than two instances.

The municipal law of the belligerent captor would decide whether the case could be brought before the court after judgment had been given in the first instance or only after an appeal. If the national courts failed to give a final judgment within two years from the date of capture, the case could be carried directly to the IPC (art. 6).

A belligerent government could not bring suit before the International Prize Court. But pursuant to articles 4 and 5 of the convention, an appeal could be brought by a neutral state if the national prize court judgment injuriously affected its property or that of its nationals, or if the capture of an enemy vessel was alleged to have occurred within its territorial waters; by a neutral individual if the national prize court judgment injuriously affected his property, subject to the reservation that his national government could forbid him to bring the case before the court or undertake the proceedings in his place; by the subject or citizen of an enemy state if the national prize court judgment injuriously affected his property on board a neutral ship or when the seizure was alleged to be in violation of a treaty between the belligerents or an enactment by the belligerent captor; and by persons belonging either to neutral states or to the enemy deriving their rights from and entitled to represent an individual qualified to appeal who had taken part in the proceedings before the national court, or persons who derived their rights from and were entitled to represent a neutral power whose property was the subject of the decision.[16] Article 51 made it clear, however, that an appeal to the International Prize Court could be brought only by a contracting power or the subject or citizen of a contracting power, or when both the owner and the person entitled to represent him were equally contracting powers or the subjects or citizens of contracting powers.

## The Individual as a Subject of International Law

Thus, one novel and innovative feature of the convention, proposed by Germany,[17] was the grant of standing to bring suit in the International Prize Court to both neutral and enemy individuals, albeit under well-defined circumstances. The creation of this right of individuals to appear before an international tribunal on their own behalf represented a radical departure from the reigning international legal positivist doctrine that only states could properly be considered the subjects of public international law endowed with international legal personality, and therefore that individuals were merely objects of international law.[18] At the Second Hague Peace Conference, the inalienable rights of human beings were accorded a preliminary foothold in the principles of international law and in the procedures of international tribunals.[19]

## U.S. Constitutional Concerns

As far as the United States was concerned, the possibility of direct appeal to the International Prize Court of a decision by its Supreme Court—which sits as America's highest prize court—raised questions as to the constitutionality of the Prize Court Convention under Article III of the U.S. Constitution.[20] Although debatable,[21] at the suggestion of Elihu Root, this objection was disposed of in 1910 by the adoption of an additional protocol to the convention providing that in the event of such constitutional difficulties, a contracting party can only be proceeded against in the IPC by a de novo action for compensation, thus in such instances eliminating the remedy of restitution set forth in article 8 of the convention as well as all other vestiges of an appellate nature.[22] Otherwise the United States was willing to follow the lead of Great Britain, the greatest naval power in the world at that time, in the ratification of the Prize Court Convention and the codification of the customary international law of prize.

Pursuant to article 7 of the convention, in the absence of a treaty the Prize Court was to apply "the rules of international law"; if no generally recognized rule existed, the court was ordered to give judgment in accordance with "the general principles of justice and equity." Due to the composition of the court, the Anglo-American judges would be in a minority, and therefore the United States and Great Britain ran a substantial risk that the Anglo-American viewpoint on certain aspects of the law of prize would be replaced by the Continental tradition. Hence, Great Britain adamantly insisted that the international law of prize first be codified into positive treaty form before it would ratify the Prize Court Convention.[23]

## The Declaration of London

After the Second Hague Peace Conference failed to codify the law of maritime warfare, Great Britain summoned a conference of representatives of the major maritime powers of the world (Germany, United States, Austria-Hungary, Spain, France, Great Britain, Italy, Japan, The Netherlands, and Russia) to meet in London toward the end of 1908 in order to determine the generally recognized principles of international law referred to in article 7 of the Prize Court Convention.[24] This meeting resulted in the 1909 Declaration of London Concerning the Laws of Naval War.[25] The Declaration of London built on the foundations established by an informal compromise on the codification of maritime warfare that had been worked out, but not adopted, at the Second Hague Peace Conference with regard to the rules concerning contraband, continuous voyage, and blockade.[26]

The Prize Court Convention, its additional protocol, and the Declaration of London all received the advice and consent of the U.S. Senate.[27] In his capacity as senator from the state of New York, Elihu Root would play a leading role in obtaining the Senate's assent to these three treaties.[28] Senate approval was readily forthcoming because a functioning International Prize Court regime would greatly benefit states, such as the United States, that anticipated being neutral in the event of another general war in Europe.

But the U.S. government was unwilling to deposit its instrument of ratification without the cooperation of Great Britain. This was never forthcoming because the British preferred to consider certain provisions and lacunae in the Declaration with reference to their potential bearing on some future naval war with Germany instead of on their merits alone as a reasonable amalgam of compromises between competing Anglo-American and Continental practices concerning various aspects of the doctrines of blockade, contraband, continuous voyage, the destruction of prizes, unneutral service, etc.[29]

Of special concern to the British was the failure of the Declaration of London to deal with the question of whether merchant ships could lawfully be converted into warships on the high seas. This issue had been previously dodged in the Second Hague Peace Conference's convention regarding the conversion of merchant ships into warships.[30] The British stridently refused to recognize a state's unrestricted right to convert merchant vessels into ships of war on the high seas for reasons of pure military expedience.[31] Of course, Great Britain had the greatest fleet of warships in the world at that time.

Even more objectionable to British public opinion was article 24 of the Declaration, which classified foodstuffs as conditional contraband, which under article 33 was liable to capture if shown to be destined for the use of the armed forces or of a government department of an enemy state.[32] The Declaration's failure to classify foodstuffs as free goods not subject to confiscation under article 28 arguably threatened to jeopardize the vital flow of foreign foodstuffs to the non-self-sufficient and isolated British Isles during wartime. Opponents of the Declaration successfully exploited the specter of mass starvation to defeat its ratification by Great Britain.

### The Naval Prize Bill

Thus, the Naval Prize Bill of 1911, purporting to amend English law relative to naval prizes of war so as to enable Britain to participate in the International Prize Court Convention, passed in the British House of Commons but failed in the House of Lords because of public opposition.[33] Since there was no point in proceeding with either the IPC or the Declaration of London without Britain, neither project subsequently came into effect of its own accord. This defeat also doomed the U.S. proposal to vest the International Prize Court with the powers and functions of the proposed Court of Arbitral Justice as well as the aforementioned four-power proposal to create the CAJ among a limited number of states on the basis of the IPC's rotational system for the appointment of judges.

Nevertheless, a preliminary provision to the Declaration of London stated that the signatory powers agreed that the rules set forth therein "correspond in substance with the generally recognized principles of international law."[34] This provision created the potential for belligerents in some future naval war to apply the rules enunciated in the Declaration by virtue of their generally recognized status as customary international law for the conduct of maritime warfare. For example, the provisions of the Declaration of London were voluntarily applied by Italy and Turkey to naval operations during their war of 1911, even though the former was a signatory that had not ratified and the latter was neither a signatory nor an adherent. An Italian royal decree required observance of the Declaration so far as consistent with Italian law. And Turkey, under pressure from Russia, stated that it intended to comply with the Declaration's provisions.[35]

### The Declaration of London and the First World War

In a similar vein, the U.S. government revised its Naval War Code in 1912 to correspond with the Declaration of London.[36] Likewise, in 1913, the British Admiralty espoused the Declaration of London as the heart of its new naval prize manual.[37] This was excellent evidence for establishing the proposition that these two governments, inter alia, considered the rules for sea warfare set forth in the Declaration to constitute customary international law (i.e., the *opinio juris*). With such weighty imprimaturs, it was not surprising that at the beginning of the First World War the Declaration of London was generally considered to constitute the most authoritative enunciation of the laws of war at sea as they stood in 1914.[38]

Thus, shortly after the outbreak of the war, the neutral U.S. government formally suggested to the belligerents that they agree to apply the laws of naval warfare set forth in the Declaration of London on condition of reciprocity in order to "prevent grave misunderstandings which may arise as to the relations between belligerent and neutral powers."[39] Germany and Austria-Hungary then agreed to promulgate the Declaration and to be bound by its provisions on condition of reciprocity by the other belligerents.[40] The Central Powers believed that an application of the Declaration's rules would favor them.[41] On the other hand, Great Britain, and following its lead Russia and France, agreed to promulgate the Declaration of London "subject to certain modifications and additions which they judge indispensable to the efficient conduct of their naval operations."[42]

The British qualifications to the Declaration of London were so severe as to prompt the U.S. government to rescind its original suggestion as to the Declaration's applicability and instead to insist on America's rights and duties under the existing rules of international law and treaties of the United States, irrespective of the Declaration of London, for the duration of the war.[43] Earning special opprobrium from the United States was the British application of the doctrine of continuous voyage to conditional contraband—at first American foodstuffs, then shortly thereafter American raw materials—in violation of article 35 of the Declaration and in contradiction to the prewar British concern that foodstuffs should be treated as free goods.[44] Somewhat ironically, it was Britain's insistence on the latter principle that resulted in the defeat of the Declaration of London, and thus the International Prize Court Convention, in the British House of Lords.[45]

The belligerents continued to apply their municipally incorporated versions of the Declaration of London for almost two years.[46] As the ferocity of the conflict intensified, however, both sides progressively adopted maritime warfare practices that flagrantly contradicted even the most elementary principles of law set forth in the Declaration of London. These practices created a vicious cycle of violations, reprisals, and counterreprisals that spiraled into a gross pattern of illegality in regard to the humanitarian laws of armed conflict and the rights of neutral states.[47] Eventually, in July 1916, the British and French governments announced their intention to withdraw from their earlier selective adherence to the provisions of the Declaration of London for reasons of pure military expedience, and thereafter to exercise their belligerent rights in accordance with existing international conventions on the laws of war and with the "law of nations."[48] The Declaration of London was alleged to have become a "dead letter" for the remainder of the war.[49]

## U.S. Intervention into the War

This fairly negative contemporaneous assessment as to the ultimate legal nullity of the Declaration of London should, in retrospect, be properly qualified to apply only in a technical legal positivist sense. For the principles of the Declaration were to serve as a bulwark for the definitional framework of international legal rules surrounding the conduct of hostilities by belligerents during the First World War. These rules of law provided a fountainhead for the generation of conceptions of legality and illegality, right and wrong, just and unjust through which neutral states—and especially the United States—perceived the unfolding of events and on which they ultimately decided whether or not to enter the war, and on whose side.[50]

For example, it was generally believed within the United States that the quality and quantity of violations against its neutral rights—set forth in part in the rules of the Declaration of London—committed by the Allied Powers were of a nature and purpose materially different from and far less heinous than those perpetrated by the Central Powers: i.e., deliberate destruction of property versus deliberate destruction of life and property.[51] Of decisive impact on U.S. public opinion and governmental decision making was Germany's wanton and indiscriminate destruction of innocent human life (American, neutral, and enemy civilian) by its policy of "unrestricted" submarine warfare against merchant vessels and passenger ships.[52]

This policy commenced with Germany's imposition of a "war zone" in the waters surrounding England and Ireland, including the entire English Channel, on February 4, 1915. Germany did not as yet assert any intention to destroy neutral ships, but it did warn of the serious dangers the latter might encounter by traversing the proscribed seas, especially in light of the British practice of misusing neutral flags.[53] The policy culminated two years later with the announcement by the German government that from February 1, 1917, all sea traffic, including neutral ships, would be stopped with every available weapon and without further notice in designated blockade zones around Great Britain, France, and Italy, and in the eastern Mediterranean.[54] Such behavior was in express violation of several provisions of the Declaration of London[55] that were generally considered not only to state the customary international law of maritime warfare but, moreover, to embody rudimentary norms of humanitarian conduct for any civilized nation.[56]

Of special concern to the U.S. government were articles 48, 49, and 50, which specifically dealt with the destruction of neutral prizes in the following language:

> Chapter IV. Destruction of neutral prizes
>
> Article 48. A neutral vessel which has been captured may not be destroyed by the captor; she must be taken into such port as is proper for the determination there of all questions concerning the validity of the capture.
>
> Article 49. As an exception, a neutral vessel which has been captured by a belligerent warship, and which would be liable to condemnation, may be destroyed if the observance of Article 48 would involve danger to the safety of the warship or to the success of the operations in which she is engaged at the time.

Article 50. Before the vessel is destroyed all persons on board must be placed in safety, and all the ship's papers and other documents which the parties interested consider relevant for the purpose of deciding on the validity of the capture must be taken on board the warship.

Quite obviously, Germany's unrestricted submarine warfare policy would be completely incompatible with these provisions of the Declaration of London, inter alia.

## Unrestricted Submarine Warfare

Tactically, German submarine warfare could only partially compensate for the surface naval supremacy of Great Britain and its allies, who were then quite successfully imposing an economic stranglehold on all neutral commerce that could possibly be destined for Germany and its allies. It was extremely dangerous for a German submarine to forgo the security afforded by undetected submersion in order to surface and comply with the rules for interdiction of merchant vessels suspected of transporting contraband that were applicable to surface warships as set forth in the Declaration of London. Indeed, it had become standard British practice to arm its merchant vessels and passenger ships with "defensive" weapons that were more than sufficient to destroy a thin-hulled submarine should it surface,[57] and also to fly neutral flags on British merchant vessels in order to deceive enemy submarine commanders.[58] Under these circumstances, application of the laws of maritime warfare as prescribed in the Declaration of London by German submarines would have essentially precluded submarine warfare for most practical purposes, and thus have provided Great Britain and its allies with a virtually uninterrupted stream of military and commercial products purchased from merchants in neutral states—most particularly from the United States—for the duration of the war.

Legally, of course, the German government justified its imposition of the war zone decree as a legitimate measure of retaliation for the grievous and repeated British violations of the Declaration of London and the generally recognized rules of international law, both of which Germany alleged it had been strictly obeying.[59] In addition, Germany complained that the neutral powers had been either unable or unwilling to exert enough pressure on Great Britain to secure its compliance with the customary and conventional laws of maritime warfare and neutrality in order to guarantee the continuation of their nationals' recognized right to trade with Germany and its allies.[60] The neutral states' collective failure to effectively prosecute their rights against Great Britain—or, in the alternative, their refusal to at least diminish proportionately the free flow of weapons, munitions, and supplies to Britain by their own merchants—worked to the substantial military and economic detriment of Germany.

### "Warfare against Mankind"

Notwithstanding the validity of these German objections, as far as U.S. public and governmental opinion was concerned, if submarines could not be effectively utilized without violating international law, then Germany should jettison its submarines, not the humanitarian laws of maritime warfare.[61] Germany's persistent refusal to relent and its consequent sinking of merchant ships and ocean liners with large loss of innocent human lives directly precipitated the U.S. decision to intervene against Germany[62] and later Austria-Hungary,[63] which had endorsed the German practices. As President Woodrow Wilson phrased it in his April 2, 1917, request to a joint session of Congress for a declaration of war against Germany:[64] "The present German submarine warfare against commerce is a warfare against mankind."[65] America's decision to abandon its neutrality and enter the war ineluctably spelled defeat for the Central Powers. It proved to be the definitive and most effective "sanction" for Germany's violation of the Declaration of London.

Indeed, that was exactly how the European system of public international law was supposed to operate before the foundation of the League of Nations. Resort to warfare by one state against another was universally considered to constitute the ultimate sanction for the transgressor's gross and repeated violations of the victim's international legal rights. With the benefit of sufficient historical hindsight, therefore, it can be determined that the laws of war at sea as codified from the Second Hague Peace Conference through the London Naval Conference were anything but a "dead letter" as far as the First World War was concerned. The United States ultimately fought in the Great War precisely to vindicate the customary and conventional international laws of maritime warfare and neutrality.[66]

### Conclusion

The international community did not succeed at its appointed task of creating an international regime to regulate maritime warfare before the Great War primarily because of British objections on grounds that were eventually reversed during the course of the war. This case study tends to substantiate the proposition that great powers should not oppose the creation of an international regime for some functional area of international relations during peacetime because of their necessarily shortsighted prognostications about what their policies might be during some future war. It would be far better to construct the international regime in the hope and expectation of preventing, limiting, and ameliorating any war or conflict.

History has repeatedly shown that governmental policies based on the assumption of war become self-fulfilling prophecies. Conversely, however, governmental policies based on the avoidance and limitation of warfare can also become self-fulfilling prophecies. All international regimes start out with defects, deficiencies, and problems. But over time they can take on lives of their own that transcend their original limitations.

In specific reference to the contemporary law of the sea, the Reagan administration was tragically shortsighted in its rejection of the 1982 UN Convention on the Law of the Sea for primarily ideological reasons. Irrespective of the alleged and questionable defects in this treaty's subregime for mining the deep seabed, the 1982 Law of the Sea Convention sought to build a new international regime that would regulate almost all significant functions relating to almost three quarters of the globe's surface. The 1982 Law of the Sea Treaty is the lineal successor to the International Prize Court Convention and the Declaration of London. Yet, once again, it was the greatest naval power in the world that played the role of spoiler to the creation of an international regime dealing with the sea.

This time, however, the rest of the world moved forward despite the greatest naval power's wishes. In direct reaction thereto, the incoming Clinton administration took a second look at the Law of the Sea Convention and decided to join and support it rather than ignore and undercut it. The Clinton administration participated in the successful negotiation of an amendment to the Law of the Sea Treaty subregime for mining the deep seabed, then signed this amended Law of the Sea Treaty on July 29, 1994, and indicated that it intends to apply the agreement pending the ratification process by the U.S. Senate and president.[67] President Clinton transmitted the amended treaty to the Senate on October 7, 1994, and there it languishes as this book goes to press.[68]

Certainly the greatest naval power in the world has the greatest interest in securing and maintaining peace and stability on and below the seas. This principle held true at the start of the twentieth century, and it holds true today at the century's end. In this regard, it is curious to note that the U.S. Senate gave its advice and consent to the International Prize Court Convention, its additional protocol, and the Declaration of London in 1912. This author doubts very seriously that the U.S. Senate would be prepared to do the same thing today. Only time will tell whether the Senate will someday give its advice and consent to the UN Law of the Sea Convention as amended. Certainly the American people deserve it.

At the outset of the twentieth century, the United States was in the fore-front of the movement to create international law, organizations, institu-tions, and regimes for the preservation of international peace and security. But toward the end of this century, America has come to distrust and under-mine the international regimes that are already in existence, and to oppose the creation of new ones that it cannot control and dominate. Today, the United States prefers to trust in its own power and its own illusions, much like Great Britain did before the First World War. Although this author can-not predict the future, if history is any guide, the United States might be destined to suffer Great Britain's fate unless America reforms its realpolitik ways.[69]

# 5 Creating a New Regime for the Peaceful Settlement of International Disputes

*Arms Limitation*

Even in 1898, American legalists observed somewhat cynically that the real reason why the Russian tsar suggested a conference devoted to "the most effective means of assuring to all nations the benefits of a real and lasting peace, and of placing before all the questions of ending the progressive development of existing armaments"[1] was in order to relieve his government of the external pressures of foreign affairs and defense budgets so that the tsarist autocracy could consolidate its internal position against mounting domestic opposition.[2] The United States decided to attend the conference even though—it said—its war with Spain rendered "impracticable" the present reduction of its armaments, which in any event "even now are doubtless far below the measure which principal European powers would be willing to adopt."[3] Consequently, Secretary of State John Hay instructed the U.S. delegation to the First Hague Peace Conference to leave the initiative on the subject of arms limitation to representatives of the states for which it possessed some relevance.[4] Generally put, the U.S. delegates did not play a constructive role in the matter of arms limitation at the 1899 conference.[5]

The First Hague Peace Conference proved totally incapable of adopting any substantive measures concerning the overall limitation or reduction of armaments.[6] Germany was adamantly opposed to a moratorium of any kind on expenditures for armaments.[7] Consequently, the conference had to content itself with adopting a unanimous resolution in favor of restricting military budgets,[8] two *voeux* (wishes) that governments examine the possibility of an agreement respecting the employment of new types and calibers of rifles and naval guns,[9] and agreements limiting armed forces on land and sea, and war budgets.[10] These meager results confirmed the conventional wisdom espoused by the majority of the U.S. international legal community that serious proposals for arms limitation and disarmament would succeed only as conditions subsequent, not precedent, to the relaxation of international tensions by means of new rules of international law and new institutions for the peaceful settlement of international disputes.[11]

To that end, the First Hague Conference proffered its Convention for the Pacific Settlement of International Disputes, which instituted the Permanent Court of Arbitration and other novel rules, procedures, and institutions for this express purpose. It can thus be argued that the 1899 convention and its 1907 successor sought to create the first international regime for the peaceful settlement of international disputes in modern history. This regime would be succeeded and supplemented—though not superseded—by the League of Nations Covenant and then later by the United Nations Charter. The two Hague Conventions for the Pacific Settlement of International Disputes still play an important role today in buttressing the contemporary regime of international law and organizations for the peaceful settlement of international disputes.

## A Positive Development for International Humanitarian Law

The First Hague Peace Conference did adopt three Declarations that forbade the use of certain types of weapons, although arms control and disarmament were not their primary purpose: (1) to prohibit, for a term of five years, the launching of projectiles and explosives from balloons or by other similar new methods;[12] (2) to prohibit the use of bullets which expand or flatten easily in the human body, etc.;[13] and (3) to prohibit the use of projectiles, the only object of which is the diffusion of asphyxiating or deleterious gases.[14]

These three Declarations specifically stated that they were "inspired by the sentiments which found expression in" the Declaration of St. Petersburg of 1868, which renounced the use in warfare "of any projectile of less weight than four hundred grammes, which is explosive, or is charged with fulminating or inflammable substances."[15] In essence, the guiding purpose of the St. Petersburg Declaration was to "reconcile the necessities of war with the laws of humanity."[16] The motivating force behind the adoption of the three 1899 Hague Declarations was attributable primarily to humanitarian considerations instead of to a genuine desire to limit or reduce armaments that were viewed as militarily significant.

## At the Second Hague Peace Conference

Although the Russian government attempted to exclude the limitation of armaments from the agenda of the Second Hague Peace Conference so as not to impede its arms buildup in the aftermath of its defeat during the

Russo-Japanese War of 1904–1905, Great Britain and the United States, inter alia, insisted that the matter be considered.[17] Nevertheless, the Second Hague Peace Conference likewise failed to adopt substantive measures concerning the overall limitation of armaments.[18] On the motion of Great Britain and with the support of the United States, the conference simply confirmed the resolution of the 1899 conference in regard to the limitation of military burdens and declared that it would be "highly desirable" for governments once again to seriously examine this question.[19]

Both its 1907 Convention Relative to the Laying of Submarine Mines[20] and its 1907 Declaration Prohibiting the Discharge of Projectiles and Explosives from Balloons,[21] which was a renewal of the expired 1899 Declaration, were primarily attributable to humanitarian considerations and were not generally perceived as genuine arms control measures. The international community would make no significant progress in regard to the limitation of armaments until well after the First World War. Then, the U.S. government would undertake the initiative to convene a conference of the Principal Allied and Associated Powers (Great Britain, France, Italy, Japan, and the United States) and other states on the subject of the limitation of armaments to be held at Washington, D.C., toward the end of 1921.[22] This meeting became known as the Washington Naval Conference; its results are discussed in chapter 8.

## The Use of Poison Gas during World War I

In addition to the submarine, the other grisly instrumentality of modern warfare to rear its ugly head and shock the conscience of the "civilized world" during the First World War was poison gas. Both sets of original belligerents eventually used poisonous gases irrespective of the fact that they had all ratified without reservation the 1899 Declaration prohibiting their use,[23] though the United States was not a contracting party. For reasons previously explained, the large-scale use of poison gas during the Great War was not, however, appropriately characterized as a failure for the general principle of arms limitation and disarmament, but rather as a setback for the development of the humanitarian laws of armed conflict.

These two bodies of international law—albeit interrelated—were and are premised on fundamentally different theoretical bases and were intended to serve distinct purposes. After World War I, the Geneva Protocol of 1925 reaffirmed the 1899 prohibition on the use in war of "asphyxiating, poisonous or other gases, and of all analogous liquids, materials or devices" and extended the ban to include the use of bacteriological methods of warfare.[24] The Geneva Protocol was generally observed by all the belligerents except

Japan during the Second World War. Later, the Geneva Gas Protocol of 1925, together with the Biological Weapons Convention of 1972, constituted a separate subregime that was nested within the overall international regime regulating the threat and use of force in contemporary international relations.[25] To this subregime must now be added the Convention on the Prohibition of the Development, Production, Stockpiling and Use of Chemical Weapons and on Their Destruction, which was ratified by the United States on April 25, 1997, and entered into force on April 29, 1997.

## Good Offices and Mediation

In addition to creating the Permanent Court of Arbitration, the 1899 Convention for the Pacific Settlement of International Disputes also established the modern practice of third parties offering their good offices and mediation to two states in conflict in order to achieve a pacific settlement of the dispute. Article 2 thereof provided that in case of serious disagreement or conflict, before an appeal to arms, the contracting powers agreed to have recourse, "as far as circumstances allow," to the good offices or mediation of one or more friendly powers.[26] Article 3 established the right of states not parties to the dispute, "on their own initiative, and as far as circumstances may allow, [to] offer their good offices or mediation to the States at variance."[27] This right could be exercised by third parties even during the course of ongoing hostilities, when the tide of battle was turning against a belligerent.

Most important, the exercise of this right could not be regarded by one of the states in conflict as an unfriendly act of intervention. Before this convention was established, a neutral state interested in peacemaking always ran that risk, and it constituted a significant deterrent to outside efforts to prevent or stop wars. However, article 7 provided that the acceptance of mediation could not, unless there was an agreement to the contrary, interrupt, delay, or hinder mobilization or other measures of preparation for war. And if mediation occurred after the commencement of hostilities, it would not interrupt the military operations in progress, unless there was an agreement to the contrary.

Article 8 was the brainchild of Frederick W. Holls, an international lawyer who was a member of the U.S. delegation to the First Hague Peace Conference.[28] It created a procedure for special mediation modeled on the choice of seconds by individuals about to engage in a private duel. The states at variance would each choose a power to which they would respectively entrust the mission of entering into direct communication with the power chosen by the other side for the purpose of preventing the rupture of pacific relations. For the period of this mandate, which could not exceed thirty days unless otherwise agreed, the states in conflict would cease all direct communication on the subject of the dispute, leaving it exclusively to the mediating powers. In case of a definite rupture of pacific relations, the mediating powers were charged with the joint task of taking advantage of any opportunity for peace.[29]

These Hague provisions for the peaceful settlement of international disputes were to bear fruit when President Theodore Roosevelt offered his good offices and mediation to Russia and Japan during their war of 1904–05.[30] Thereafter, representatives of both belligerents met in the United States and concluded the so-called Peace of Portsmouth on September 5, 1905, terminating the war on terms favorable to Japan, the military victor.[31] For the success of his initiative, Roosevelt was awarded the Nobel Peace Prize for 1906.[32]

### International Commissions of Inquiry

Title III of the 1899 Convention for the Pacific Settlement of International Disputes[33] created a voluntary procedure for the formation of international commissions of inquiry to investigate, ascertain, and report on international differences involving neither honor nor vital interests, and arising from disputed points of fact that could not be settled by means of diplomacy (art. 9). International commissions of inquiry were to be constituted by a special agreement between the parties in conflict, which would define the facts to be examined and the extent of the commissioners' powers (art. 10). Unless otherwise stipulated, the international commissions of inquiry were formed in the manner fixed by article 32 of the 1899 convention, which specified the procedure to be used for the constitution of a tribunal from the Permanent Court of Arbitration.

The parties in dispute were obligated to cooperate with the commission "as fully as they may think possible" (art. 12). On completion of its investigation, the commission would communicate a report signed by all its members to the parties in dispute (art. 13). The report was limited to a statement of the facts and in no way possessed the character of an arbitral award (art. 14), and it left the conflicting parties entire freedom of action as to the effect to be given to it (art. 14). Nevertheless, the theory behind the procedure was that once the facts had been impartially ascertained, authenticated, and communicated to the parties in dispute, a pacific settlement of the conflict on the basis of the commission's report should be readily forthcoming.

### The Dogger Bank Incident

At the suggestion of France, an international commission of inquiry was successfully employed to resolve the Dogger Bank controversy between

Great Britain and Russia, which arose out of the Russo-Japanese War.[34] In this case, the Russian Baltic fleet, on its way to the Pacific, fired on British fishing vessels in the North Sea, killing two fishermen, injuring others, and causing substantial property damage. Nonresolution of this dispute could have resulted in a very serious conflict, if not war, between the parties.[35] The successful resolution of the Dogger Bank incident in favor of Britain by an international commission of inquiry demonstrated to the entire international community that even disputes between great powers concerning their honor and vital interests could be subjected to some procedure for their peaceful settlement.[36] This experience led the Second Hague Peace Conference to revise the 1899 Convention for the Pacific Settlement of International Disputes in order to improve and expand on the operating procedures for international commissions of inquiry. Twenty-two additional articles on this subject were added to the 1907 convention.[37]

Hence, two new procedures for the peaceful settlement of international differences that had been instituted by the First Hague Peace Conference proved their usefulness during the Russo-Japanese War. Prior to the First World War, two other international commissions of inquiry were organized under the terms of the Hague Conventions, each charged with investigating a wartime incident between a belligerent and a neutral state.[38] Likewise, mechanisms for the creation of international commissions of inquiry to promote the peaceful settlement of international disputes later constituted the centerpiece of the so-called Bryan peace treaties, which are analyzed in chapter 8. This device was also to figure prominently in article 15 of the Covenant of the League of Nations, which enabled the Council and the Assembly to discharge the functions of an international commission of inquiry in the event of a dispute "likely to lead to a rupture" between members that was not submitted to arbitration or, later, adjudication.

Eventually, United Nations Charter article 34 gave the Security Council the expansive power to "investigate any dispute, or any situation which might lead to international friction or give rise to a dispute, in order to determine whether the continuance of the dispute or situation is likely to endanger the maintenance of international peace and security." Such a determination could then lead to "enforcement action" by the Security Council under the terms of Chapter VII of the Charter. So the Security Council has the authority to investigate even a "situation" and to act effectively in order to prevent it from becoming a "dispute."

## Convention on the Opening of Hostilities

Another major substantive and procedural innovation concerning international disputes that was instituted by the Second Hague Peace Conference was its 1907 Convention Relative to the Opening of Hostilities.[39] Consistent with the reigning philosophy of the day that war was not illegal, but rather an unfortunate fact of international life, the convention did not attempt to regulate the reasons for going to war, but only its modalities. However, hope was expressed that the convention might create both the time and the opportunity for third states to offer their good offices or mediation to the parties in dispute, or to convince the latter to submit the matter for decision to the Permanent Court of Arbitration.[40]

The contracting parties agreed that hostilities between them would not begin without explicit notice either in the form of a reasoned declaration of war or an ultimatum with a conditional declaration of war. The state of war must be made known to neutral powers without delay and was not effective in regard to them for purposes of the laws of neutrality until they received notice or it was clearly established that they knew in fact of the state of war. The convention was intended to apply to both naval operations and land warfare.[41]

Up to the time of this convention, a declaration of war or an ultimatum that preceded the opening of hostilities was the exception, not the rule, of international belligerent practice.[42] This axiom had been demonstrated most recently by the Japanese surprise attack on the Russian naval fleet at Port Arthur in February 1904, which signaled the start of the Russo-Japanese War. That experience indicated that this convention might tend to favor a weak power over a strong one because the former usually obtains the greater relative strategic benefit from the element of surprise.

Consequently, proposals at the conference to fix a mandatory interval between delivery of the declaration or ultimatum and the commencement of hostilities failed.[43] The convention essentially left each signatory free to fix whatever interval was best suited to its own interests, even though tactically the interval would be so short as to take the enemy by surprise. Nevertheless, at the outset of the First World War, most of the major belligerents dutifully complied in good faith with the terms of this 1907 treaty.[44]

## Pearl Harbor

Indeed, despite its behavior at Port Arthur, Japan attempted to comply with the terms of the 1907 Convention on the Opening of Hostilities more than thirty-five years later, before its December 7, 1941, attack on Pearl Harbor. Japan instructed its diplomatic representatives in Washington to deliver its declaration of war on the United States shortly before the hostilities were scheduled to commence.[45] Delays in the extended transmission process from Tokyo resulted in a late delivery of the declaration.[46] So, against its wishes, the Japanese government ended up violating the terms of the convention.

The 1907 Convention on the Opening of Hostilities became a significant part of the definitional framework of international legal rules surrounding the Second World War in the bureaucratic perceptions of the U.S. government. Japan's "sneak attack" at Pearl Harbor in explicit violation of international law exerted a profound impact on American public opinion toward Japan throughout the war, as well as on the Allied governments' formulation of their ultimatum for Japan's unconditional surrender or "prompt and utter destruction" enunciated by the Potsdam Proclamation of July 26, 1945.[47] Most regrettably for all humanity, Hiroshima and Nagasaki became the ultimate "sanction" for Japan's violation of this 1907 convention.[48]

## The Cuban Missile Crisis

Certainly the most profound contribution to the maintenance of international peace and security made by the 1907 Convention on the Opening of Hostilities occurred, albeit indirectly, some fifty-five years after its adoption by the Second Hague Peace Conference. At the onset of the Cuban missile crisis in October 1962, a substantial majority of the members of the U.S. governmental decision-making team established to handle the matter (the so-called Executive Committee) believed that a "surprise surgical air strike" against Soviet missile sites in Cuba was the only viable course of conduct to take in response to Khrushchev's surreptitious emplacement of these extraordinarily dangerous and threatening weapons just a short distance off the coast of the continental United States.[49] Notification of Khrushchev or Castro prior to the bombardment was ruled out "for military or other reasons."[50]

On hearing general support for launching a surprise attack during the initial deliberations of the Executive Committee, Attorney General Robert Kennedy passed a note to his brother, the president, that said: "I now know how Tojo felt when he was planning Pearl Harbor."[51] Robert Kennedy adamantly opposed a sneak attack because it was entirely inconsistent with the moral values on which the United States was founded and was supposed to represent around the world:[52] "We spent more time on this moral question during the first five days than on any other single matter."[53] Primarily for this reason, Robert Kennedy joined ranks with Secretary of Defense Robert McNamara in advocating the imposition of a naval blockade around Cuba, followed by U.S. resort to the Organization of American States for its endorsement.[54]

One major advantage a blockade had over a surprise attack was that the former would permit the United States to present a plausible legal justification for its conduct before the Organization of American States and the United Nations in a bid to obtain their support for or at least lack of opposition to U.S. action. A sneak attack would have been legally indefensible before any international forum.[55] Eventually the blockade alternative prevailed over the surprise attack scenario, and the United States did receive the unanimous support of the OAS for its "quarantine" of Cuba.[56] In the opinion of Robert Kennedy, "the strongest argument against the all-out military attack, and one no one could answer to his satisfaction, was that a surprise attack would erode if not destroy the moral position of the United States throughout the world."[57] Solid Western hemisphere support for the arguably legal U.S. position proved to be a key factor in convincing Khrushchev to withdraw Soviet missiles and bombers from Cuba.

## A Legal-Moral Imperative

During the historical interim between the Second Hague Peace Conference and the Cuban missile crisis, the 1907 Convention on the Opening of Hostilities successfully performed a complete transposition of governmental attitudes toward the acceptability of sneak attacks as a means to signal the commencement of international hostilities. The convention had entered into the definitional framework of international legal rules from which modern governmental decision makers consciously and unconsciously derive their conceptions of legality and illegality, right and wrong, just and unjust. In this manner, the 1907 rule shaped the perceptions that conditioned the responses by U.S. governmental decision makers to the Cuban missile crisis more than fifty years later.

Unanimous and fervid American repugnance at the "treachery" of the Japanese sneak attack on Pearl Harbor in 1941 thereafter transformed the 1907 Convention on the Opening of Hostilities into a phenomenon that was far more binding, effective, and significant than any principle of international law ever could be: a legal-moral imperative. As far as the U.S. government was concerned, a rule of international law that was qualified and ambiguous at its origin had become, by virtue of time and tragic experience, an absolute legal-moral obligation that must be obeyed even during a severe international crisis when the very survival of the state itself was deemed to be at stake. As a legal-moral imperative, the rule of the 1907 convention was able to head off the initially favored "surprise surgical air strike" on Soviet missile sites in Cuba.

Of course, the 1907 Convention on the Opening of Hostilities was not primarily intended or designed to deter or forestall the outbreak of war.

But its proscription on sneak attacks indirectly contributed to the prevention of the Third, and perhaps Last, World War in October 1962 through the medium of Pearl Harbor. Hence, the 1907 Convention on the Opening of Hostilities has already proven to be a monumental contribution by the Second Hague Peace Conference to the maintenance of international peace and security in the post–World War II era.

### The Porter Convention

The final mechanism for the peaceful settlement of international disputes instituted by the Second Hague Peace Conference was the Convention Respecting the Limitation of the Employment of Force for the Recovery of Contract Debts.[58] This treaty is commonly referred to as the Porter Convention in honor of General Horace Porter, U.S. delegate to the 1907 conference, who proposed it on behalf of the U.S. government and labored strenuously to obtain its adoption.[59] Pursuant to the terms of this convention, the contracting powers agreed not to have recourse to armed force for the recovery of "contract debts"[60] claimed from the government of one country by the government of another country as being due its nationals. However, this undertaking was rendered expressly inapplicable when the debtor state refused or neglected to reply to an offer of arbitration, or, after accepting the offer, prevented any *compromis* from being agreed on, or, after the arbitration concluded, failed to submit to the award (art. 1).

Such arbitration was to be conducted in accordance with part IV, chapter III of the 1907 Convention for the Pacific Settlement of International Disputes, which pertained to the Permanent Court of Arbitration. Except as otherwise agreed by the parties, the award by the PCA would determine the validity of the claim, the amount of the debt, and the time and mode of payment (art. 2). Most significantly, however, the convention did not contain the usual reservations of vital interests, honor, independence, and the interests of third parties for such arbitrations. The U.S. government did, however, enter an "understanding" to the Porter Convention to the effect that recourse to the PCA could only be had by conclusion of a general or special *compromis* with the party in dispute.[61]

With the entry into force of the Porter Convention, creditor states had to be willing to submit their nationals' contract claims against debtor states to international arbitration. This requirement created a means whereby fraudulent, spurious, or inflated claims could be identified and denied or reduced in an impartial manner, thus deterring the undeniable abuses that had been perpetrated by the nationals of powerful creditor states. Conversely, the Porter Convention established the right of a debtor state to insist on international arbitration of contractual claims against it by citizens of foreign states. The implication was clear, however, that in the event the debtor state was unwilling to adhere to the terms of the PCA arbitral procedure, the creditor state would retain whatever freedom of action it allegedly possessed under customary international law to use force to collect on the debts.

Despite this loophole, subsequent history has proven the Porter Convention a phenomenal success. It virtually put an end to the generally tolerated practice of stronger—invariably European—creditor states threatening or using military force to collect on contract debts owed to their nationals by weaker—typically Latin American or Caribbean—debtor states. Thereafter, the only major use of force in international relations principally for the purpose of recovering on governmental debts was the occupation of the Ruhr by Belgium and France in 1923 after Germany defaulted on the payment of its First World War reparations. However, France defended this action on the grounds that it was supposedly permitted by the terms of the Treaty of Versailles.[62]

## The Drago Doctrine

The impetus behind U.S. sponsorship of the Porter Convention at the Second Hague Peace Conference came from a 1902 controversy surrounding the default on its public debts by Venezuela. Great Britain, Italy, and Germany attempted to collect their nationals' claims through the use of military force, which included the blockade of Venezuela's coastline, the capture of its fleet, and the bombardment of some forts.[63] On December 29, 1902, Luis M. Drago, the Argentine minister of foreign affairs, sent a note to Washington in which he argued that the United States should insist on the principle that the public debt of an American state could not serve as the pretext for armed intervention or military occupation of its territory by a European power.[64] This note was the genesis for the so-called Drago Doctrine to the effect that physical force cannot be used to compel the collection of public debt under any circumstances.

The Drago Doctrine was premised on the theory that nonintervention is a necessary corollary to the freedom, independence, and equality of all states in a modern system of public international law. Otherwise, recognition of such a right to intervene creates a pretext for strong states to intervene against militarily weaker states in order to establish spheres of influence or advance other imperialist enterprises. Drago also pointed out that for the United States to follow a contrary rule would be tantamount to sanctioning a violation of the Monroe Doctrine. For obvious reasons, Drago felt that the

United States had made a mistake at the Second Hague Peace Conference in pushing the Porter Convention because it effectively legalized war as a means for the collection of debts.[65]

## The Venezuelan Debt Controversy

President Roosevelt was more acutely concerned with the potential for violation of the Monroe Doctrine arising from a possible occupation of Venezuelan territory by European creditor states seeking to satisfy their nationals' debts. Unless the United States somehow rectified the situation, it could easily establish an unfortunate precedent for European creditor states' continued intervention into the turbulent political and economic affairs of debtor states in Latin America and the Caribbean. Roosevelt, therefore, decided to intervene diplomatically into the Venezuelan dispute by convincing the creditor states to allow their claims to be settled by a series of mixed commissions and to have the blockading powers present their demands for preferential treatment in the payment of debts to the PCA for arbitration, which resulted in the aforementioned *Venezuelan Preferential Case*.[66]

This peaceful resolution of the Venezuelan debt controversy created the precedent eventually enshrined in the Porter Convention that the United States successfully advocated at the Second Hague Peace Conference. Of course, the Porter Convention did not go as far as the Drago Doctrine did because the treaty did not prohibit the use of force to collect on public debts under all circumstances. Nevertheless, the Porter Convention was proclaimed a victory for U.S. foreign policy. The conclusion of a multilateral pact essentially designed to protect Latin American states from European military intervention was interpreted as an implicit recognition by all its signatories of the validity of the Monroe Doctrine as partially incarnated in this new principle of public international law.[67]

## The Third Hague Peace Conference

The fifth and final element of the American legalists' war-prevention program for world politics during the twenty-five years after the Spanish-American War was the institution of a mechanism for the periodic convocation of peace conferences among the nations of the international community for the purpose of completing, perfecting, and advancing the work of the First and Second Hague Peace Conferences. The First Hague Peace Conference was convoked on the initiative of Tsar Nicholas II of Russia. Several provisions of its Final Act contemplated the convening of a subsequent conference in order to deal with a variety of unresolved issues, but nothing specific was said concerning who had the right to initiate its convocation or when this should be done. The outbreak of the war between Japan and Russia over Manchuria in 1904 rendered it awkward, if not politically infeasible, for the tsar to assume the initiative in calling for the convocation of a second peace conference. This raised the general question of whether some other state possessed the legal right, and should undertake the political obligation, to summon another Hague peace conference in default of a Russian diplomatic initiative.

In September 1904, the Interparliamentary Union held its meeting in St. Louis, Missouri, and adopted a resolution requesting the president of the United States to sound out the states of the world concerning their willingness to attend a second peace conference.[68] Shortly thereafter, President Theodore Roosevelt undertook this initiative by issuing a circular note to that effect to the signatories of the First Hague Conference Acts.[69] The note pointed out that at the time the tsar issued his invitation in 1898, the United States and Spain had not concluded a peace treaty ending their war, and yet the First Hague Conference did not attempt to intervene in the determination of peace terms between them. Roosevelt argued that the Russo-Japanese War should likewise not interrupt the world's progress toward the realization of universal peace and that a subsequent conference would not seek to interfere with the Russo-Japanese War.

With the conclusion of that conflict, however, Tsar Nicholas asked Roosevelt to surrender the initiative for the convocation of the second conference to him, and Roosevelt readily acquiesced. The Second Hague Peace Conference commenced its deliberations on June 15, 1907.[70] The Final Act and Conventions of the Second Peace Conference were signed on October 18, 1907.

Among these documents was a recommendation that the holding of a third peace conference should take place within a period of time similar to that which had elapsed since the first conference (i.e., eight years, or in 1915), on a date to be set by joint agreement among the powers.[71] The Final Act also stated that it would be desirable that a preliminary committee be charged by the governments, about two years before the probable date of the meeting, with the duty of collecting various propositions to be considered by the conference, to prepare a program for it, and to determine the mode of organization and the procedure for the third conference.[72] U.S. legalists argued that the language of the Second Hague Peace Conference's Final Act concerning a third conference was specific enough to indicate that any state represented at the First or Second Hague Peace Conferences could undertake the initiative to convene the Third Hague Peace Conference, thus implicitly repudiating any putative claims that Russia possessed the exclusive right of priority to do so.[73] At the Second Hague Peace Conference, the U.S. delegation was in the vanguard of the movement to terminate the tsar's proprietary interest in calling for the convocation of future Hague Peace Conferences.[74]

In preparation for the Third Hague Peace Conference, the American Society of International Law decided to devote the entire program of its sixth annual meeting in April 1912 to discussing the conference's program, organization, and procedure.[75] Some of the topics considered were the conclusion of general arbitration treaties, the codification of the laws of naval warfare, the effects of war on international conventions and private contracts, the marine belt and territorial waters, and, of course, the creation of a permanent court of international justice. At this time, American international lawyers expressed a great deal of optimism that a plan for the proposed Court of Arbitral Justice could be placed into operation before the convocation of the Third Hague Peace Conference.[76]

Shortly after the conclusion of the 1912 presidential election, outgoing President Taft appointed a governmental advisory committee to consider proposals for a program for the Third Hague Peace Conference.[77] In 1913, the nineteenth annual Lake Mohonk Conference on international arbitration adopted a declaration of principles that included a recommendation that the U.S. secretary of state urge the nations of the world to form immediately the international preparatory committee for the third conference that was called for by the Final Act of the Second Hague Peace Conference.[78] At that time, however, certain countries objected to a meeting of the third conference before Great Britain had ratified the Declaration of London and the International Prize Court was established, both of which projects had been rejected by the British House of Lords in December 1911.

On January 31, 1914, Woodrow Wilson's secretary of state, William Jennings Bryan, dispatched an identical circular note to the diplomatic officers of the United States accredited to the governments that participated in the Second Hague Peace Conference suggesting that the latter entrust the duties of the international preparatory committee for a third peace conference to the Administrative Council of the Permanent Court of Arbitration at The Hague (which consisted of The Netherlands minister of foreign affairs and the diplomatic representatives of the contracting powers accredited to The Hague), and that the third conference be held in 1915.[79] In light of the various responses received from some of the powers, Bryan issued a follow-up circular note on June 22 revising his prior proposal by suggesting that the third conference meet at The Hague in June 1916, and that the duties of the international preparatory committee be entrusted to a committee to be selected from the members of the PCA Administrative Council by them-selves.[80] Shortly thereafter, on June 26, 1914, The Netherlands government invited the contracting powers that had participated in the Second Hague Peace Conference to name one member of a preparatory committee to meet in 1915 to consider the questions to be brought before the Third Hague Peace Conference.[81] Two days later, Archduke Francis Ferdinand of Austria-Hungary and his wife were assassinated at Sarajevo by a Serbian nationalist, thus precipitating the First World War.[82] The ubiquitous James Brown Scott, who had been chosen as the U.S. representative on the international prepa-ratory committee for the Third Hague Peace Conference, canceled his trip to Europe for that purpose when the war broke out.[83]

## Conclusion

This simultaneity of developments indicates the surprise and suddenness with which the First World War descended on the great powers of Europe.[84] The 1919 Paris Peace Conference to end the Great War had to serve in de-fault of the never-realized Third Hague Peace Conference.[85] Yet, the long-standing U.S. legalist objective of establishing some means for the periodic convocation of peace conferences among all nations of the international community was ultimately achieved, and indeed, far exceeded, by the cre-ation of the League of Nations.

## 6 U.S. Legalist Imperial Policy toward Latin America, the Caribbean, and the Far East

### International Law and U.S. Imperial Policy

The history of U.S. foreign policy toward international law and organizations from the Spanish-American War through the establishment of the League of Nations and the Permanent Court of International Justice would be substantially incomplete, if not materially misleading, if it did not include a brief analysis of U.S. legalist attitudes and policies toward Latin America and the Caribbean during this crucial period. To be sure, the U.S. government pioneered and promoted a war-prevention program for the Western hemisphere that essentially consisted of the same five legalist elements that constituted its contemporaneous foreign policy toward Europe: arbitration, adjudication, codification, other legalist devices for the peaceful resolution of international disputes, as well as the periodic convocation of regional conferences. Nevertheless, by the end of the nineteenth century, the material difference between U.S. foreign policies toward the Old and New Worlds, respectively, was predicated on the unavoidable historical fact that the United States had become an active participant, and the acknowledged predominant power, in Western hemisphere geopolitics. For example, in 1895 President Cleveland's secretary of state, Richard Olney, stated quite forthrightly: "Today the United States is practically sovereign on this continent, and its fiat is law upon the subjects to which it confines its interposition."[1]

As a result of its easy victory over Spain in 1898, the United States quickly came to act as if Latin America and the Caribbean constituted its rightful sphere of influence, akin to those carved out by the major European imperial colonial powers on the continents of Africa and Asia. In the Western hemisphere, the U.S. war-prevention program based on considerations of international law and organizations was confronted head-on by the political realities of U.S. imperial power and pretensions. This direct confrontation between two competing—if not antithetically opposed—ideologies for the conduct of international relations created an insoluble set of dilemmas for the U.S. foreign policy decision-making establishment.

For the next three decades, the U.S. government would try to cope with the problem of curing political and economic instability in Mexico, Central America, and the Caribbean by using the crude techniques of actual and threatened military intervention and armed occupation. This interventionist foreign policy expressly contravened the emotional sentiments, philosophical principles, and international legal conventions that the U.S. government had actively promoted for general application within the worldwide system of international relations, as well as within the separate inter-American system of international law, organizations, and institutions that it was actively seeking to create. Interventionism's ramifications have chronically plagued and hopelessly perplexed U.S. foreign policy decision making toward Latin American and Caribbean countries since that time. For the most part, it is fair to say that throughout the twentieth century, the U.S. government has attempted to create a "regime" of international law and organizations in the Western hemisphere that would consolidate, advance, and legitimate its hegemonial position in the region.

## The Monroe Doctrine

The focal point for all U.S. foreign policy toward Latin America and the Caribbean between 1898 and 1922 became the proper interpretation of the Monroe Doctrine, a policy originally designed by the U.S. government to prevent the Holy Alliance in Europe from helping Spain regain its territorial possessions in Latin America.[2] As stated by President James Monroe in his message to Congress of December 2, 1823, this doctrine proclaimed that the American continents were no longer considered by the U.S. government to be appropriate subjects for future colonization by any European powers; that the countries of Europe must not seek to extend their political systems to the Western hemisphere; that the United States would not interfere in the affairs of any current European colony or dependency in the Western hemisphere; that the United States would remain neutral in the war between Spain and the newly independent governments of South America, but not to the point of permitting a reimposition of Spanish rule; and, finally, that the United States would continue to obey the dogma of Washington's Farewell Address by preserving its neutrality in the affairs of Europe except when its rights were seriously jeopardized.[3] The so-called Polk Corollary to the Monroe Doctrine subsequently created an additional prohibition that a European power could not acquire territory in the Western hemisphere by means of cession from another European power.[4]

At the turn of the twentieth century, American international lawyers forthrightly admitted that the Monroe Doctrine had not been elevated to the level of constituting a general principle of public international law recognized by the nations of the world. Rather, the Monroe Doctrine merely professed an official statement of international political policy by the U.S. government that was tacitly respected by European states for reasons of political, diplomatic, and military expediency.[5] From the U.S. perspective, this was an advantage. The recognition of the Monroe Doctrine as a matter of policy instead of law meant that questions or disputes related to it could not properly become the subject of international arbitration or adjudication pursuant to the various obligatory arbitration treaties and dispute settlement schemes then advocated by the U.S. government.[6]

Despite its commitment to the general principle of the arbitration or adjudication of international disputes, the United States firmly avowed its intention to preserve intact its ability unilaterally to interpret and act on the Monroe Doctrine in whatever manner it deemed fit.[7] Legalists claimed this to be essential because the Monroe Doctrine was founded on the sovereign right of the U.S. government to self-defense, a prerogative that was recognized by public international law. In a system of international relations in which war was not yet outlawed but simply tolerated, the ultimate guarantee for self-defense was not arbitration or adjudication, but brute military power. According to this U.S. legalist logic, the same axiom must hold true for the Monroe Doctrine.

### The Roosevelt Corollary

From a Latin American perspective, the Monroe Doctrine as originally defined was not theoretically objectionable because it was well understood that this U.S. policy position was in part responsible for the ability of Latin American states to maintain independence from their respective former European colonial powers.[8] The real problem arose from the so-called Roosevelt Corollary to the Monroe Doctrine, announced by President Theodore Roosevelt in his annual message to Congress on December 6, 1904:

> Chronic wrongdoing, or an impotence which results in a general loosening of the ties of civilized society, may in America, as elsewhere, ultimately require intervention by some civilized nation, and in the Western Hemisphere the adherence of the United States to the Monroe Doctrine may force the United States, however reluctantly, in flagrant cases of such wrongdoing or impotence, to the exercise of an *international police power.*[9] (Emphasis added.)

Although phrased in somewhat general terms to apply to any international delict committed by a Western hemisphere state, the essence of this precept meant that the U.S. government alleged a right of preemptive intervention into the domestic affairs of Latin American and Caribbean countries delinquent in the payment of their public debts, in order to forestall intervention by European creditor states, by means of establishing a regime for the proper administration of the former's public finances and retirement of the debts under direct U.S. supervision. If deemed necessary, this objective would be accomplished by means of the forceful seizure and occupation of foreign territory and customs houses by armed U.S. troops.

In effect, the practical success of the aforementioned Porter Convention at preventing European intervention into the Western hemisphere for economic reasons was to a great extent deemed to be predicated on the enforcement of the Roosevelt Corollary to the Monroe Doctrine. As the Porter Convention reduced the grounds for European intervention into the domestic affairs of Latin American and Caribbean countries, the Roosevelt Corollary increased the number of ostensible reasons that purported to justify U.S. intervention. So in this sense, as well, the Porter Convention must also be appropriately interpreted as an adjunct of U.S. imperial policy toward Latin America and the Caribbean.

### The International Policeman
From a Latin American perspective, the Roosevelt Corollary was perceived to announce a unilateral policy of hegemonial imperialism by the United States toward the Western hemisphere akin to the balance-of-power politics and spheres-of-influence system pursued around the world by the great powers of Europe. Luis Drago—author of the Drago Doctrine discussed above—argued quite vigorously that the United States should not assume the functions of a public debt collector on behalf of Europe as it was then doing in the Dominican Republic.[10] Latin America was not a U.S. sphere of influence, and the United States had no right to exercise "international police functions" throughout the region.

From this Latin American perspective, the Roosevelt Corollary explicitly contradicted the underlying principles of nonintervention, state equality, and sovereign independence fundamental to the Monroe Doctrine. Even former U.S. secretaries of state Richard Olney and Elihu Root—the first to President Cleveland, the latter to Theodore Roosevelt—eventually joined in these Latin American protestations to assert that the true essence of the Monroe Doctrine did not require the United States to become the "international policeman" of the Western hemisphere or a debt collection agent for the benefit of foreign creditor states and their nationals.[11] On this point they were in full agreement with the positions advocated by such notable Latin Americans jurists as Luis Drago and Alejandro Alvarez.[12]

Yet, the majority viewpoint in the U.S. international legalist community favored Roosevelt's newly decreed interventionist interpretation of the Monroe Doctrine.[13] With the creation of a U.S. "sphere of influence" over the Western hemisphere by virtue of its victory over Spain, it was generally believed that the U.S. government must now assume an activist role in "enforcing" the Monroe Doctrine by economic, diplomatic, and military intervention into the domestic affairs of Latin American and Caribbean countries that became delinquent in the performance of their international legal responsibilities toward European states. Otherwise, the latter might in turn seek to redress alleged violations of their rights in a manner inconsistent with the Monroe Doctrine by means of military intervention and occupation. According to this U.S. legalist imperial logic, by virtue of the Roosevelt Corollary, the U.S. government had become the "policeman" for the enforcement of international law in the Western hemisphere.

## The Panama Canal

At that particular time, the U.S. government felt a special need to play the role of policeman in Central America and the Caribbean because it had recently acquired a supposed "vital national security interest"[14] in protecting the approaches to the proposed Panama Canal. U.S. marines had served in the capacity of midwife to the 1903 birth of the Republic of Panama from the womb of Colombia and in the negotiation of the Hay–Bunau Varilla Treaty of that year.[15] This treaty granted to the United States in perpetuity a ten-mile-wide canal zone across the isthmus of Panama with all the rights, power, and authority therein to be exercised as "if it were the sovereign of the territory."[16]

There was no debate over the more recently controversial question whether this peculiar phraseology of article 3 actually meant that the United States was not in law the sovereign over the Canal Zone because, at the time, the United States was deemed to be the "practical sovereign" for all essential purposes.[17] There were, however, some severe criticisms of the Panamanian intervention as a serious violation of the fundamental principle of public international law concerning state equality and as an instance in which the United States had not, contrary to prior practice, upheld the rights of a weaker nation in its foreign affairs.[18] Former secretary of state Richard Olney went so far as to suggest that the United States should have compensated Colombia for the seizure of the Canal Zone. Eventually, the United States would pay a $25 million indemnity to Colombia "to remove all the misunderstandings growing out of the political events in Panama in November 1903."[19]

On the other hand, some American international lawyers attempted to justify the Panamanian intervention on the grounds of "permanent national or international interests of far-reaching importance,"[20] which presumably permitted a derogation from the basic proscriptions of public international law against military intervention. The majority of U.S. international lawyers in this era essentially accepted the forceful creation and permanent occupation of an "American" Panama Canal as an inevitable necessity of geopolitical life that existed beyond the domain of public international law.[21] This attitude was consistent with their general predilection for concocting transparent legal justifications for U.S. interventionism throughout the Western hemisphere on such patently spurious grounds.[22]

The Roosevelt administration tried to justify its intervention in Panama on the grounds of the 1846 treaty with New Grenada (later Colombia). Thereby the United States had guaranteed the rights of sovereignty and of property of New Grenada as well as free transit on the isthmus of Panama.[23] The U.S. government rejected Colombia's request to submit this interpretation of the treaty to the Permanent Court of Arbitration at The Hague.[24]

Military interventionism became the keystone of U.S. foreign policy toward Latin America and the Caribbean from the time of the Spanish-American War until well after the conclusion of the First World War. Politically, the policy was justified by the Roosevelt Corollary to the Monroe Doctrine. Legally, the policy was justified either by the terms of some treaty that had been imposed on the targeted state or else by the asserted right under customary international law for the U.S. government to intervene militarily in order to protect the lives and property of its nationals abroad from dangerous civil conditions allegedly degenerating beyond the control of the host government—usually a pretext at best.[25] Strategically, the fulcrum of U.S. interventionist foreign policy toward Latin America and the Caribbean turned on the Panama Canal, which linked the two American coasts and served as the highway for political, military, and economic communications between the U.S. mainland and its recently acquired possessions in the Far East.

## The Dominican Republic Loan Convention

The formal promulgation of the Roosevelt Corollary to the Monroe Doctrine had been precipitated by the chaotic situation in the Dominican Republic. There the government had literally fallen into a state of international bankruptcy and was faced with the imminent prospect of military intervention by European powers in order to enforce collection on debts owed to their nationals. The situation raised again the specter of the volatile Venezuelan debt controversy that has already been discussed above.[26]

Pursuant to a convention concluded between the United States and the

Dominican Republic in 1907, the president of the United States was authorized to appoint a general receiver for the collection and proper administration of all Dominican customs duties revenues.[27] The U.S. receiver was to apply these funds to the orderly payment of interest on and the amortization and redemption of $20 million in new bonds issued and sold by the Dominican Republic. The proceeds of the new bonds, together with the customs revenues, were to be paid to the government's creditors, who had already agreed to a substantial reduction in the nominal amount of their claims as part of the financial rearrangement. Writing thirty years later, one American historian concluded: "The assertion that the United States initiated the receivership by means of military force would be approximately correct."[28]

The 1907 convention with the Dominican Republic did not explicitly grant the United States the right to intervene militarily in order to secure the discharge of any of its obligations, although pursuant to article 2 the United States could provide the general receiver and his assistants "such protection as it may find to be requisite for the performance of their duties."[29] In the shadow of the Great War in Europe, however, on November 29, 1916, President Woodrow Wilson decided to intervene and placed the Dominican Republic under military occupation over an alleged failure to fulfill the terms of the convention.[30] The marines were withdrawn in 1924, but the customs receivership was not terminated until 1940.[31]

The Dominican Republic Loan Convention proved to be a rough-and-ready model for the negotiation of economic receivership agreements between the United States and Honduras in 1911 (not ratified);[32] between the United States and Nicaragua in 1911 (not ratified)[33] and 1914 (ratified);[34] and between the United States and Haiti in 1915.[35] U.S. marines intervened in Nicaragua in 1912, occupied the country until 1925, returned the next year, and finally withdrew in 1933.[36] Marines occupied Haiti from 1915 through 1934, although the receivership was maintained until 1947.[37] The marines landed in Honduras in 1924 and were not withdrawn until the following year.[38] "Dollar diplomacy" and "gunboat diplomacy" were to merge and proceed hand in hand in the formulation of U.S. foreign policy toward Central America and the Caribbean during the first three decades of the twentieth century.[39]

## Cuba and the Platt Amendment

The ostensible cause for the war of 1898 was the abuses committed by Spain during its repression of the Cuban revolution for independence. Consequently, in its Joint Declaration of War against Spain, the U.S. Congress disclaimed any intention to exercise sovereignty or control over Cuba and expressly stated that the United States would ultimately leave the government and control of Cuba to its own people.[40] According to the Treaty of Paris ending the war, Spain relinquished all claims of sovereignty to Cuba and the United States assumed responsibility under international law for the occupation of Cuba.

The U.S. government imposed the Platt Amendment on Cuba as a condition for its independence and for the ultimate withdrawal of U.S. occupation forces left in the aftermath of the Spanish-American War. The Platt Amendment, a harbinger of the Roosevelt Corollary, stated:

> That the government of Cuba consents that the United States may exercise the right to intervene for the preservation of Cuban independence, the maintenance of a government adequate for the protection of life, property, and individual liberty, and for discharging the obligations with respect to Cuba imposed by the treaty of Paris on the United States, now to be assumed and undertaken by the government of Cuba.[41]

This language originally was included as part of an amendment to the Army Appropriation Act of 1901; then in article 3 of an appendix to the Cuban Constitution of February 21, 1901;[42] and finally in article 3 of the U.S.-Cuban Treaty of May 22, 1903.[43] The Platt Amendment was the brainchild of then Secretary of War Elihu Root, who deemed it essential to the protection of the U.S. strategic position in Panama.[44]

The Platt Amendment served as the legal pretext for a series of actual or threatened U.S. military and diplomatic interventions into Cuba from 1906[45] until its formal abrogation in 1934 as part of President Franklin Roosevelt's "good-neighbor" policy toward Latin America.[46] The U.S. government actually sent troops into Cuba in 1906, 1912, 1917, and 1920.[47] The doctrine of intervention enunciated by the Platt Amendment was considered so salutary that it was generally recommended to serve as a comprehensive basis for the conduct of U.S. foreign policy throughout the Caribbean basin.[48] One or another of its conditions warranting intervention can be found scattered throughout the various international agreements that the U.S. government attempted to impose on the countries of Central America and the Caribbean during this era.

## The U.S. Imperial Protectorate over Central America and the Caribbean

In addition to the Platt Amendment, the Roosevelt Corollary, the supposed right of self-defense, and the alleged need to protect the approaches to the Panama Canal, U.S. international lawyers purported to justify armed interventions into and prolonged occupations of sister American republics on such specious grounds as "the abatement of an international nuisance" and "in the defense of special rights and the general interests of international law and order."[49] Another superficial rationale invented by U.S. international lawyers became the supposed moral obligation of the U.S. government to rescue the peoples of such backward nations from their generally despotic, corrupt, and inefficient rulers, who threatened to propel the region into a condition of interminable anarchy and chaos.[50] According to this U.S. legalist imperial logic, the U.S. government had to assist its fellow American nations to advance toward a higher level of civilization and self-government in both their international relations and their domestic affairs. Until they reached that stage, however, the fundamental rule of international law dictating nonintervention simply did not apply to protect Central American and Caribbean states from the imposition of what was tantamount to a U.S. imperial protectorate. The idea that such an allegedly beneficent and supposedly altruistic policy might have been motivated principally by considerations of international power politics, military strategy, and economic greed was dismissed out of hand by many U.S. international lawyers.[51]

### U.S. Imperial Policy in the Americas and Japanese Imperial Policy in the Far East

Such specious justifications for U.S. imperial behavior in the Western hemisphere set into motion a deleterious process of interaction between U.S. foreign policies toward Central America and the Caribbean, on the one hand, and toward the Far East, on the other, that served as an ominous prelude to the Japanese attack on Pearl Harbor almost forty years later. The acquisitions of Hawaii,[52] as well as of Guam and the Philippines in 1898, signaled the opening thrust of U.S. imperialism into the easternmost rim of the Pacific Ocean. Here the United States soon came into serious conflict with another rapidly expanding imperial power, Japan, flush from its recent military victories over China in 1895 and Russia in 1905. The latter venture resulted in the creation of a Japanese protectorate over Korea in 1905, and Korea's annexation by Japan in 1910.

U.S. legal commentators on the eastern side of the Pacific accorded Japan's blatant conquest of Korea a shortsightedly benign interpretation as constituting merely part of Japan's effort to obtain a degree of equality with the great powers of the New and Old Worlds, thereby assuming its legitimate "place in the sun" with them.[53] Of course, this quest was similar to the contemporaneous imperial pursuits undertaken by the United States in the Western hemisphere as well as in the Far East, using the purloined Panama

Canal, buttressed by the interventionist Roosevelt Corollary, to serve as the strategic link between the twin portions of the U.S. empire. It would have been glaringly hypocritical for generally approbative American international lawyers to have excoriated Japan for likewise exploiting seductive targets of opportunity in its purported "sphere of influence" on the continent of Asia. As the American legalists saw it, just as the United States was currently engaged in the process of consolidating its hegemonial position in the Western hemisphere, Japan was destined to become the leader of an Asian empire encompassing much of the western Pacific basin.[54] Consequently, the Roosevelt administration formally acquiesced in the Japanese takeover of Korea in return for a free hand in the Philippines and an agreement to bar Japanese immigration to the United States.[55]

### The Open Door to China
Granting Japan imperial deference in the Pacific, however, did not gainsay the geopolitical fact that the promotion of U.S. possessions in the Far East depended on preventing Japan from obtaining any additional territory on the Asian mainland.[56] In particular, the inestimable strategic and economic value of China's territory, population, and resources must not fall under the domination of Japan. Nor, for that matter, must China be further divided into additional zones of exclusive economic or political control exercised by the great powers of Europe, which had already staked out imperial beachheads in China and Southeast Asia.

Consequently, the cornerstone of U.S. foreign policy toward the Far East at the turn of the century became the preservation of what remained of the territorial integrity and political independence of China.[57] These considerations induced the United States to specifically endorse the British government's "open-door" policy toward China.[58] This policy was designed to ensure equality of treatment for commerce and navigation by all the Western imperial powers in China within their respective "spheres of influence or interest"[59]—in other words, it was the rules of the road for a de facto, but not de jure, carve up of China.

### The Boxer Rebellion
The U.S. interpretation of the open-door policy toward China was expanded on in a July 3, 1900, circular note sent by Secretary of State John Hay to the various European powers then contemplating the formation of an international expedition (including U.S. troops) for the relief of their legations currently besieged in Peking as a result of the so-called Boxer rebellion against Western colonial imperialism.[60] As stated by Hay, the purpose of U.S. for-

eign policy toward China was to ensure the permanent safety and peace of the Chinese empire, to maintain its territorial and administrative integrity, to protect all rights of foreigners under treaty or international law, and to safeguard the principle of equal and impartial trade for all powers throughout China.[61] The principles enunciated in the Hay circular note were eventually endorsed by the major imperial powers in several important conventions concluded between them prior to the outbreak of the First World War.

Among these, of primary significance were the agreement between Great Britain and Germany defining their mutual policy in China of October 16, 1900;[62] the treaty of alliance between Great Britain and Japan of January 30, 1902,[63] replaced by a convention of August 12, 1905,[64] which was revised and extended by another treaty of alliance of July 13, 1911;[65] articles 3 and 4 of the Peace of Portsmouth of September 5, 1905, between Russia and Japan,[66] as well as the St. Petersburg Convention between them of July 17 (30), 1907;[67] an arrangement concluded between Japan and France of June 10, 1907;[68] and finally the Root-Takahira Agreement on Pacific possessions of November 30, 1908, concluded between the United States and Japan.[69]

A principal American legalist expressed hope that this general agreement on the Chinese open-door policy among the world's great powers in the Far East, together with the interlocking of Great Britain, France, and Russia in the Triple Entente, and the alliance between Japan and Great Britain—all of which states were further interconnected with the United States through a series of bilateral arbitration treaties—might create conditions ripe for the negotiation of some worldwide "peace pact" that could embrace the continents of Europe, Asia, and America.[70]

## The Mexican Revolution

On the other side of the Pacific Ocean, after the severance of Mexican sovereign territory north of the Rio Grande by the Treaty of Guadalupe-Hidalgo in 1848,[71] the primary U.S. concern in Mexico prior to the First World War was not strategic but rather economic in nature because of the large amounts of American capital invested in Mexico, the main repository of U.S. funds invested abroad.[72] The security of these investments was irreparably threatened by the outbreak of the Mexican Revolution in 1910, an event precipitated by President Porfirio Díaz's decision to renege on his promise not to seek reelection in that year and the consequent amendment of the Mexican constitution to permit him to do so.[73]

After instigating an armed revolt against Díaz with tacit support from the U.S. government, Francisco Madero was elected president in 1911.[74] On March 14, 1912, a joint resolution by the U.S. Congress authorized the president to forbid the exportation of arms or munitions of war to any American country in which he should find conditions of domestic violence to exist.[75] Pursuant thereto, President Taft promulgated an arms embargo against Mexico in order to strengthen the Madero government against its internal adversaries.[76]

## U.S. Recognition Policies

Madero was nevertheless overthrown and murdered in 1913 by General Victoriano Huerta, who ruled without the benefit of a constitutional imprimatur.[77] This supposed defect provided the grounds for the incoming Wilson administration to refuse to recognize the Huerta regime, even though the U.S. ambassador in Mexico had supported Huerta in his overthrow of Madero, although apparently without approval from Washington.[78] Although not without precedent in U.S. dealings with Latin American states,[79] refusal to accord diplomatic recognition because a government was not established in accordance with its formal constitutional procedures contravened the usual U.S. diplomatic practice extending all the way back to President Thomas Jefferson's 1792–1793 correspondence with Governeur Morris, U.S. minister to France, in regard to the French Revolution.

Jefferson's injunction was to the effect that the United States would "acknowledge any government to be rightful which is formed by the will of the nation, substantially declared."[80] As subsequently explained by Jefferson, this principle meant that the United States considered every nation to have the right to govern itself by whatever form of institution it desired, to change those institutions as it saw fit, and to conduct its foreign relations through whatever organs it thought proper.[81] For the United States to operate in accordance with some other principle of diplomatic recognition would be tantamount to an act of intervention into the sovereign affairs of another people.

By contrast, the U.S. failure to extend diplomatic recognition to the Huerta regime was calculated to produce a change of governments in Mexico. Thereafter, the Wilson administration would pursue a policy of nonrecognition toward governments not created in accordance with their respective constitutional procedures throughout Central America and the Caribbean as a purposeful instrument of diplomatic intervention supposedly designed to promote peace and stability in the strategic region adjacent to the Panama Canal.[82] The U.S. government has persistently pursued such a purposefully interventionist recognition policy toward Central American and Caribbean countries throughout the twentieth century.

### The Dolphin Incident

When President Wilson later surmised that the arms embargo had in fact worked in favor of Huerta and against the Constitutionalist party of Venustiano Carranza, the embargo was lifted on February 3, 1914.[83] Yet, neither diplomatic intervention nor manipulation of U.S. neutrality laws was enough to achieve the desired objective of replacing Huerta with Carranza. This goal was ultimately accomplished, however, by means of U.S. military intervention. Here, the pretext was to obtain amends from Mexico for its refusal to offer an unconditional twenty-one-gun salute to the U.S. flag as an apology for the arrest and prompt release of U.S. marines who had come ashore from the warship Dolphin then anchored at Tampico.[84]

Huerta proposed that the Dolphin incident be referred to international arbitration at The Hague or arbitration by means of article 21 of the 1848 Treaty of Guadalupe-Hidalgo. The latter mandates arbitration between the two states concerning any matter related to the treaty or other matters concerning the political or commercial relations of the two states. Secretary of State William Jennings Bryan rejected the Hague arbitration proposal. And President Wilson decided to use force rather than refer the Dolphin incident to arbitration as required by article 21 of the Treaty of Guadalupe-Hidalgo.[85] So much for the peaceful resolution of inter-American disputes when it conflicted with U.S. imperial policy.

On the request of President Wilson, Congress passed a joint resolution on April 22, 1914, giving the president the authority to use the armed forces of the United States to enforce his demand for unequivocal amends from the Mexican government over the Dolphin incident.[86] An amendment offered by Senator Henry Cabot Lodge to broaden the reasons for the authorization to refer more generally to the failure of the Mexican government to protect the lives and property of U.S. nationals during the revolution was defeated.[87] Nevertheless, Congress did expressly disclaim any hostility against the Mexican people as well as the desire to make war on Mexico.

### The Vera Cruz Intervention

The day before receiving legislative authorization, however, Wilson had already ordered the landing of marines at Vera Cruz in order to seize the customs house for the purpose of preventing a shipment of German arms and ammunition destined for Huerta's forces. This intervention prompted Carranza to declare the seizure an act of hostility, whereupon Wilson decided, on April 23, to reimpose the Mexican arms embargo.[88] Two days later, however, at the annual banquet of the American Society of International Law, Secretary of State Bryan took the occasion to announce the offer—as well as the U.S. acceptance—of the good offices of the envoys from Argentina, Brazil, and Chile (ABC) to mediate the dispute. Huerta accepted the ABC offer the very next day.[89]

Meetings among representatives of the numerous governments were held at Niagara Falls, Canada, where the negotiations quickly proceeded beyond mere settlement of the *Dolphin* incident into consideration of elaborating some modus operandi for full-scale termination of the Mexican civil war. An agreement by Huerta to step aside as part of an overall settlement led to the signature of a protocol on June 24, 1914. By means of this agreement, it was determined that a provisional government would be established in Mexico that would be recognized by the United States and the three mediating ABC governments.[90]

In return, the provisional Mexican government agreed to negotiate for the creation of international commissions for the settlement of claims by foreigners for damages sustained during the civil war "as a consequence of military acts or the acts of national authorities."[91] On its face, this restrictive language seemed tacitly to accept, by what it omitted, the Mexican assertion that a government was not responsible for injuries to aliens in time of civil war or internal disturbances, or resulting from mob violence for which the government was not directly responsible.[92] Hence, this appeared to represent a U.S. concession to Mexican sensitivities on the eve of the First World War.

When the Great War was over, however, in 1923, Mexico was forced to agree to the establishment of a mixed claims commission to decide how much Mexico should pay the United States for claims by U.S. citizens that arose during the Mexican Revolution.[93] Article 3 of this convention seemed to render Mexico liable for almost all harm done to American citizens during the civil war. Despite this, all claims submitted to the commission were disallowed. Eventually, Mexico paid a lump-sum settlement to the United States.

## Pancho Villa's Raid at Columbus

By late August 1914, Carranza had taken the oath of office as the chief executive of Mexico; some three weeks later, President Wilson ordered the withdrawal of U.S. troops from Vera Cruz. Nevertheless, the American pullout was delayed by continued revolutionary disturbances throughout Mexico.[94] It was not until October 19, 1915, that the United States recognized the Carranza government as the de facto government of Mexico.[95]

Yet, Carranza still exerted no real control over the forces of General Pancho Villa, which had consolidated their military position in the northern states of the country. Reacting to U.S. recognition of Carranza, on March 9, 1916, General Villa launched his notorious raid into Columbus, New Mexico,[96] during which seventeen U.S. civilians and soldiers were killed.[97]

### The Pershing Expedition

On March 10, President Wilson issued a statement that a military force would be sent at once in pursuit of Villa while, in the process, the United States would somehow maintain "scrupulous respect" for the sovereignty of Mexico.[98] On that same day, in a vain attempt to forestall what seemed inevitable, the Mexican government offered to conclude an agreement with the United States giving each country the reciprocal right for the passage of troops to pursue cross-border bandits on the territory of the other in the event an incident similar to Columbus recurred.[99] The U.S. government quite disingenuously treated this undoubted proposal to negotiate as a formal offer to permit the entry of the U.S. expedition against Villa under the command of General J. J. Pershing, and then promptly accepted it as such—only to have this interpretation quickly disavowed by the Mexican government and, ultimately, coupled with a demand for the immediate withdrawal of U.S. troops.[100]

### The Supposed Doctrine of Hot Pursuit

The Mexican government challenged the U.S. military intervention as a violation of its territorial sovereignty that could only be construed as an act of hostility directed against Mexico warranting forceful measures of legitimate self-defense.[101] In response, the United States insisted on its alleged right under international law to undertake "hot pursuit" of the Columbus raiders into Mexico because the Mexican government had proven itself totally incapable of preventing depredations against U.S. lives and property launched across the border by so-called Mexican bandit groups.[102] Until the Mexican government could give sufficient guarantees of its willingness and ability to discharge its undeniable obligations under international law in this regard, the United States would continue to act in order to abate what it asserted was tantamount to an international nuisance.[103]

### The Mexican-American Joint Commission

There matters stood between the two governments until late June 1916, when Mexican troops engaged General Pershing's expedition in combat on the direct order of the Carranza government in order to impede their further movement into the country.[104] The situation could have easily degenerated into all-out warfare between the two states had cooler heads not prevailed on both sides of the border. On July 4, the Carranza government expressed its desire to resolve the dispute peacefully,[105] and on July 12 proposed the formation of a joint commission for the negotiation of a complete settlement of the Columbus affair, including withdrawal of U.S. forces from Mexico, an agreement between the two states on the reciprocal passage of troops in pursuit of bandit raiders across the border, and an investigation and determination of responsibility for past and future incidents.[106]

Later that month, the United States accepted the idea of a joint commission.[107] The joint commission opened its sessions at New York City on September 4, 1916.[108] The creation of the commission transpired in accordance with the aforementioned article 21 of the Treaty of Guadalupe-Hidalgo, which created such a device for the arbitration of disputes between the two countries in order to preserve their peaceful relations.[109]

On November 24, the members of the joint commission signed a protocol providing for the withdrawal of U.S. forces from Mexico so long as the border was made safe by Mexican troops.[110] The protocol was preceded, however, by a statement from the American commissioners that the United States reserved the right to pursue bandits into Mexico if necessary.[111] The Carranza government objected to this additional statement because otherwise it would appear to be sanctioning the presence of foreign troops in Mexico.[112]

## The U.S. Evacuation from Mexico

Failing to obtain a modification of this protocol, the Carranza government refused to ratify it,[113] and the joint commission dissolved on January 15, 1917.[114] Nevertheless, under the pressure of impending U.S. entry into the European war, President Wilson ordered the withdrawal of U.S. forces from Mexico on January 28, 1917, and returned the U.S. ambassador to Mexico on February 17.[115] The Wilson administration finally accorded the Carranza government de jure recognition on August 31, some four months after his election as president under the newly proclaimed Mexican constitution.[116]

There was little discussion among U.S. international lawyers regarding whether or not the U.S. punitive raid into Mexico violated the letter or at least the spirit of that same article 21 of the Treaty of Guadalupe-Hidalgo. The general sentiment was that the United States had a right under international law to enter a foreign state in order to pursue and punish cross-border raiders who had retreated into their own country for refuge when the territorial government proved completely ineffective at suppressing them.[117] Yet, it was argued that since the United States had recognized the Carranza government, it should not have intervened with troops without the latter's knowledge and express permission.[118] To take the enforcement of international law into its own hands under these circumstances was deemed an act of bad policy on the part of the U.S. government.

## Conclusion

Regretfully, no conclusion to this chapter can be written because the history of U.S. military interventionism into the domestic affairs of Latin American and Caribbean states under one pretext or another has continued apace after the Second World War in Guatemala, Cuba, Panama, Dominican Republic, Haiti, Nicaragua, El Salvador, Honduras, Costa Rica, Grenada, Brazil, Chile, etc. Toward the end of the twentieth century, the U.S. government is committing the same mistakes in this region of the world that it committed at the start of the century.[119]

No point would be served here by trying to sum up or make sense of U.S. military interventionism in the Western hemisphere throughout the course of the twentieth century. Nothing has changed. No lessons have been learned. No progress has been made.

All that can be said about the future of U.S. foreign policy toward the Western hemisphere at the dawn of the next millennium is to paraphrase Socrates: We know that we do not know. That candid admission must be at the heart of any serious and fundamental revision of U.S. foreign policy toward Latin America and the Caribbean basin. Perhaps the time has come for the U.S. government to do the one thing it has not done for the past century in the Western hemisphere: Pack up, go home, and allow these tormented peoples to sort out their own destinies.[120]

## 7 The Foundation of the Inter-American System of International Relations and Its Central American Subsystem

### Philosophical Bonds

Even those American international lawyers who generally supported the interventionist foreign policy of the U.S. government in Mexico and throughout Central America and the Caribbean during the first three decades of the twentieth century recognized that unilateral intervention by the United States under any legal and political justifications or pretexts was in itself undesirable over the long run, and far less preferable than founding a system for collective intervention, when necessary, that was sanctioned by all states in the Western hemisphere in order to ensure that each lived up to its international responsibilities.[1] Such notions were the motivating force behind the formation of an inter-American system of international legal, political, and economic relations that was intended to be distinct from and superior to the European balance-of-power system.

After all, the U.S. system of international relations purported to be essentially different from, if not antithetical to, the European system of public international law and politics that was irremediably grounded in monarchism, the balance of power, spheres of influence, war, conquest, imperialism, and the threat and use of force. The fact that such policies might also be practiced at times by the U.S. government in its relations with certain Latin American countries could never detract from the spirit underlying the Monroe Doctrine as originally proclaimed, which was infused with the principles of sovereign equality, state independence, noninterventionism, peaceful settlement of disputes, mutual cooperation, and a fundamental commitment to democracy as the ideal form of government.

These philosophical bonds among sister American republics found their common origin in the intellectual ferment of the European Enlightenment and were tempered by the shared experience of revolutions for independence against the Old World colonial countries. This similar heritage created a profound awareness that all states in the inter-American region possessed a mutual interest in the advancement of superior rules for international behavior applicable to their own relations that at some time in the not-too-distant future might be extended to relations between all states in the international community. For these reasons, it seemed possible to create an actual "system"[2] of international law and politics in the inter-American region that would be governed by a set of principles more exacting, humane, enlightened, liberal, and moral than those currently in operation between the states of the Old World, especially when it came to the threat and use of transnational force, and notwithstanding the fact that American states might have to continue to adhere to such regressive and bankrupt rules in their relations with non-American states.

Despite its imperialist foreign policy in the region, the government of the United States did not at all dissent from the validity of these propositions, but instead constituted itself as the vanguard for the movement to create a distinctively inter-American system of international law, politics, and economics. In this manner, the Manichaean tension between its perceived national interests in the Western hemisphere and its professed moral, legal, and political ideals could perhaps be effectively alleviated, if not altogether dissipated. The U.S. policy of fostering the creation of a formal inter-American system in the Western hemisphere coincided with and reinforced the nation's contemporaneous promotion of international law and organizations as part of a war-prevention program for the great powers of Europe and Japan based on international law and organizations. Simultaneously, the existence of a viable and discrete inter-American system would advance the U.S. government's perceived vital national security interest of getting and keeping the European powers out of the affairs of the Western hemisphere for good.[3]

### The First International American Conference

Plans for the "confederation" of Latin America go back to the Liberator himself, Simon Bolívar. In 1826, he called for a conference of the newly independent American states to be held in Panama. Although little came of the conference, it can accurately be said to constitute the beginnings of the phenomenon known as Pan-Americanism.[4]

The formal start of an organizational structure for the inter-American system can be traced to the November 29, 1881, call by Secretary of State James Blaine for the convocation of a conference of American states to be held in Washington, D.C., in 1882 for the purpose of discussing means for the prevention of warfare among them.[5] The primary motivation was to better promote U.S. economic penetration of the economies of Latin America.[6] The project was sidetracked by Blaine's resignation after President James Garfield's assassination. It was on the initiative of President Cleveland's secretary of state, T. F. Bayard, that the First International American Conference eventually met at Washington in 1889.[7]

That conference was followed by a second conference in Mexico City in 1901, a third in Rio de Janeiro in 1906, and a fourth in Buenos Aires in 1910. The fifth inter-American conference, scheduled for 1914, was postponed because of the world war and did not convene until 1923 in Santiago. These various conferences and their postwar successors were to serve as the institutional framework for the creation of the inter-American system of international politics, organizations, law, and economic relations, which, after the Second World War, culminated in the foundation of the Organization of American States.[8]

### Obligatory Arbitration in America

Among other projects,[9] the First International American Conference adopted a plan of arbitration for the settlement of disputes among American nations.[10] According to article 1 of the model treaty, the American republics adopted arbitration "as a principle of American international law for the settlement of the differences, disputes, or controversies that may arise between two or more of them." Article 2 created obligatory arbitration for all controversies concerning diplomatic and consular privileges; boundaries; territories; indemnities; the right of navigation; and the validity, construction, and enforcement of treaties.

Article 3 was a general catchall provision that established obligatory arbitration for all other cases, "whatever may be their origin, nature, or object," subject to the single exception stated in article 4. Article 4 created an exemption from obligatory arbitration for questions which in the judgment of any nation involved in the controversy may endanger its independence. In such a case arbitration would be optional for that nation but obligatory for its adversary.

Article 5 provided that all controversies pending or thereafter arising would be submitted to arbitration, even though they originated in occurrences antedating the treaty. Article 6 made it clear, however, that the arbitration treaty could not revive any question concerning which a definite agreement had already been reached. In these cases arbitration could be resorted to only to settle questions concerning the validity, interpretation, and enforcement of such agreements.

Article 8 provided that the court of arbitration could consist of one or more persons selected jointly by the nations concerned; in the event of disagreement, each nation involved had the right to appoint one arbitrator on its own behalf. Whenever the court consisted of an even number of arbitrators, the nations concerned would appoint an umpire, whose only function was to decide all questions on which the arbitrators might disagree (arts. 9 and 11). If the nations in dispute failed to agree on an umpire, the umpire would be selected by the arbitrators already appointed (art. 9).

The absence or withdrawal of a minority of arbitrators could not impede the majority from the performance of their duties (art. 14). The decision of a majority of the arbitrators would be final unless unanimity on an issue was expressly required in the agreement to arbitrate (art. 15). Thus, in accordance with normal arbitral practice, this model obligatory arbitration convention between American republics contemplated the conclusion of a separate *compromis* between the parties in dispute that specifically submitted the matter to arbitration.

Article 18 provided that the treaty would remain in force for twenty years from the date of the exchange of ratifications. Thereafter, it was to continue in operation until one of the contracting parties had notified all the others of its desire to terminate. The nation giving such notice was obliged to abide by the treaty for one year, and the withdrawal of one or more nations would not invalidate the treaty with respect to the other nations concerned.

Shortly after the conclusion of the First International American Conference, a formal treaty with wording almost identical to this model arbitration convention was signed by Bolivia, Brazil, Ecuador, El Salvador, Guatemala, Haiti, Honduras, Nicaragua, United States, Uruguay, and Venezuela. But the treaty never came into force because its signatories failed to exchange instruments of ratification within the stipulated time.[11]

## The Illegality of Conquest

The First International American Conference also took up a proposal by Argentina and Brazil that acts of conquest should thereafter be considered a violation of the public law of America.[12] The United States wanted to condition this principle on the conclusion of the aforementioned proposed treaty of obligatory arbitration of disputes containing an exemption for matters concerning a state's independence.[13] A compromise plan that was unanimously adopted by the conference (with the abstention of Chile) recommended the adoption of the following declarations: (1) that the principle of conquest shall not, during the continuance of the treaty of arbitration, be recognized as admissible under American public law; (2) that all cessions of territory made during the continuance of the arbitration treaty shall be void if made under threats of war or the presence of armed force; (3) that any nation from which such cessions shall be exacted may demand that the validity of the cessions shall be submitted to arbitration; and (4) that any renunciation of the right to arbitration made under threats of war or the presence of armed force shall be null and void.[14]

Since the treaty of arbitration recommended by the conference never came into force, the plan to declare conquest illegal did not take formal effect. Nevertheless, the principle behind this early American ideal for international law and politics would eventually be espoused by the entire international community in article 1 of the Kellogg-Briand Pact (or Pact of Paris) of 1928, which stated: "The High Contracting Parties solemnly declare in the names of their respective peoples that they condemn recourse to war for the solution of international controversies, and renounce it as an instrument of national policy in their relations with one another."[15]

Despite the isolationist tenor of U.S. foreign policy at that time, the Paris peace pact had been jointly promoted around the world by the governments of the United States and France. The pact sought to repudiate the teachings of Carl von Clausewitz in his classic book *On War* (1832) to the effect that war is an instrument of national policy. It was generally believed that this philosophy was responsible for the First World War and had to be expressly condemned and repudiated by the states of the world community as an important step toward preventing another world war.

The U.S. government later sought to effectuate the Kellogg-Briand Pact proclaiming the illegality of conquest with reference to the Japanese invasion of Manchuria by means of promulgating the so-called Stimson Doctrine on January 7, 1932. Pursuant thereto, the U.S. government would not recognize as valid any legal effects flowing from a violation of the Kellogg-Briand Pact.[16] The Stimson Doctrine was unanimously adopted and approved by the Assembly of the League of Nations on March 11, 1932. According to this resolution, the Assembly declared it "incumbent upon the Members of the League of Nations not to recognise any situation, treaty or agreement which may be brought about by means contrary to the Covenant of the League of Nations or the Pact of Paris."[17]

The Stimson Doctrine was later upheld by the Nuremberg Tribunal in its 1945 Judgment.[18] This originally inter-American principle of international law and politics making conquest illegal is now expressly recognized by the entire international community in article 2(4) of the United Nations Charter: "All Members shall refrain in their international relations from the threat or use of force against the territorial integrity or political independence of any state, or in any other manner inconsistent with the Purposes of the United Nations."

## Origins of the Pan-American Union

In retrospect, certainly the most significant, immediate, and practical result of the First International American Conference was its recommendation that the participating countries form "The International Union of American Republics" for the purpose of collecting and distributing commercial information.[19] The union was to be represented at Washington, D.C., by the Commercial Bureau of the American Republics under the supervision of the U.S. secretary of state, which would be charged with overseeing all translations, publications, and correspondence pertaining to the union. The U.S. government would advance a maximum of $36,000 to the International Union for the expenses of the Commercial Bureau during its first year, and a similar sum for each subsequent year of its existence.

The United States would be reimbursed by the other members in accordance with a table of assessments determined by their respective population ratios. The union would continue in force for ten years from the date of its organization, during which period no member could withdraw, and then for successive periods of ten years each unless a majority of its members should give a twelve-month notice of their wishes to terminate the union. The Commercial Bureau of American Republics was established in 1890,[20] and when the period of notification expired without any notices of withdrawal by members, continued automatically for another ten years.[21]

## Functional Integration in America

The First International American Conference adopted a Recommendation to the countries of Europe that controversies between them and American states be settled by means of arbitration.[22] It also adopted formal Recommendations[23] concerning the adoption of a uniform (i.e., metrical-decimal) system of weights and measures; the adoption of a common nomenclature for merchandise; the creation of an intercontinental railway; the adoption of a sanitary convention; the adoption of the Montevideo treaties for the protection of patents and trademarks; the adoption of the Montevideo conventions on private international law, civil law, commercial law, and procedural law; the establishment of steamship service between the ports of the Gulf of Mexico and the Caribbean Sea, as well as between the United States and Brazil; the promotion of maritime, telegraphic, and postal communications between countries bordering the Pacific Ocean; the establishment of an International American Monetary Union; the negotiation of commercial reciprocity treaties, which eventually led to the conclusion of some twenty such treaties between the United States and governments in South America, Europe, and the West Indies;[24] the simplification of port dues; the establishment of an International American Bank; adhesion to the Montevideo treaty on penal international law and the conclusion of extradition treaties with the United States; the adoption of the so-called Calvo Doctrine as a principle of American international law; and freedom of navigation on shared rivers for riparian states. Yet, despite this plethora of formal recommendations, the reports, recommendations, and resolutions adopted by the First International American Conference were silent on the matter of convening a second conference.

## The Calvo Doctrine

According to the teachings of Argentine jurist and diplomat Carlos Calvo, aliens in a foreign country had the same rights to protection as nationals, but no more. Hence, foreign states had no right to exercise diplomatic intervention on behalf of their citizens against the state of residence unless a "denial of justice" toward the latter was manifest. As Calvo saw it, recognition of this doctrine flowed inevitably from the principle of the sovereign equality of states. Latin America's adherence to the Calvo Doctrine was intended to put an end to the abuses of diplomatic protection inflicted by the United States and the stronger states of Europe against the weaker states of Latin America.

By contrast, the United States argued that aliens were entitled to a basic minimum standard of rights under international law that if not protected by the state of residence, would justify diplomatic intervention by the U.S. government after the U.S. citizen had exhausted the domestic remedies, assuming these were available and effective. Quite obviously, the U.S. position was designed to protect the economic investments and interests of U.S. citizens abroad. Even today, the validity of the Calvo Doctrine is generally adhered to by the republics of Latin America and rejected by the United States.[25]

## The Second International American Conference

On the initiative of President William McKinley, the Second International American Conference met at Mexico City from October 1901 to January 1902.[26] In response to a related suggestion by the United States, this conference adopted a protocol recognizing the principles set forth in the three conventions signed at the First Hague Peace Conference as a part of public international American law.[27] Notice here the implication that the American republics had developed their own system of public international law that was distinct from and inherently superior to, but nevertheless part of, the rules of international law practiced by the rest of the world.

The three aforementioned 1899 Hague treaties were (1) the Convention for the Pacific Settlement of International Disputes, (2) the Convention with Respect to the Laws and Customs of War on Land, and (3) the Convention for the Adaptation to Maritime Warfare of the Principles of the Geneva Convention.[28] The protocol also conferred authority on the governments of Mexico and the United States—which were American states in attendance at the First Hague Peace Conference—to negotiate with the other Hague convention signatories for the adherence of the American states to the 1899 Convention for the Pacific Settlement of International Disputes.[29]

Consequently, at the Second Hague Peace Conference, the U.S. government secured the assent of the parties to the 1899 convention to adopt a protocol permitting the adherence to the convention of nonsignatory states not represented at the first conference that were invited to attend the second,[30] as required by article 60 of the 1899 convention. Pursuant to this protocol, The Netherlands minister of foreign affairs opened a *procès-verbal* to receive the adhesions of the Latin American states to the 1899 convention.[31] Eventually, Argentina, Bolivia, Brazil, Chile, Colombia, Cuba, Dominican Republic, Ecuador, El Salvador, Guatemala, Haiti, Nicaragua, Panama, Paraguay, Peru, Uruguay, and Venezuela adhered to the 1899 Convention for the Pacific Settlement of International Disputes.[32]

## Obligatory Arbitration Revisited

The Second International American Conference also requested the president of Mexico to ascertain the views of the participating governments on the most advanced form of a general arbitration convention that could be drawn up and meet approval, and to prepare a plan for such a convention with the necessary protocols to carry it into effect.[33] Toward the end of the conference, Argentina, Bolivia, the Dominican Republic, El Salvador, Guatemala, Mexico, Paraguay, Peru, and Uruguay signed a convention for the obligatory arbitration of disputes.[34]

Article 1 of this convention bound the parties to submit to arbitration all disputes that existed or might arise between them that could not be settled by diplomacy, unless it affected the national independence or the national honor of an interested party as determined by itself. Article 2, however, made it clear that this exemption did not include any dispute about diplomatic privileges; boundaries; rights of navigation; or the validity, interpretation, and fulfillment of treaties. Article 3 designated the Permanent Court of Arbitration at The Hague as the arbitral tribunal, unless any of the parties preferred to organize a special tribunal.

Following the 1899 Convention for the Pacific Settlement of International Disputes, article 7 of this 1902 arbitration convention conferred a right on each contracting power to offer its good offices or mediation to two or more parties in dispute, even during the course of hostilities, without this being considered an unfriendly act. Likewise, articles 13–19 of this 1902 arbitration convention established a procedure for the creation of international commissions of inquiry to investigate and report on disputes of an international character arising from differences over facts. The treaty would take effect as soon as at least three of its signatories expressed their approval to the Mexican government. It was eventually ratified by the Dominican Republic, El Salvador, Guatemala, Mexico, Peru, and Uruguay.[35]

## Contract Debts

Spurred into action by the Venezuelan debt controversy, the nine signatories of the 1902 Treaty of Obligatory Arbitration were joined by the United States, Colombia, Costa Rica, Chile, Ecuador, Haiti, Honduras, and Nicaragua in signing a treaty at the Second International American Conference calling for the submission to the Permanent Court of Arbitration at The Hague of all claims for pecuniary loss or damage presented by their respective citizens that could not be settled by diplomacy and were of sufficient importance to warrant the costs of arbitration.[36] The treaty was to come into effect for a term of five years after ratification by five of its signatories. This occurred in 1905 as a result of ratifications by El Salvador and Guatemala (1902), Peru (1903), Honduras (1904), and the United States (1905).[37] The 1902 Treaty for the Arbitration of Pecuniary Claims was also ratified by Colombia, Costa Rica, Ecuador, and Mexico.[38]

The Third International American Conference, held in 1906, agreed to celebrate a convention extending the life of the 1902 treaty until December 31, 1912.[39] The 1906 convention was subsequently ratified by Chile, Colombia, Costa Rica, Cuba, Ecuador, Guatemala, Honduras, Mexico, Nicaragua, Panama, El Salvador, and the United States.[40] Later, the Fourth International American Conference of 1910 adopted a Convention on the Arbitration of Pecuniary Claims, which would come into force immediately after the expiration of the extended 1902 treaty in 1913, and remain in force indefinitely.[41] It was subsequently ratified by Brazil, Costa Rica, Dominican Republic, Ecuador, Guatemala, Honduras, Nicaragua, Panama, Paraguay, the United States, and Uruguay.[42]

## Reorganization of the Inter-American Bureau

Among other projects,[43] the Second International American Conference also undertook a reorganization of the Commercial Bureau of American Republics.[44] The management of the bureau was entrusted to a board of directors comprising the diplomatic representatives of the signatory countries accredited to Washington, D.C., with the U.S. secretary of state becoming its chairman. The bureau was also given the explicit authority to correspond with the executive departments of the American republics through their diplomatic representatives in Washington.

### More Functional Integration in America

Continuing the social, economic, and humanitarian work of the First International American Conference, the second conference at Mexico City adopted a series of resolutions, recommendations, and conventions[45] on subjects such as the Pan-American Railway and Bank, a customs congress, codes on public and private international law, copyrights, patents and trademarks, extradition, international sanitary police, and a controversial convention on the rights of aliens incorporating the Calvo Doctrine, which the United States refused to sign.[46] Unlike its predecessor, the Second International American Conference did adopt a resolution calling for the convocation of the next conference within five years.[47]

### The Third International American Conference

Pursuant to the above recommendation, the Commercial Bureau of the American Republics determined that the Third Conference of American states would meet at Rio de Janeiro on July 21, 1906.[48] On the important matter of international arbitration, this conference approved a resolution ratifying its adherence to the principle of arbitration and recommending that the participants instruct their delegates to the upcoming Second Hague Peace Conference to secure the celebration of a worldwide general arbitration convention.[49] At the instance of the U.S. government, the conference also approved a resolution inviting the Second Hague Peace Conference to examine the question of the compulsory collection of public debts and, in general, the best way to reduce international disputes of a purely pecuniary nature.[50]

The latter inter-American resolution led directly to the adoption of the 1907 Convention Respecting the Limitation of the Employment of Force for the Recovery of Contract Debts by the Second Hague Peace Conference.[51] The Porter Convention was ratified with reservations by El Salvador, Guatemala, and the United States; by Haiti, Mexico, and Panama without reservations; adhered to by Nicaragua with reservations; and never ratified by Chile, Cuba, Paraguay, Argentina, Bolivia, Colombia, Dominican Republic, Ecuador, Peru, and Uruguay, all of which had signed it, although only the first three without reservations.[52] The fact that the Porter Convention did not explicitly prohibit the use of force for the collection of public debts under all circumstances rendered it objectionable to those Latin American governments that fully subscribed to the undiluted version of the Drago Doctrine.

## The American System of International Law and Politics

The Third International American Conference continued the life of the Commercial Bureau of the American Republics for another ten years and significantly expanded its functions.[53] The conference also expressed support for the construction of a building to house the bureau's activities in Washington, D.C.[54] In addition to continuing the work of previous conferences in social, economic, and humanitarian matters, the third conference adopted a convention calling for the creation of an International Commission of Jurists to prepare draft codes of public and private international law "regulating the relations between the Nations of America" for consideration by the Fourth International American Conference.[55]

This commission met in 1912, five years behind schedule, at Rio de Janeiro. There it divided itself into six committees for the preparation of draft codes on subjects such as maritime war, war on land and civil war, international law in times of peace, the pacific settlement of international disputes, and the organization of international tribunals, the rights of aliens, and other matters of private international law.[56] The outbreak of the First World War interfered with the deliberations of the commission, though it did resume its work after the war.[57]

These efforts by governmental experts to codify public and private international law were supplemented by the labors of the First Pan-American Scientific Congress in Santiago, Chile (December 1908–January 1909),[58] and the Second Pan-American Scientific Congress in Washington, D.C. (December 1915–January 1916).[59] The Second Pan-American Congress was held in conjunction with the annual meeting of the American Society of International Law and the newly founded American Institute of International Law.[60] The latter organization was the brainchild of Alejandro Alvarez of Chile and the ubiquitous James Brown Scott, managing editor of the *American Journal of International Law*, and was designed to consist of national societies of international law in every American republic brought into affiliation with the institute.[61]

On January 6, 1916, the American Institute of International Law adopted its seminal Declaration of the Rights and Duties of Nations, which was intended to epitomize the inter-American attitude toward international law and politics.[62] The declaration recognized that every nation had a right to exist; rights to independence and equality; a right to territory and exclusive jurisdiction over it; a right to the respect of its rights by other nations; and, finally, that international law was at one and the same time both national and international. After the First World War, President Warren G. Harding's secretary of state, Charles Evans Hughes, speaking before the American Academy of Political and Social Science on the occasion of the centenary of the Monroe Doctrine in 1923, commented favorably on the American Institute's declaration and stated that it was "supported by decisions of the Supreme Court of the United States" and "embodies the fundamental principles of the policy of the United States in relation to the Republics of Latin America."[63]

### The Fourth International American Conference

Pursuant to the terms of a resolution adopted by the Third International American Conference,[64] the fourth in the series was held at Buenos Aires in 1910. Among other projects,[65] the fourth conference adopted conventions on copyrights,[66] pecuniary claims,[67] inventions and patents,[68] and trademarks.[69] The fourth conference continued the life of the International Union of American Republics—created by the first conference and continued at the second and third—but changed its name to the Union of American Republics. The Commercial Bureau was renamed the Pan American Union and given significantly broader functions.[70] The Pan American Union was given another ten-year lease on life. The fourth conference did, however, adopt a resolution recommending the celebration of a convention that would organize the Pan American Union on a permanent basis.[71]

The next volume of this study will have to detail the histories of the fifth inter-American conference held in Santiago in 1923, the sixth inter-American conference at Havana in 1928, the seventh inter-American conference held in Montevideo in 1933, the Inter-American Conference for the Maintenance of Peace held at Buenos Aires in 1936, and the Eighth International American Conference held at Lima in 1938.[72] Suffice it to say here that all of these endeavors eventually culminated at the Ninth International American Conference at Bogotá in 1948, which adopted the Charter of the Organization of American States.[73] Thus, with the active participation and leadership of the U.S. government, a structural framework for the inter-American system of international political, institutional, legal, and economic relations was soundly built before the First World War. In the words of one consistently astute and prophetic U.S. international law professor of that earlier era: "The International Conference of American Republics has assumed a well-defined and dignified position among the great *international organizations* of the world" (emphasis added).[74]

## The Central American Subsystem

In addition to sponsoring the foundation of a formal inter-American system encompassing most of the Western hemisphere, the U.S. government actively supported attempts to create an organized subsystem within this structure that would incorporate the states of Central America: Costa Rica, El Salvador, Guatemala, Honduras, and Nicaragua. The primary U.S. motivation was to establish a zone of peace and stability within the Central American isthmus to protect the U.S. strategic and economic investment in the Panama Canal. Since the Republic of Panama was placed under a virtual U.S. protectorate by its 1903 treaty with the United States,[75] there was little reason to bother integrating Panama into various U.S. schemes for the creation of a separate Central American subsystem of inter-American relations. This accounts for the fact that for a long time Panama remained relatively aloof from the internecine turmoil that has engulfed Central America for most of the twentieth century. As of 1998, Panama remained under de facto U.S. military occupation.

## The Marblehead Peace

When war broke out in 1906 between Guatemala, on the one hand, and Honduras and El Salvador, on the other, President Theodore Roosevelt and President Díaz of Mexico offered their good offices to settle the dispute.[76] This led to the conclusion of a peace agreement among the belligerents on the U.S. warship Marblehead.[77] Pursuant to the Marblehead peace convention, a conference of Central American states was to be held within two months at San José for the purpose of celebrating a general treaty of peace, amity, and navigation. The conference did meet, but its labors were doomed to failure because Nicaragua refused to participate and instead renewed its war with Honduras and stirred up trouble in El Salvador.[78] Mexico and the United States offered their good offices once again, and in September 1907, the five Central American republics signed a protocol for the convocation of a peace conference in Washington, D.C., later that year.[79]

## The Central American Peace Conference

On December 20, 1907, the five participants in the Central American Peace Conference signed eight conventions: a ten-year general treaty of peace and amity, article 3 of which established the absolute neutrality of Honduras;[80] an additional convention to the general treaty establishing the principle of nonrecognition of governments coming to power without popular endorsement by coup d'état or revolution, the principle of nonintervention in civil wars, and the principle of alternation in power for governments;[81] a convention for the establishment of the Central American Court of Justice;[82] and conventions on extradition,[83] communications,[84] the establishment of the Central American Bureau[85] and the Central American Pedagogical Institute,[86] and on the convocation of future Central American conferences.[87] Of all these projects, the crowning achievement of the 1907 Central American Peace Conference was generally deemed to be its successful establishment of the Central American Court of Justice.

### The Central American Court
The Central American Court, proposed by the U.S. government, basically followed the U.S. plan for the Court of Arbitral Justice recommended for adoption by the Second Hague Peace Conference.[88] The Central American Court possessed compulsory jurisdiction over all controversies or questions, without exception, arising between the contracting powers that could not be settled through diplomacy.[89] It was therefore the modern world's first permanently constituted tribunal for the compulsory adjudication of disputes between states.[90]

Similar to the International Prize Court Convention adopted by the Second Hague Peace Conference, the Central American Court was also given jurisdiction over questions that a national of one Central American country might raise against any of the other contracting governments over the violation of a treaty or questions of an international character irrespective of the wishes of his or her government, provided that the individual had exhausted local remedies or demonstrated a denial of justice.[91]

During its ten years of existence, from 1908 to 1918, the court rendered only two affirmative judgments and declared all five claims brought by individuals inadmissible.[92] Nevertheless, its first decision—Honduras v. Guatemala & El Salvador (December 19, 1908)[93]—is generally credited with preventing the outbreak of a major war throughout Central America.[94] The successful prevention of just this one war proved the establishment of the Central American Court of Justice well worth the efforts of its founders.

The Wilson administration's heedless insistence on the ratification of the Bryan-Chamorro Treaty with Nicaragua[95] seven years later was directly and deliberately responsible for the destruction of the Central American Court of Justice.[96] Pursuant to this agreement, the U.S. government attempted to provide for an alternative interoceanic canal through Nicaragua and obtained rights to establish a naval base in Nicaragua on the Gulf of Fonseca in order to protect it. Both Costa Rica and El Salvador took Nicaragua before the court on the grounds that the Bryan-Chamorro Treaty was incompatible with their legal rights under preexisting treaties and general principles of law. The court ruled against Nicaragua in both cases, but Nicaragua refused to accept the two decisions. So when the court's convention expired in 1918 in accordance with its own terms, all efforts to revive it proved fruitless.[97]

## A Central American Union

The first Central American conference held pursuant to the terms of the 1907 convention (the second in the series started by the Washington conference) met in Tegucigalpa in January 1909, and was followed by another conference at San Salvador in February 1910. The second conference adopted conventions dealing with the unification of currency, the unification of weights and measures, commerce, consular service, the Central American Pedagogical Institute, and the Central American Bureau.[98] The next conference, held in Managua in January 1912, continued the momentum toward Central American unification with the adoption of seven more conventions dealing with similar functionally related subjects.[99]

This dramatic progress toward legal, economic, and political integration led to a confident prediction that the foundation of a Central American union was inevitable.[100] This prediction was partially fulfilled by the signing of the Pact of Union of Central America by Guatemala, El Salvador, Honduras, and Costa Rica on January 19, 1921.[101] Nicaragua failed to join, however, so the plans for the "Federal Republic of Central America" were abandoned[102]—at least for the time being.

## Another Central American Peace Conference

In yet another effort to stabilize the situation in Central America, the presidents of Honduras, El Salvador, and Nicaragua met on August 20, 1921, aboard the USS *Tacoma*, anchored in Fonseca Bay. This meeting, reminiscent of the so-called *Marblehead* Peace of 1907, led directly to the convocation of another Central American peace conference within about a year's time.

At the invitation of the U.S. government, the Conference on Central American Affairs was held in Washington, D.C., from December 4, 1922, to February 7, 1923, with the participation of Honduras, Nicaragua, El Salvador, Costa Rica, and Guatemala.[103] Notably, Mexico was not the co-host of this Central American peace conference, as it had been in 1907. The outstanding disputes left over from the Mexican Revolution had led the United States to act on its own initiative to sponsor this conference, and to exclude Mexico.

Under strong pressure from the United States, the five Central American republics concluded twelve treaties and conventions as well as three protocols and declarations.[104] All five Central American republics signed an extradition convention along the lines of their 1907 extradition convention; the Convention Relative to the Preparation of Projects of Electoral Legislation; the Convention for the Unification of Protective Laws for Workmen and Laborers; the Convention for the Establishment of Stations for Agricultural Experiments and Animal Industries; the Convention for the Reciprocal Exchange of Central American Students; the Convention on the Practice of the Liberal Professions; and the Convention for the Establishment of Permanent Central American Commissions on finance and communications. Also, Guatemala, El Salvador, Honduras, and Nicaragua concluded the Convention for the Establishment of Free Trade amongst themselves, with a provision for Costa Rica to join in the future.

In addition, all five Central American republics signed the General Treaty of Peace and Amity, which built on their Treaty of Peace and Amity of 1907, with certain additional provisions, among them:

> The recognition by the Central American Republics that their first duty is the maintenance of peace; the declaration of the five Republics that the violent or illegal alteration of the constitutional organization in any one of them is a menace to the peace of all and the assumption by each Republic of the obligation not to recognize in another a government resulting from a coup d'état or a revolution against a recognized Government, or from the election to power of a person disqualified by the Constitution from being elected; the obligation, in case of civil war, not to intervene in favor of or against the Government of another Republic; the obligation to seek constitutional reforms which would make impossible the reelection of the President or Vice President; the obligation on the part of each Government not to intervene in the internal political affairs of any other Republic and not to permit within its territory the organization of revolutionary movements against the recognized Government of any other Central American Republic; and, finally, the obligation not to enter into secret treaties.[105]

Obviously, these provisions constituted a laundry list of the problems that had traditionally plagued Central America—and, one could say in retrospect, have continued to do so through the rest of the twentieth century.

The five Central American republics also signed the Convention for the Establishment of an International Central American Tribunal, which replaced the defunct Central American Court of Justice.[106] This convention provided for the establishment of an international tribunal for the adjudication of all controversies arising between the Central American republics that could not be resolved by means of diplomacy, provided that such controversies did not affect the sovereign and independent existence of the nations concerned. In an effort to make amends for the role it had played in the dissolution of the Central American Court of Justice, the U.S. government signed a protocol with the five Central American republics declaring its "full sympathy with the purposes" of the new international Central American tribunal, and expressing its willingness to designate fifteen of its citizens for service on the tribunal.[107] In a similarly conciliatory move, the U.S. government also signed the Convention for the Establishment of International Commissions of Inquiry with the five Central American republics, which would function along the lines of the Hague international commissions of inquiry[108] discussed in chapter 5.

Finally, in the spirit of the recently concluded Washington Naval Conference of 1921–22, the five Central American republics signed the Convention for the Limitation of Armaments, which limited the number of enlisted men in their standing armies and national guards for a period of five years in accordance with the following schedule:[109] Guatemala, 5,200; El Salvador, 4,200; Honduras, 2,500; Nicaragua, 2,500; and Costa Rica, 2,000. The arms limitation convention required the five Central American republics to establish national guards "organized in accordance with the most efficient modern method," including the employment of foreign officers as instructors toward that end.[110] This convention opened the door for U.S. participation in the training and control of the national guard forces that have actually ruled most of the Central American republics for the subsequent course of the twentieth century.

## Conclusion

Certainly a good argument can be made that the processes of Central American unification, democratization, and economic development cannot and will not succeed unless and until the U.S. government is prepared to withdraw all of its military forces, national guard trainers, political advisers, and covert operatives from the region. In this regard, a crucial test of the supposed good faith of the United States toward Central America will come on December 31, 1999, when the United States must withdraw its military forces from Panama pursuant to the terms of the Panama Canal Treaties of 1977.[111] The Bush administration's illegal invasion of Panama in 1989 cast serious doubt on the sincerity and viability of that commitment.[112]

Similar considerations apply to the future of the overall inter-American system of international politics, law, organizations, and economics. Articles 15, 16, 17, and 18 of the Charter of the Organization of American States signed at Bogotá on April 30, 1948, were supposed to have represented the

U.S. government's definitive repudiation of the Roosevelt Corollary, "gunboat diplomacy," "dollar diplomacy," as well as all other pretexts, justifications, and supposed rationales for U.S. military intervention into, as well as political and economic coercion against, Latin American states:

> Article 15. No State or group of States has the right to intervene, directly or indirectly, for any reason whatever, in the internal or external affairs of any other State. The foregoing principle prohibits not only armed force but also any other form of interference or attempted threat against the personality of the State or against its political, economic and cultural elements.
>
> Article 16. No State may use or encourage the use of coercive measures of an economic or political character in order to force the sovereign will of another State and obtain from it advantages of any kind.
>
> Article 17. The territory of a State is inviolable; it may not be the object, even temporarily, of military occupation or of other measures of force taken by another State, directly or indirectly, on any grounds whatever. No territorial acquisitions or special advantages obtained either by force or by other means of coercion shall be recognized.
>
> Article 18. The American States bind themselves in their international relations not to have recourse to the use of force, except in the case of self-defense in accordance with existing treaties or in fulfillment thereof.[113]

These provisions of the OAS Charter constituted a distinct advance in the rights and protections afforded to American states in their relations with each other that were and still are considerably more humane, liberal, progressive, detailed, and ironclad than those found in the United Nations Charter itself. Nothing should have been clearer than that by signing the OAS Charter the United States agreed to abandon its imperial history of political, diplomatic, military, and economic interventionism into the internal and external affairs of Latin American states.

Nevertheless, in 1954, soon after the outbreak of the cold war between the United States and the Soviet Union, which heated up in Korea, the U.S. government expressly violated the solemn commitments it had just made to all the states of Latin America by overthrowing the democratically elected Arbenz government in Guatemala. The U.S. government then proceeded to manipulate and abuse the Organization of American States as an instrument for the conduct of its realpolitik, cold war, anticommunist foreign policy in the Western hemisphere, especially during the course of its numerous self-induced confrontations with Fidel Castro in Cuba. This manipulative policy culminated in direct U.S. military intervention into the Dominican Republic with the supposed imprimatur of the OAS in 1965.

After that venture, the United States's manipulation and abuse of the OAS became so illegal, blatant, and repugnant for all states and peoples in the Western hemisphere that the organization lost all credibility as an independent institution for the peaceful resolution of international disputes. The collective Latin American resentment was such that the U.S. government could no longer control the OAS. At that point, the United States proceeded to undercut, undermine, and exclude the OAS from active and effective participation in the peaceful resolution of inter-American disputes.

To be sure, in 1979 the Carter administration attempted to convince the OAS to send an international peacekeeping force to Nicaragua to prevent the Sandinistas from assuming power in light of their impending victory over the U.S.-backed dictator, Anastasio Somoza. The Latin American states refused to go along with this U.S.-concocted plan to rob the Sandinistas of their final victory under the auspices of the OAS. And even though it was unsuccessful, this U.S. stratagem created legitimate suspicions about the independence, credibility, and fairness of the OAS in the eyes of the Sandinista government.

Thereafter, the OAS proved to be completely incapable of doing anything to stop the Reagan administration's contra-terror war against the people of Nicaragua; the Reagan administration's illegal invasion of Grenada; the Reagan administration's unilateral military intervention into El Salvador's civil war; the Reagan administration's militarization of Honduras; the Reagan administration's bullying of Costa Rica; and the Bush administration's 1989 invasion of Panama, as well as its concurrent attempts to militarize Peru, Bolivia, and Colombia in the name of fighting its self-proclaimed "war" against drugs. The same can be said for the Clinton administration's politically motivated invasion of Haiti in September 1994.

Indeed, starting with the Bush administration, the U.S. government has been perpetrating yet another round of direct, indirect, and covert interventions in Latin American states on the alleged grounds of the need to fight its self-styled war against drugs. Coupled with these efforts, the U.S. government has tried to revive, resuscitate, and reinvigorate the OAS in order to serve as a pillar for its so-called New World Order in the Western hemisphere. This author doubts very seriously that the Latin American states will go along with the patently bogus effort by the U.S. government to use the OAS to reimpose a North American imperial order on the Western hemisphere under whatever guise or pretext.

Be that as it may, it is fair to say that the Pan-American movement launched more than a century ago by the United States has been killed by its own progenitor. The corpse of the OAS has been preserved for display at its headquarters in Washington, D.C., but certainly the life of the Pan-American movement as originally envisioned by Bolívar has expired.

*The Knox Treaties*

On April 23, 1913, President Woodrow Wilson's secretary of state, William Jennings Bryan, issued a circular note to the governments of the world proposing a series of bilateral treaties that would establish standing international commissions of inquiry for the peaceful settlement of disputes that might arise between the contracting powers.[1] This "Bryan Peace Plan" built on the foundations laid by two unratified arbitration conventions negotiated by Secretary of State Knox during the Taft administration on behalf of the United States with France and the United Kingdom.[2] The Knox treaties would have represented a distinct advance over the above-mentioned Root arbitration conventions because the former did not contain the typical express exemptions from obligatory arbitration.

Article 1 of the Knox treaties provided that all differences arising between the parties that could not be adjusted by means of diplomacy, relating "to international matters in which the High Contracting Parties are concerned by virtue of a claim of right made by one against the other under treaty or otherwise, and which are *justiciable* in their nature by reason of being susceptible of decision by the application of the principles of law or equity,"[3] shall be submitted to the Permanent Court of Arbitration at The Hague in accordance with the PCA procedures except as otherwise agreed by the parties in the *compromis* (emphasis added). Knox had borrowed the word *justiciable* from a U.S. Supreme Court case between Kansas and Colorado over water rights.[4]

In addition, article 2 of the Knox treaties provided for the institution of a Joint High Commission of Inquiry for the investigation of any controversy between the parties within the scope of article 1 before its submission to arbitration, and also any other controversy even if the parties were not agreed that it fell within the scope of article 1, provided that such reference to the commission could be postponed for one year by either party in order to give diplomacy an opportunity to adjust the controversy. The proposed Joint High Commission of Inquiry would operate in accordance with the rules of procedure applicable to international commissions of inquiry under the 1907 Hague Convention for the Pacific Settlement of International Disputes.

Article 3 established a novel procedure: in cases where the parties disagreed as to whether a difference was subject to arbitration under article 1, that question would be submitted to the Joint High Commission of Inquiry. If all or all but one of the members of the commission agreed and reported that the difference was within the scope of article 1, the matter would be referred to arbitration under the Knox treaty. This provision proved particularly unacceptable to the U.S. Senate, which amended the treaties to provide that decisions concerning the "justiciability" of a controversy should be made by the president and the Senate together. Although other amendments were also attached to the Knox treaties by the Senate, in President Taft's opinion article 3 was the heart of the treaties, so he decided not to proceed with their ratification.[5]

### The Bryan Peace Plan

William Jennings Bryan was responsible for the idea of including the one-year cooling-off period in the Knox treaties. Before he had accepted Wilson's offer to become secretary of state, Bryan had obtained Wilson's consent to go forward with his peace treaties plan.[6] A typical Bryan peace treaty provided that all disputes between the parties, "of whatever nature they may be," that were not subject to arbitration and could not be settled by means of diplomacy were to be referred for investigation and report to a preexisting five-member international commission of inquiry.[7] As soon as possible after exchanging ratifications of the treaty, one member was to be chosen from each country by its respective government; one member was to be chosen by each government from a third country; and the fifth member was to be chosen by agreement between the two governments but should not be a citizen of either country. Thus, a majority of the commission would be composed of members who were not nationals of parties to the dispute.

In the event of an unsettled dispute, each party had the right to ask the commission to undertake an investigation. The commission was charged with preparing a report within one year after its investigation had commenced, and the report had to be adopted by a majority of the commission members. The commission would as far as possible be guided by the procedures set forth in articles 9–36 of the 1907 Convention for the Pacific

Settlement of International Disputes, which pertained to the Hague international commissions of inquiry.

The parties to the treaty agreed not to declare war or begin hostilities during the investigation and before the report was submitted. In essence, this created a one-year cooling-off period for the parties in dispute. Thereafter the parties reserved full liberty to act independently on the subject matter of the dispute, presumably including the threat or use of force and resort to war. Nevertheless, the theory behind the Bryan peace treaties was that an impartial investigation and report would be tantamount to a peaceful settlement of the dispute because compliance with the report by the parties would be demanded by their respective domestic constituencies and world public opinion.[8]

The Bryan peace treaties were not intended to replace, but only to supplement, general arbitration treaties already in existence between the contracting powers. Consequently, Bryan also had to simultaneously undertake the negotiation of renewals for the Root arbitration treaties of 1908, which had expired in accordance with their terms after five years.[9] Unlike the Root arbitration conventions, however, the Bryan peace treaties did not contain the typical exemptions concerning matters affecting the independence, honor, or vital interests of either party or the interests of third states.

Thus, Bryan's international commissions of inquiry would possess jurisdiction to investigate and report on even those matters generally excepted from obligatory arbitration. Between a Bryan peace treaty and a renewed Root arbitration convention, every possible source of dispute between the United States and another state would be subject to some formal mechanism for its peaceful settlement. This would enable the United States either to refrain from going to war with another contracting power in the first place, or to stay out of an ongoing war between other states, provided they were all contracting powers.

During 1913 and 1914, Secretary of State Bryan concluded thirty-one of these "Treaties for the Advancement of General Peace" on behalf of the United States, only nine of which failed to go into force.[10] On August 13 and 20, 1914, almost immediately after the outbreak of the general war in Europe, the U.S. Senate gave its advice and consent to the ratification of eleven of the twenty Bryan peace treaties that had so far been submitted to it for consideration.[11] On September 15, 1914, Bryan used the occasion of signing such treaties with China, Spain, France, and Great Britain to utter his conviction that "they will make armed conflict between the contracting nations almost, if not entirely, impossible."[12] Eventually the United States entered into Bryan treaty relations with all of the major Allied

Powers (France, Great Britain, Russia, and Italy), but, despite repeated over-tures, none of the major Central Powers (Germany, Austria-Hungary, and the Ottoman Empire). One legal commentator felt that the treaties would at least prevent war between the United States and any one or all of the Allied Powers over any disputes arising out of the Great War.[13]

The principles for the peaceful settlement of international disputes set forth in the Bryan peace treaties would later be incorporated into the terms of the Covenant of the League of Nations.[14] In particular, the so-called cooling-off period was incorporated in article 12 and the procedure for the League Council to investigate and settle international disputes was found in article 15.[15] Although the United Nations Charter did not establish a formal cooling-off period for international disputes, chapters VI and VII gave the Security Council the power to investigate and settle an international dis-pute or even a "situation" that might lead to international friction or a dispute, as previously explained.

## Bryan's Resignation

In an ominous portent of U.S. entry into the war, however, on June 8, 1915, Bryan resigned as secretary of state in disagreement with President Wilson's hard-line approach toward Germany over the sinking of the British passen-ger ship *Lusitania* with a heavy loss of American lives.[16] He was replaced by Robert Lansing, previously counselor of the State Department and a found-ing member of the American Society of International Law.[17] Bryan wanted Wilson to propose to Germany the creation of an international commission of investigation along the lines of the Bryan peace treaties, and wanted the U.S. government to warn against, if not prevent, American citizens from traveling on belligerent vessels or with cargoes of ammunition even though they might have the perfect right under the international laws of neutrality to do so.

Instead of following Bryan's advice, Wilson chose to reiterate a previous U.S. demand for an official disavowal of the *Lusitania* sinking and other illegal sinkings of merchant ships by German submarines, for the payment of reparations, and for assurances by the German government that it would prevent the recurrence of similar gross violations of the humanitarian prin-ciples of sea warfare by its submarines.[18] In Bryan's opinion, Wilson's ap-proach to the problem was similar in tone and substance to the Austrian ultimatum to Serbia that had started the Great War in 1914. As far as Bryan was concerned, Wilson's insistence on Germany adhering to the punctilio of the international laws of neutrality and sea warfare could only propel the United States into Europe's war.

## The International Laws of Neutrality

Since the subject of neutrality was not on the Russian agenda for the First Hague Peace Conference, the latter did not adopt any conventions on the laws of neutrality per se, but rather just a *voeu* to the effect that the next conference should consider the question of the rights and duties of neutrals in warfare.[19] Pursuant to that wish, the Second Hague Peace Conference adopted the Convention Respecting the Rights and Duties of Neutral Powers and Persons in Case of War on Land[20] as well as the Convention Respecting the Rights and Duties of Neutral Powers in Naval War.[21] In addition, the 1907 Convention Relative to the Laying of Submarine Mines[22] was primarily designed to protect neutral shipping, and the 1907 Convention Relative to Certain Restrictions on the Exercise of the Right of Capture in Maritime War contained protections for neutral postal correspondence.[23]

When the Great War erupted in Europe in the summer of 1914, the United States was a party to these four Hague conventions. Indeed, since the time of that conflagration, the two major 1907 Hague neutrality conventions governing land and sea warfare, respectively, have been universally considered to enunciate the basic rules of customary international law on this subject that bind parties and nonparties alike. For this reason alone, the two 1907 Hague neutrality conventions on land and sea warfare represent yet another major contribution by pre–World War I U.S. legalist foreign policy to the maintenance of international peace and security into the post–World War II era. It is appropriate to think of the international laws and institutions of neutrality as a subregime nested within the overall regime of international law and organizations controlling the threat and use of force in international relations today.

## U.S. Domestic Neutrality Legislation

On the domestic front, extant U.S. neutrality legislation dated back to the first Neutrality Act of June 5, 1794,[24] which expired after two years, was renewed in 1797 for two more years,[25] and was eventually made permanent with amendments by an Act of April 20, 1818.[26] The 1818 act made it a crime for a U.S. citizen within U.S. territory to accept and exercise a commission in the military forces of a foreign government engaged in a war against another foreign government with which the United States was at peace; for any person within U.S. territory to enlist or to procure the enlistment of another person, or proceed beyond U.S. territory with the intent to be enlisted in the forces of a foreign sovereign, subject to a proviso for transient foreigners; for any person in U.S. territory to fit out and arm a vessel for the purpose of engaging in hostilities on behalf of a foreign sovereign against another foreign sovereign with which the United States was at peace; for any U.S. citizen outside U.S. territory to fit out and arm a vessel of war for the purpose of committing hostilities on U.S. citizens or their property; for any person within U.S. territory to increase or augment the force of foreign armed vessels at war with another foreign government with which the United States was at peace; and, finally, for any person in U.S. territory to set on foot any military expedition or enterprise against the territory of a foreign sovereign with which the United States was at peace. The president was authorized to employ the land or naval forces or the militia for the purpose of carrying the provisions of the 1818 act into effect, or to compel any foreign ship to depart from the United States when so required by the laws of nations or treaty obligations.

## The Alabama *Claims Arbitration*

Historically, the U.S. government had played a leading role in the development of the international laws and institutions of neutrality by endeavoring to obtain general acceptance of its policy pronouncements on such matters from the countries of Europe throughout the late eighteenth, nineteenth, and early twentieth centuries.[27] Such active support for and promotion of this subregime of "neutrality" was due to the fact that during this isolationist period of its history, the United States anticipated being neutral in the event of another general war in Europe. For example, the aforementioned proscriptions of U.S. domestic neutrality legislation and practice found their way into the three great principles of the seminal 1871 Treaty of Washington concluded between the United States and Great Britain that dealt with the famous *Alabama* Claims arising out of England's provision of assistance to Confederate raiders during the American Civil War.[28]

The Treaty of Washington provided for an international arbitration tribunal to which each party presented claims relating to various violations of neutral rules by the other party. Moreover, in this case the Washington agreement actually set forth the rules to be applied by the tribunal itself. Technically, Britain agreed to the rules, but always maintained that they were not rules of customary international law. These three great rules, found in article 6, provided that:

> A neutral Government is bound
> First, to use due diligence to prevent the fitting out, arming, or equipping, within its jurisdiction, of any vessel which it has reasonable ground to believe is intended to cruise or to carry on war against a power with which it is at peace; and also to use like diligence to pre-

vent the departure from its jurisdiction of any vessel intended to cruise or carry on war as above, such vessel having been specially adapted, in whole or in part, within such jurisdiction to war-like use.

Secondly, not to permit or suffer either belligerent to make use of its ports or waters as the base of naval operations against the other, or for the purpose of the renewal or augmentation of military supplies or arms, or the recruitment of men.

Thirdly, to exercise due diligence in its own ports and waters, and, as to all persons within its jurisdiction, to prevent any violation of the foregoing obligations and duties.

A revised version of these rules would later find their way into articles 5 and 8 of the 1907 Hague Convention Respecting the Rights and Duties of Neutral Powers in Naval War,[29] and thus into customary international law.

Simply put, Britain was anxious to avoid a war with the United States over events that had occurred during the Civil War. At the time, U.S. domestic public opinion was strongly against what was regarded as unneutral British support for the defeated Confederacy. Shrewdly, both great powers decided to submit this dispute to international arbitration in order to avert a war that neither government really wanted. The remarkable success of the *Alabama* Claims arbitration was generally considered to have ushered in the modern era of international arbitration as already discussed above.

## U.S. Neutrality toward the Great War

The evolving attitudes of the U.S. government toward determining the precise contents of the customary international laws of neutrality would eventually find their way into the numerous provisions of the two major 1907 Hague neutrality conventions on land and sea warfare, respectively. On the outbreak of the Great War, these two Hague neutrality conventions, together with the protections afforded neutral shipping and commerce by the unratified Declaration of London, would constitute the basic framework of legal rights and duties that governed the multifarious relations between the neutral United States of America, on the one hand, and each set of European belligerents, on the other. In addition, a joint resolution of Congress approved by the president on March 4, 1915, was designed to better enforce and maintain U.S. neutrality during the European war. This legislation authorized the president to direct customs collectors to withhold clearance from any vessel that there was reasonable cause to believe was about to carry certain materials and men to ships of a belligerent nation in violation of U.S. obligations as a neutral state.[30]

It was originally thought that the 1818 act together with this 1915 joint resolution were sufficient to bring the U.S. government into full compliance with its obligations of neutrality under international law.[31] By 1916, however, as the ferocity of the conflict intensified, the U.S. government felt the need to pass additional legislation in order to better protect its neutrality from the ravages of the war.[32] Somewhat ironically, these proposed amendments were eventually enacted into law as the so-called Espionage Act after the United States had abandoned its neutrality and entered the war on the side of the Triple Entente.[33]

### Philosophical Foundations of Neutrality

Taken as a whole, the international subregime of neutrality was designed to operate in a system of international relations in which war was considered to be an inescapable fact of international life, and yet the outbreak of war between even major actors did not automatically precipitate a total systemic war among all global powers. According to the international laws and institutions of neutrality, the conduct of hostilities by a belligerent was supposed to disrupt the ordinary routine of international intercourse between neutral nationals and the belligerent's enemy to the minimal extent required by the dictates of military necessity.[34] Such arrangements were intended to permit the neutral state to stay out of the conflict while at the same time allowing its nationals to take advantage of international commerce and intercourse with all belligerents.

The political and strategic dimensions of the international laws of neutrality were complicated by the fact that they operated on the basis of a legal fiction concerning the neutral government's reputed nonresponsibility for what were intrinsically nonneutral acts committed by its citizenry against a belligerent during wartime.[35] Generally put, a belligerent state could not hold a neutral government accountable for the private activities undertaken by the neutral's citizens, even if these worked directly to the detriment of the belligerent's wartime security interests.[36]

The laws of neutrality were essentially predicated on Lockean assumptions concerning the nature of government and its proper relationship to the citizen: namely, that the political functions of government must impinge on the private affairs of the citizen to the least extent possible, especially in the economic realm, where the right to private property and its pursuit were deemed to be fundamental.[37] Typical of this Lockean attitude was the prohibition on the confiscation of private property found in article 46 of the Regulations annexed to both the 1899 and 1907 Hague Conventions with Respect to the Laws and Customs of War on Land.[38] Into the same Lockean category fell the futile attempts by the U.S. government at both the First and the Second Hague Peace Conferences to secure international agreement on the principle of immunity from capture and confiscation of noncontraband private property during warfare on the high seas.[39]

## The Two Hague Neutrality Conventions

The primary duty of a neutral state was to maintain strict impartiality in its governmental relations with all belligerents. Yet, the laws of neutrality specifically denied that the neutral government had any obligation to guarantee that its nationals would conduct their affairs with belligerents in a similar fashion—or indeed, in accordance with any but the most rudimentary rules. For example, according to the 1907 Hague Convention Respecting the Rights and Duties of Neutral Powers and Persons in Case of War on Land, the territory of neutral powers was "inviolable" (art. 1), and belligerents were forbidden to move troops or convoys of either munitions of war or supplies across the territory of a neutral power (art. 2).

Nevertheless, a neutral power was not required to prevent the exportation or passage through its territory, on account of either belligerent, of arms, ammunition, or anything useful to an army or navy (art. 7)—or to forbid or restrict the use, in behalf of belligerents, of telegraph or telephone cables or wireless telegraph apparatus belonging to it or to companies or private individuals (art. 8)—provided that all restrictive or prohibitive measures taken by a neutral power in regard to these matters be applied uniformly to both belligerents, and this rule must be respected by companies or individuals owning such telecommunication facilities (art. 9). Also, the national of a neutral power would not compromise his neutrality by furnishing supplies or loans to one of the belligerents, provided he did not reside in the territory of the other belligerent or territory occupied by it, and the supplies did not come from these territories (art. 18). Finally, article 10 made it clear that it would not be considered a hostile act for a neutral power to take measures, even forcible ones, to prevent violations of its neutrality.

In a similar vein, according to the 1907 Hague Convention Respecting the Rights and Duties of Neutral Powers in Naval War, belligerents were bound to respect the sovereign rights of neutral powers and to abstain, in neutral territory or neutral waters, from any act that would, if knowingly permitted by any power, constitute a violation of neutrality (art. 1). Any act of hostility committed by belligerent warships in the territorial waters of a neutral power was deemed to constitute a violation of neutrality and was strictly forbidden (art. 2). In return, a neutral government could not supply warships, ammunition, or war materials of any kind to a belligerent under any circumstances (art. 6).

Yet, the neutral government was under no obligation to prevent the export or transit, for the use of either belligerent, of arms, ammunition, or, in general, of anything that could be of use to any army or fleet (art. 7). Nevertheless, the neutral power must apply equally to the two belligerents any conditions, restrictions, or prohibitions made by it in regard to the admission into its ports, roadsteads, or territorial waters of belligerent warships or their prizes. Finally, article 26 made it clear that a neutral government's exercise of its rights under the convention could never be considered an "unfriendly act" by any belligerent that was a contracting power.

## The Realities of Neutrality

Contraband of war shipped by neutral nationals to a belligerent was properly subject to capture and confiscation by the offended belligerent. Yet even these actions had to be undertaken by the belligerent in accordance with the laws of war at sea and the international law of prize. Historically, the U.S. government had opposed the imposition of a mandatory embargo on trade in contraband of war between belligerents and neutral nationals in order to ensure the economic well-being of its own citizens during wartime.[40]

U.S. legalists argued that this arrangement offered a residual benefit: the existence of neutral nations during a war would permit states to refrain from arming excessively in anticipation of hostilities, because they knew that as belligerents they could readily do so from neutral merchants in the event of war.[41] Legalists said that the freedom of neutral nationals to trade with belligerents during warfare would create a disincentive for major powers to engage in massive, wasteful, and unnecessary arms races between themselves in times of peace. Presumably, in this manner the international laws of neutrality could contribute to the preservation of world peace. In their advocacy of this argument, however, early twentieth-century American international lawyers and statesmen were attempting to elevate a consideration of pure economic expedience into one of legal and moral virtue.

More important, however, without the recognition of a formal subregime such as neutrality by international law and politics, nonbelligerents would be virtually compelled by circumstances to choose sides in a war so as to maintain political and economic relations with at least one set of belligerents. In theory, the neutral state had an economic disincentive to participate in the war because its citizens could greatly prosper from an increasing degree of moderately restricted international trade with all belligerents in desperate need of goods. Conversely, a belligerent would supposedly not act to violate the neutral state's rights or those of its nationals in order to keep the neutral state from entering the war on the side of its enemy. Another theory held that since the number and strength of neutral states in a future war would be proportionately greater than those of belligerents, the community of neutral states could compel the belligerents to obey the laws of neutrality.[42]

In practice, however, each neutral's normal international trading patterns invariably worked to the greater advantage of one set of belligerents.[43] The disadvantaged belligerent thus had to engage in a complicated cost-benefit analysis to decide whether the greater harm was the continued sufferance of this strategic disadvantage in trade or its termination through outright destruction of the neutral commerce, with the consequent risk that the neutral power would enter the war against it. Also, instead of acting as part of some international community of neutrals, each neutral state constantly assessed the relative advantages and disadvantages of maintaining its own neutrality as opposed to belligerency on one side or the other throughout the war in accordance with quite selfish calculations of its own vital national security interests. Unless guaranteed by treaty, the violation of one neutral's rights did not obligate another neutral to declare war or even to undertake measures of retorsion against the violator.

For example, the United States did not enter the First World War in order to defend the international laws of neutrality in the abstract. This was evidenced by its failure to consider the German invasions of either neutral Belgium or neutral Luxemburg as a *casus belli*. It was only when Germany's gross and repeated violations of U.S. citizens' neutral rights of trade and intercourse with Great Britain seriously interfered with their ability to engage in international commerce and resulted in the large-scale destruction of American lives and property that the U.S. government invoked the sacred cause of neutrality as one of the primary justifications for its entry into the war.[44] As mentioned above, it was generally believed within the United States that the quality and quantity of violations against U.S. neutral rights committed by the Allied Powers were of a nature and purpose materially different from, and far less heinous than, those perpetrated by the Central Powers—i.e., deliberate destruction of property as opposed to deliberate destruction of both life and property.[45]

## Benevolent Neutrality

Typically, the U.S. international legal community approved of the attitude of strict and impartial neutrality taken by the U.S. government at the start of the European war.[46] Yet, as international lawyers, they could reach no other conclusion than that Germany and Austria-Hungary must assume full legal responsibility for the outbreak of the war.[47] In their opinion, the German invasions of neutral Belgium[48] and neutral Luxemburg[49] in explicit violation of international treaties represented completely reprehensible behavior for which there was no valid excuse.[50]

Deserving especial opprobrium in the eyes of American international lawyers was the infamous speech by Chancellor Bethmann Hollweg of Germany to the Reichstag publicly admitting the German invasions of Belgium and Luxemburg to be in violation of international law, but arguing that Germany was "in a state of necessity, and necessity knows no law."[51] Later that same day he uttered his notorious statement to the British ambassador that the 1838 treaty guaranteeing the neutrality of Belgium was a "scrap of paper."[52]

The need to uphold the rules of international law made it crystal clear to American international lawyers on which side they should personally stand on the war even if their government remained formally neutral. As far as they were concerned, the egregious violations of international law by Germany made continued U.S. neutrality a highly dubious proposition.[53] Such legalist perceptions would exert a profound impact as the U.S. government's strict neutrality policy evolved into a stance of "benevolent neutrality" in favor of the Allies and against the Central Powers.[54]

These legalist arguments would also exercise an important influence on President Wilson's own perceptions of the war.[55] After all, Wilson had taught international law when he was a professor of political science at Princeton University.[56] Indeed, from the outbreak of the war in 1914 until the United States entered the war in 1917, Wilson's entire policy toward the conflagration was based on international law.[57] For reasons already explained, the extant international laws of neutrality and sea warfare were ideally suited to the U.S. national security interests of staying out of the war, profiting from it, and yet effectively assisting the Allies to conduct it.

As the intensity of the war heightened and the Allies imposed their stranglehold over commerce shipped from the United States to the continent of Europe,[58] the Central Powers took the position that the U.S. government was under an obligation to take measures to rectify the developing imbalance of trade in arms, munitions, and supplies that U.S. nationals were quite successfully transporting to the Allies but not to them. Both the U.S. government and the American international legal community were quite emphatic in their rejection of this complaint: If one belligerent was militarily unable to secure the safe passage of neutral commerce to its shores because of the misfortunes of war, that was its problem, not that of the neutral government, which possessed the right under international law to permit its citizens to continue trading with the militarily more powerful belligerent.[59] For a neutral government to discriminate in favor of the weaker belligerent in order to compensate for the military imbalance would constitute an unneutral act that could precipitate a declaration of war on it by the stronger belligerent. Moreover, it was argued that even if the neutral government were to embargo all trade in contraband of war by its citizens with both sets of belligerents, this affirmative departure from the normal rules of neutral practice during the course of an ongoing war could compromise its neutrality.[60]

### The U.S. Decision to Enter the War

Of course, the arms trade from the United States went almost exclusively to Britain and France. And loans from private U.S. financial institutions became critical to keeping the Allies afloat during the war.[61] Consistent with Lockean philosophy, nongovernmental war loans were not considered to violate the international laws of neutrality.[62] But as the German government would come to see the situation, the United States had already become a vital participant in the war on the side of the Allies even if it remained technically "neutral" in accordance with the standards of international law. Germany calculated that unrestricted submarine warfare would bring Britain to its knees before America could effectively bring to bear its full weight on the war.

The U.S. government's insistence on the international legal right of its citizens to trade with the Allies would play a significant part in the decision by the Central Powers to resume their policy of waging unrestricted submarine warfare in order to destroy this vital neutral commerce, irrespective of the international laws of neutrality and the laws of war at sea.[63] The U.S. government would respond by entering the Great War in order to secure those rights of its nationals and thus uphold the international laws of neutrality and armed conflict. Once again, that was exactly how the European system of public international law was supposed to operate before the foundation of the League of Nations and its system of collective security.

Resort to warfare by one state against another state was universally considered to constitute the standard and appropriate response to a transgressor's gross and repeated violations of the victim's international legal rights. Hence, consistent with its legalist approach to international relations, the United States did not enter the First World War for some nebulous reason such as "upholding" or "restoring" the European balance-of-power system.[64] Instead, America abandoned its neutrality for the very realistic purpose of redressing egregious violations of its fundamental rights under international law committed by the Central Powers, and relied on the usual and most effective recourse sanctioned by the international community at that time to prosecute its rights: war.[65]

The laws and institutions of neutrality and sea warfare formed the most substantial part of the definitional framework of international legal rules whose gross, repeated, and wanton violation by the Central Powers was responsible to a great degree for the decision by the United States to enter the First World War on the side of the Triple Entente.[66] This proved to be the definitive and most effective "sanction" for Germany's violation of the international laws of neutrality and sea warfare. Whether rightly or wrongly, Germany would pay the ultimate price for its passionate embrace of international legal nihilism: the Treaty of Versailles.

## Legalism versus Wilsonianism

Of course, coupled with the legal justification for America's entry into the Great War was President Wilson's political rationalization and propagandistic moralization that by abandoning its neutrality the United States thereby joined a great universal moral crusade on behalf of the forces of good (i.e., democracy) against the forces of evil (i.e., autocracy).[67] Autocratic governments were thereafter presumed to be inevitably warlike by nature, and democratic governments inherently peaceful. Therefore the peace of the entire international community required the utter destruction of autocracy and its replacement by democratic forms of government throughout the world. In the words of President Woodrow Wilson: "The world must be made safe for democracy."[68]

In his April 2, 1917, address to a joint session of Congress, Wilson (who was both a lawyer and a political scientist) attempted to fuse the classic U.S. "legalist" approach to international relations with these newly invented "moralistic" elements in his request for a declaration of war against Germany. But this fusion violated the cardinal tenet of the founders of the U.S. "legalist" approach to international relations, that all considerations of moralizing should be excluded from the "science" of positivist international legal studies.[69] The moralistic elements of Wilsonianism were completely incompatible with the U.S. international "legalism" that had been developed between 1898 and 1917 by the U.S. international legal community within its scholarly writings and in its formulation of foreign policies at the White House and the U.S. Department of State. As classically defined and articulated, U.S. legalism was antithetical to Wilson's moralizing about the inherent superiority of democratic forms of government. Both at the time and in retrospect, members of the pre–World War I U.S. international law community would most appropriately be categorized as staunch "legal realists"; they would have been proud to bear such an appellation had it been in vogue then.[70]

## Neutrality versus Collective Security

The incongruous suppositions underlying the international subregime of neutrality could not withstand the rigors of twentieth-century "total warfare" with its all-encompassing political, military, economic, and propagandistic dimensions. The First World War demonstrated the abject failure of the laws and institutions of neutrality to perform their intended purpose of constricting the radius of the war. This tragic experience led many American international lawyers, diplomats, and statesmen to the unavoidable conclusion that in the postwar world the international community had to abandon neutrality as a viable concept of international law and politics and instead create a system of international relations in which some organization would be charged with the task of enforcing international law against recalcitrant nations.[71]

Henceforth, the international legal rights of one state must be treated as rights pertaining to all states. National security could no longer be a matter of just individual concern; it must be a collective responsibility shared by the entire international community organized together. So although the pre–World War I U.S. international legal community did not expend much energy promoting the formation of an executive "international police power," the experience of the First World War and the failure of the subregime of neutrality to protect the United States from the scourge of war induced many powerful international lawyers both in and out of the U.S. government to support the creation of the League to Enforce Peace, and later to champion the foundation of the League of Nations.[72] In other words, they sought to actually build a global regime of international law and institutions for the express purpose of controlling, reducing, and progressively eliminating the threat and use of force by states in their conduct of international relations.

It was the opinion of many (though certainly not all) American international lawyers of that era that the U.S. government must at last definitively repudiate its traditional policies of isolationism in peace and neutrality in war in order to become a formal participant in the new worldwide system of collective security established by the League of Nations. Admittedly, this new balance of power had been wrought by brute military force; yet its continued existence could nevertheless be legitimized, if not sanctified, by the adoption and effective enforcement of the principles of international law set forth in the Covenant of the League of Nations. America's vital national security interests, on the one hand, and its professed philosophical and moral ideals, on the other, could most successfully be reconciled, and indeed would coincide and reinforce each other by joining the League.

## Differing Legalist Attitudes toward the League of Nations

Despite this majority sentiment, however, the question of whether or not the United States should join the League, and if so on what terms, provoked a sharp and irreparable divergence of viewpoints among the members of the U.S. international law community. A strong minority opposed U.S. membership in the League precisely because this step would constitute a definitive repudiation of America's classic position of isolationism in peace and neutrality in war that had served U.S. national security interests so well since Washington's Farewell Address. Others argued that whatever the merits of continued isolationism, the League of Nations as then currently proposed was fatally defective because article 10 of its Covenant guaranteed the preservation of an essentially unjust status quo in favor of France and against Germany that was not entitled to U.S. support during peace or war.[73] Specifically, article 10 stated that: "The Members of the League undertake to respect and preserve as against external aggression the territorial integrity and existing political independence of all Members of the League. In case of any such aggression or in case of any threat or danger of such aggression the Council shall advise upon the means by which this obligation shall be fulfilled." Elihu Root and James Brown Scott took the intermediate position that the United States should join the League, but enter a reservation as to article 10.[74]

As far as President Wilson was concerned, article 10 of the Covenant was the very heart of the League. The territorial guarantee in that article was Wilson's idea, and it had been included in the Covenant at Wilson's insistence.[75] Likewise, for Wilson the Covenant of the League was the very heart of the Treaty of Versailles. So at Paris he made it impossible for the two to be separated, against the wishes of some prominent members of the Republican party.[76]

Senator Henry Cabot Lodge and the Republican opponents to the Treaty of Versailles in the Senate relied on Elihu Root to advise them on developing a package of proposed amendments to the League of Nations Covenant.[77] Under their influence and pressure, Wilson felt compelled to secure the revision of a draft Covenant that would explicitly recognize the Monroe Doctrine in article 21, a right of withdrawal from the League after two years notice in article 1(3), and the reservation of matters within domestic jurisdiction from the competence of the Council found in article 15(8).[78] For the reasons explained above, however, Wilson did nothing about article 10, and this proved to be an insuperable obstacle to the ratification of the treaty in the U.S. Senate.[79]

## Neutrality under the League

Whatever its merits, the fight over the ratification of the Treaty of Versailles split the U.S. international law community into a pro-League majority[80] and an influential anti-League minority. From this point in time on, it was no longer possible to speak about the existence of one relatively homogeneous U.S. legalist approach to international relations. From either legalist perspective, however, the successful creation of the League of Nations was supposed to have sounded the death knell for the international subregime of neutrality, and thus for the customary and conventional international laws and institutions of neutrality. This supposed watershed in international legal and political relations was made quite clear by Covenant article 10 as well as by article 11(1): "Any war or threat of war, whether immediately affecting any of the Members of the League or not, is hereby declared a matter of concern to the whole League, and the League shall take any action that may be deemed wise and effectual to safeguard the peace of nations. In case any such emergency should arise, the Secretary-General shall on the request of any Member of the League forthwith summon a meeting of the Council."

Nevertheless, these contemporaneous prognostications concerning the imminent demise of "neutrality" proved to be quite premature. This was because the U.S. government never joined the League of Nations, but instead returned to its previous foreign policies of isolationism in peace and neutrality in war. Shorn of U.S. participation, the League of Nations arrived into the world stillborn. So it should have come as no surprise that the congenitally defective League was ultimately incapable of preserving world peace against the onslaughts of fascist and communist dictatorships during the 1930s. Needless to say, the international and domestic laws and institutions of neutrality ultimately proved to be ineffective at keeping American out of the Second World War, and especially against the express wishes of the imperial President Franklin Roosevelt to the contrary.[81]

## Neutrality under the United Nations

The shocked reaction of the U.S. government and the American people to the conflagration of the Second World War produced a profound realization of the extreme dangers of continuing a foreign policy premised on the interrelated principles of isolationism in peace and neutrality in war. Whether accurate or not, the thesis developed that if the willfully obstructionist U.S. Senate had ratified the Treaty of Versailles, which contained the League of Nations Covenant, the Second World War might never have occurred. Hence, the argument went, in order to avoid a suicidal Third World War, the United States must not repeat the same near fatal mistake it had made after the termination of the First World War by retreating into its cocoon of isolationism in peace and neutrality in war. These perceptions convinced the U.S. government of the compelling need to sponsor, found, and join the United Nations.

Thus, under the regime of the United Nations Charter, neither the organization itself nor any of its member states was supposed to remain "neutral" in the face of an unjustified threat or use of force (article 2(4)), nor when confronted by the existence of a threat to the peace, breach of the peace, or act of aggression by one state against another state (Chapter VII and article 39). According to article 2(5), all UN members were to give the organization every assistance in any action it took in accordance with the Charter, and they must refrain from giving any assistance to any state against which the organization took preventive or enforcement action. Article 2(6) even empowered the organization to act against nonmembers "so far as may be necessary for the maintenance of international peace and security." This arrogation of power by UN member states, and its overt threat to nonmember states, constituted the exact antithesis to the principle of neutrality.

Furthermore, article 24 gave the Security Council "primary responsibility" for the maintenance of international peace and security, and article 25 required all members of the UN "to accept and carry out" the decisions of the Security Council. This injunction included their mandatory adoption of Security Council "enforcement measures" under articles 41, 42, and 43, though the special agreements needed to bring this last article into effect were never concluded. Finally, Charter article 51 permitted, but did not obligate, UN members to come to the assistance of any state that was the victim of an armed attack or armed aggression by another state pursuant to the international legal right of "collective" self-defense.

Clearly, the continued existence of the international laws and institutions of neutrality did not fall within the contemplation of the drafters of the United Nations Charter. Nevertheless, and once again, reports of the death of the international subregime of neutrality proved to be greatly overexaggerated. At the time of the founding of the United Nations, the most that could have been reasonably expected was that the Security Council would somehow preserve and extend the uneasy wartime alliance among the five great powers into the postwar world on the basis of its fundamental underlying condition—unanimity. To the degree that the five permanent members of the Security Council (viz., the United States, United Kingdom, USSR, France, and China) could maintain, or at least selectively reinstitute, their World War II coalition in order to handle postwar international crises, then the UN Security Council would provide a mechanism to enforce the peace of the world in a manner basically deemed to be legitimate by the remainder of the international community.

The atomic bombings of Hiroshima and Nagasaki, however, occurred shortly after the UN Charter had been signed in San Francisco on June 26, 1945, and even before the organization itself came into existence on October 24, 1945. The ensuing cold war between the United States and the Soviet Union, each supported by its respective allies, led to a breakdown of the World War II coalition that was formally and legally known as the "United Nations." This created a stalemate at the UN Security Council because of the veto power over substantive matters accorded to its five permanent members by Charter article 27(3).

Hence, if the Security Council should fail to act in the event of a threat to the peace, breach of the peace, or act of aggression, and the state members of the United Nations choose not to exercise their right of collective self-defense to come to the assistance of the victim of an armed attack or armed aggression as permitted by article 51, then the international laws and institutions of neutrality would come into effect to govern the relations between the neutral states, on the one hand, and each set of belligerents, on the other. Thus, even under the reign of the intrinsically nonneutral United Nations Charter, in default of the Security Council taking measures "necessary to maintain international peace and security," the international subregime of neutrality still plays an important role in the preservation of international peace and security by constricting the radius and intensity of an ongoing war. So, the international laws and domestic statutes pertaining to the subregime of neutrality analyzed above are still valid, and continue to exercise a substantial impact on the formulation and conduct of U.S. foreign policy toward ongoing hostilities when the U.S. government has chosen not (yet) to take sides.

Most recently, for example, the international laws of neutrality played an important role in shaping U.S. foreign policy toward the Iraq-Iran War of 1979–88.[82] Domestic U.S. neutrality legislation is still on the books and is periodically (though selectively) enforced against U.S. citizens who involve themselves in foreign conflicts while using U.S. territory as a base of operations. For example, this author has personally been involved for the defense in two such federal criminal prosecutions concerning the conflicts in Nicaragua and Northern Ireland.

## The Washington Naval Conference

Obviously, there were many issues left over from the First World War that the U.S. government needed to deal with. But with the definitive rejection of the Treaty of Versailles by the Senate, these issues could not be handled within the context of the League of Nations. Consequently, the Harding administration decided to convene the so-called Washington Naval Conference on November 11, 1921—not coincidentally the third anniversary of the armistice ending the Great War. Included on the agenda of the conference were both naval armaments and Far Eastern questions.[83] Not surprisingly, Elihu Root attended on behalf of the U.S. government.

A detailed analysis of the actual proceedings and overall significance of the Washington Naval Conference falls outside the defined scope of this volume. Indeed, in fairness it can be said that the Washington Naval Conference began the new era of a U.S. foreign policy that promoted international law and organizations for the entire world community of states, but without participating in the League of Nations: e.g., the Kellogg-Briand Pact, the Stimson Doctrine, various disarmament conferences, neutrality legislation, and the inter-American conferences.[84] Indeed, that became the overall objective and dilemma of U.S. foreign policy during the interwar period.

But in order to provide some degree of closure for this volume and continuity with the next, let us briefly consider the net results of the Washington Naval Conference. The keynote address by U.S. secretary of state Charles Evans Hughes would ultimately lead to the conclusion of the so-called Five-Power Treaty of February 6, 1922, that would require the United States, Britain, Japan, France, and Italy to limit the tonnage of their aircraft carriers and capital ships, and establish a ratio of capital ships among them on the basis of 5:5:3:1.67:1.67, respectively. Another Five-Power Treaty of February 6, 1922, made the rules of warfare applying to surface ships applicable to submarines and outlawed the use of poison gas. Since not all of the five signatories ratified the second five-power treaty, it never came into force. Eventually, the London Naval Conference of 1930 would adopt a treaty declaring that submarines were bound by the usual rules of visit and search applicable to surface vessels that came into general acceptance.[85]

A Four-Power Pact would end the 1902 Alliance between Japan and Britain and put in its place an agreement whereby Britain, Japan, France, and the United States pledged to respect their respective possessions in the Pacific and to consult with each other in case of any threats.[86] The Nine-Power Treaty of February 6, 1922, among the United States, Great Britain, France, Italy, Japan, Belgium, China, The Netherlands, and Portugal bound the contracting powers except China to accept the principle of equal commercial and industrial opportunity in China as well as to uphold the independence and territorial integrity of that nation.[87] The latter agreement would multilateralize the open-door policy for the exploitation of China.

The Geneva Protocol of 1925, concluded under the auspices of the League of Nations, expressly recognized the universal prohibition on "the use in war of asphyxiating, poisonous or other gases, and of all analogous liquids, materials or devices." The Protocol also agreed "to extend this prohibition to the use of bacteriological methods of warfare." Unfortunately, the United States would not become a contracting party to this so-called Geneva Gas Protocol until April 10, 1975.[88]

# Conclusion

## *Still Seeking World Order*

The dominant interpretation among historians, political scientists, and international lawyers is that during the period between the First and Second World Wars, the U.S. government simply retreated to its traditional foreign policies of isolationism in peace and neutrality in war vis-à-vis the rest of the world that went all the way back to Washington's Farewell Address. But the situation was far more complicated than that. During the interwar period, the U.S. government continued to pursue a foreign policy based on the active promotion of international law and organizations for the rest of the world. In this regard, there was a remarkable degree of continuity between U.S. legalist foreign policy during the 1898–1922 era and the interwar period of its history.

One of the overall objectives and dilemmas of U.S. foreign policy during the interwar period became how to advance the nation's perceived vital national security interest in promoting international law and organizations around the world without participating in the League of Nations. This interpretation of U.S. interwar diplomacy can account for the Kellogg-Briand Pact, the Stimson Doctrine, the Washington Naval Conference, U.S. neutrality legislation, the inter-American conferences, etc. The U.S. government simply continued to pursue the legalist approach to international relations that was classically defined and articulated during the pre–World War I era into and throughout the interwar period, though without dealing with the League.

To recapitulate: This pre–World War I U.S. legalist approach to international politics sought to create an actual "regime" of international law and organizations that would prevent, reduce, and regulate the threat and use of force in international relations. In particular, its war-prevention program for world politics consisted of obtaining the following concrete objectives:

(1) the creation of a general system for the obligatory arbitration of disputes between states; (2) the establishment of an international court of justice; (3) the codification of important areas of customary international law into positive treaty form; (4) arms reduction, but only after the relaxation of international tensions by means of these and other legalist techniques and institutions; and (5) the institutionalization of the practice of convoking periodic peace conferences for all states in the recognized international community. A subsidiary element of this war-prevention program was to strengthen the well-established international legal institution of neutrality and the humanitarian laws of armed conflict in order to further isolate the bulk of the international community, and especially the United States, from some future war in Europe that might erupt despite the enactment of these preventive legalist devices.

The fifth legalist objective of creating some mechanism for the convocation of periodic international peace conferences was attained and far exceeded by the creation of the League of Nations. Nevertheless, for reasons already explained, the United States never joined the League. Moreover, after the definitive repudiation of the Treaty of Versailles by the Senate, the U.S. government made no further attempt to join the League by negotiating on some other terms.

Although joining the League of Nations never again became an objective of U.S. foreign policy, the government nonetheless remained committed to joining the Permanent Court of International Justice (PCIJ). Since the creation of a world court had been an objective of U.S. foreign policy going all the way back to the First Hague Peace Conference, the Senate's rejection of the Treaty of Versailles was not tantamount to a rejection of the PCIJ. Indeed, a strong element of partisan politics can account for the fact that although the U.S. government rejected the League of Nations, it did not reject the World Court.

Prior to Woodrow Wilson's ascent to power, the most prominent members of the U.S. international legal establishment had been staunch Republicans. To some extent, therefore, they looked down their noses at President Wilson and his supposedly inexperienced advisers—at least as compared with them. In their opinion, Wilson's League was a "Democrat" institution that had been devised by amateurs. But with the rejection of the League by the Senate and the return of the Republican party to the White House under President Harding in 1921, these Republican international lawyers used their influence with the new administration and its successors to continue pressing for U.S. membership in the World Court. This was made possible when the League was formally separated from the Court by means of formulating the Protocol of Signature for the PCIJ Statute, which was done for the express purpose of allowing the United States to join the World Court without having to join the League.

Concerning the legalist objective of establishing the obligatory arbitration or adjudication of international disputes, after the meetings of the Advisory Commission of Jurists set up to establish the Permanent Court of International Justice, the great powers repudiated the long-standing U.S. objective of creating some system for the obligatory adjudication of disputes by a world court. In effect, the First World War had exerted a chastening influence on American international lawyers and had weakened their long-standing belief that the obligatory adjudication of international disputes by some world court could make a positive contribution to the maintenance of international peace and security.

Moreover, after the First World War, the United States was clearly the most powerful state in the world, something that had not been so obvious before the outbreak of the war. Therefore, it was no longer perceived to be within the vital national interest of the United States to submit all of its disputes with other states to the World Court on an obligatory basis. The Protocol of Signature for the PCIJ Statute had to receive the advice and consent of the U.S. Senate, but the Senate would have been highly unlikely to approve joining a world court with compulsory authority to adjudicate international disputes to which the U.S. government might become a party.

Nonetheless, in a concession to upholding the principle of the obligatory adjudication of disputes, the Protocol of Signature of the PCIJ Statute did include an "optional clause" that would allow parties thereto to accept ipso facto the compulsory jurisdiction of the world court for certain categories of disputes on the basis of reciprocity. Thus, according to the U.S. legalist strategy, the Senate could reject the League, accept the World Court, and leave the acceptance of the obligatory adjudication of some disputes to a later day. Unfortunately, the United States never joined the Permanent Court of International Justice on any terms. But in 1945 the United States did create and join its successor—the International Court of Justice.

The codification of customary international law still remained an important objective of U.S. foreign policy during the interwar period. Despite the fact that the United States was not a party to the League Covenant, it nevertheless perceived its vital national interests as requiring participation in various efforts to codify certain areas of customary international law for the entire world. However, since many of these codification efforts took place under the auspices of the League, it became quite difficult for the U.S. government to associate itself with these codification efforts while at the same time not formally associating itself with the League.

Arms control and disarmament remained an objective of U.S. foreign policy during the interwar period. It was the U.S. government that played the leading role in convoking the Washington Naval Conference of 1921. The United States also participated in the London Naval Conference of 1930. The significance of these two conferences for arms limitation and some degree of disarmament with respect to certain types of weapons will have to be discussed at a later time.

Finally, despite the fact that the U.S. government was hindered by its nonparticipation in the activities of the League of Nations, it nevertheless sought to trump the League by promoting a new concept of international law and politics: the outlawry of war. As previously mentioned, that principle of international law and politics goes all the way back to the inter-American conferences held before the First World War. This idea was resurrected by the U.S. government and ultimately enshrined in the Kellogg-Briand Peace Pact of 1928, which outlawed war as an instrument of national policy. This was followed up by the Stimson Doctrine of 1931, whereby the U.S. government refused to recognize any legal results flowing from a violation of the Kellogg-Briand Pact with respect to the Japanese invasion of China. The general principle of law and policy enunciated by the Stimson Doctrine would ultimately be endorsed by the League of Nations Assembly. The outlawry of war would later find its way into article 2(4) of the United Nations Charter, the cornerstone of the post–World War II world order: "All Members shall refrain in their international relations from the threat or use of force against the territorial integrity or political independence of any state, or in any other manner inconsistent with the Purposes of the United Nations." Finally, some of the major Nazi war criminals would be tried, convicted, and sentenced to death by the Nuremberg Tribunal for waging an aggressive war or a war in violation of international treaties such as the Kellogg-Briand Pact. This Nuremberg Crime against Peace would become another pillar of the post–World War II legal and political world order.

## The Realist Critique
Today, in the post–World War II era, with the enlightened but uninspiring benefit of historical hindsight, it would be easy, yet simplistic, for international political realists to argue that pre–World War I American international lawyers and statesmen should have foreseen that the national interests of the newly imperial United States demanded its active participation in the European balance-of-power system after 1898; that America had succeeded to the geopolitical position of Great Britain by effectively becoming the "holder" of a worldwide balance of power that now only radiated from and around Europe; that the primary obligation of the holder of the balance

was the willingness to abandon its "splendid isolation" when necessary in order to "restore" the balance in the event the latter was threatened or disrupted; that the moment had come for the United States to countermand its traditional policies of isolationism in peace and neutrality in war by allying itself with the two other major Western democracies, France and Great Britain,[1] in time to forestall the development of a general war in Europe, or else, immediately after the war broke out in 1914, to throw in its lot with the Triple Entente; and that after the war, America's global interests required it to be willing to guarantee the existence of even an arguably unjust status quo in Europe by joining the League of Nations in order to enforce world peace.[2]

## The Legalist Response

In retrospect, contemporary political scientists, lawyers, historians, and realists of all stripes are certainly entitled to raise the general question whether the Second World War decisively proved that the 1898–1922 U.S. legalist war-prevention program for world politics was an abysmal failure because it was essentially predicated on naive, idealistic, and utopian assumptions concerning the inherent utility of international law and international organizations for the attenuation of the use of force by states. Yet, before this question can be properly answered, it is first necessary to consider a different set of questions drawn from a counterfactual historical perspective:[3]

–What if Germany had not objected to the principle of obligatory arbitration at the First Hague Peace Conference? Or to the conclusion of a multilateral obligatory arbitration treaty at the Second?

–What if the Latin American states had not opposed the formation of the Court of Arbitral Justice at the Second Hague Peace Conference over the issue of its composition, which did not impede the conference's adoption of the plan for the International Prize Court?

–What if the British House of Lords had not rejected the Declaration of London and the International Prize Court in 1911?

–What if the nations of the world had proceeded on schedule in 1913 to enter into preliminary preparations for the convocation of the Third Hague Peace Conference in 1915?

–What if the states of the world community had established some system for the automatic convocation of an international conference in the event of tensions or hostilities?[4]

–Would there have been a First World War over Sarajevo if one or more of these international legal developments had occurred beforehand?

–Even then, what if Austria had accepted Serbia's offer to submit the entire dispute arising out of the assassination of Francis Ferdinand to "the International Tribunal of The Hague"[5] or to a Hague international commission of inquiry?

–Could the United States have succeeded at its appointed task of staying out of the Great War by means of an operative International Prize Court adjudicating in accordance with a Declaration of London that was ratified by all the belligerents? Or by means of a Bryan peace treaty with Germany?[6] Or at least by virtue of both mechanisms working in conjunction with each other for the peaceful settlement of America's major disputes with Germany arising from the war?

The historical record adduced above substantiates the proposition that with just a little more support from a few obstreperous actors at key moments, the elements of the pre–World War I U.S. legalist war-prevention program could have fallen into place soon enough to create a reformed structure of international relations in which conditions propitious for the outbreak of a general systemic war in Europe could have been substantially ameliorated. In any event, there is no evidence that the U.S. legalist approach to international relations was to any extent responsible for the eruption of the Great War. Furthermore, it would be difficult to maintain that the adoption of any one or more of these U.S. schemes and devices for international law and organizations rendered the First World War more likely to occur.

The breakdown of world order in 1914 was definitely not caused by international law and international organizations, let alone by a U.S. legalist foreign policy that promoted them. Indeed, a good historical argument could be made that the First World War occurred in substantial part because there were too few, and certainly not too many, international laws and organizations. When the Great War among the European powers finally broke out, it occurred in spite of—not because of—America's perspicacious efforts to prevent, forestall, and ultimately confine a feared global conflagration through preemptive implementation of this legalist approach to international relations.

### The Causes of the Second World War

A similar rationale can be developed to refute the political realists' claims that U.S. reliance on international law and organizations was somehow responsible for the outbreak of the Second World War. In the aftermath of the First World War, to the extent that U.S. nonparticipation in the work of the League of Nations and the Permanent Court of International Justice vitiated the effectiveness of these organizations, and to the extent that their inefficacy can accurately be said to have contributed to the development of historical conditions ripe for the eruption of the Second World War, then responsibility for this situation must be placed squarely on the shoulders of the isolationist members of a U.S. Senate that was controlled by a Republican party with both eyes firmly fixed on the 1920 presidential election.[7] If the habitually cantankerous and traditionally partisan Senate had implemented those constituent elements of the U.S. international law community's 1898–1922 war-prevention program that were embodied in the League of Nations Covenant by means of giving its advice and consent to the Treaty of Versailles as well as to the PCIJ Protocol of Signature,[8] there is perhaps a good possibility that the Second World War might not have occurred.

The foundation of the League of Nations and the Permanent Court of International Justice was the direct result—if not the ultimate consummation—of the pre–World War I U.S. legalist approach to international relations. Both well before and immediately after the First World War, American international lawyers and statesmen had astutely led the way in promoting support for the creation of these international organizations and their lineal predecessors among the states of the international community. It was certainly not their fault that after the Great War the Senate chose to repudiate the fundamental elements of their war-prevention program for world politics.

Furthermore, the alleged "failure" of the League of Nations to "prevent" the Second World War should be attributed in substantial part to the fact that the United States adamantly refused to participate in its activities. The League of Nations was Woodrow Wilson's Fourteenth Point. The League was supposed to be America's gift to the Old World for the preservation of its international peace and security into the indefinite future. The entire structure of the League of Nations had been designed and constructed at the Paris Peace Conference on the elemental premise that the United States would become its foremost member.

Disowned by its own parent, and thus devoid of any support from the world's most powerful and principled state at that time, it was not surprising that the League could do little to prevent Hitler from overthrowing the Treaty of Versailles. After all, the Covenant of the League of Nations was both in fact and in law Part I of the Treaty of Peace signed at Versailles on June 28, 1919, as well as of the other peace treaties that were signed in 1919 and 1920. If the Treaty of Versailles really was an unjust peace that had been imposed on Germany at France's insistence, in violation of Wilson's Fourteen Points, then the League could not have worked successfully to support the Versailles status quo without vigorous backing from the United States, whose entry into the Great War had made the Versailles victory possible in the first place.

If anything, the European states—not the United States—must be faulted for relying on the shell of the League to protect their Versailles gains from a predictably revanchist Germany.[9] But, of course, an impressive facade at Geneva was all that America had left to Europe. Be that as it may, certainly after the First World War the U.S. government did not look to the League of Nations to protect its national security interests to any extent. Rather, whether rightly or wrongly, America simply defined its national interest to exclude the preservation of the Versailles status quo, including the League of Nations. Despite the best efforts of the U.S. international law community to the contrary, the cardinal principles of interwar U.S. foreign policy would become—once again—isolationism in peace and neutrality in war, but still seeking world order by means of promoting international law and international organizations.

## The Legalist Origins of the United Nations

During the period between the First and Second World Wars, America's innate isolationist tendencies reasserted themselves and restrained the nation's relatively more recent internationalist foreign policies promoting international law and organizations. Thus, the U.S. legalist approach to international relations that was classically defined and articulated from the Spanish-American War through the establishment of the League of Nations and the Permanent Court of International Justice cannot fairly be held responsible for either the First or the Second World War. If anything, both world wars occurred in spite of, and not because of, the best efforts by American international lawyers and statesmen to prevent them through the creation of new rules of international law and new institutions for the peaceful settlement of international disputes.

Eventually, during the course of the Second World War, Americans gained a better comprehension of the essential wisdom of the pre–World War I U.S. legalist approach to international relations. The shocked reaction of the U.S. government and the American people to the horrors of this second worldwide conflagration produced a profound realization of the extreme dangers that would flow from continuing an isolationist foreign policy. On October 30, 1943, the United States, the United Kingdom, the Soviet Union, and China proclaimed the Moscow Declaration, which recognized "the necessity of establishing at the earliest practicable date a general international organization, based on the principle of the sovereign equality of all peace-loving States, and open to membership by all such States large and small, for the maintenance of international peace and security."[10] Pursuant thereto, the U.S. Senate would readily give its advice and consent to the Charter of the United Nations on July 28, 1945, by a vote of 89 to 2.[11] And when the U.S. Senate grudgingly accepted the compulsory jurisdiction of the International Court of Justice in 1946, the pre–World War I U.S. legalist approach to international relations finally attained its full fruition.[12]

To be sure, almost forty years later, on October 7, 1985, the Reagan administration decided to repudiate the compulsory jurisdiction of the International Court of Justice in reaction to an adverse jurisdictional ruling in the *Nicaragua* case.[13] But despite this serious setback for both the United States and the World Court, ever since 1945 the United Nations has substantially contributed to the maintenance of international peace and security, and thus to the prevention of a suicidal Third World War.[14] A significant percentage of the international institutions and an enormous degree of the world order that humankind benefits from today are directly attributable to the legalist approach to international relations that was designed and partially implemented by the U.S. government between the First Hague Peace Conference of 1899 and the Paris Peace Conference of 1919. These matters are discussed in the Appendix.

### Lessons from the Past

In 1898, the United States purposefully chose to emulate the imperial countries of the Old World and set out to become a major global power by performing a series of naked acts of military, political, and economic expansion. Since that time, America has struggled to come to grips with the irreversible consequences of those fateful decisions, which directly contradicted several of the most fundamental normative principles on which the United States was supposed to have been founded. During this imperialist era of its history, the promotion of international law and international organizations has usually provided the United States with the means for reconciling the idealism of American values and aspirations with the realism of world politics and historical conditions. The U.S. government's resolute dedication to pursue a legalist approach to international relations has proven to be critical for the preservation of America's internal psychic equilibrium, which in turn has historically been a necessary precondition for the successful advancement of its global position.

Both well before and immediately after the First World War—as well as immediately after the Second World War—the United States established an excellent track record for pioneering innovative rules of international law and novel institutions for the peaceful settlement of international disputes. Drastic departures from the 1898–1922 tradition of U.S. legalist diplomacy in order to follow a foreign policy based essentially on isolationism in peace and neutrality in war after the Senate's rejection of the Treaty of Versailles— or, under the influence of the modern political realists, on Machiavellian power politics soon after the Second World War—produced only unmitigated disasters for the U.S. government both at home and abroad. One of the primary lessons to be learned from the history of the 1898–1922 era of U.S. foreign policy is that the states of the contemporary world—and especially the United States of America—must grow to possess a little more courage and foresight, and a little less selfishness and fear, when it comes to the promotion of international law and organizations as impediments to nuclear Armageddon.[15]

From 1898 to 1922, the American legalist founders of world order stepped boldly into the future with a grand design for preventing war and ensuring peace over the long-haul course of international relations that was solidly based on international law and international organizations. Because of their vision, plans, and efforts, the world is a much safer place for humanity today. We must do no less for the sake of our children and the children of tomorrow's world.

# Appendix.
## International Law and the Use of Force:
## Beyond Regime Theory

*I. Right versus Might*

In recent years, Stanley Hoffmann developed a resounding critique of the so-called Reagan Doctrine, while in the process—and more importantly—analyzing the ethical foundations of international law and world order, particularly with respect to superpower relations.[1] According to Hoffmann, from this broader perspective, the "rules" of the "game" between the then superpowers do not constitute a "regime" as that has been defined in the literature of international political science. Hoffmann was certainly correct to argue that there currently is no such thing as an international security regime between the United States and the Soviet Union, or Russia, its successor state. Nevertheless, there does indeed exist such a phenomenon known as a "regime" concerning the threat and use of force in international relations. The existence of such a regime is made possible by the fact that whatever their respective differences *inter se* may be, both superpowers during the cold war did share a common interest in regulating and then reducing the transnational threat and use of force by other actors in the international system, if not even oftentimes by themselves.

Hoffmann concluded his chapter by noting the "seachange" in Soviet international behavior under Mikhail Gorbachev that was designed to produce more superpower cooperation. Gorbachev's initiatives were certainly worth U.S. reciprocation. Realistically speaking, cooperation seemed the only alternative for America in today's world of "existential deterrence."

In any event, a good deal could be learned from the application of regime theory in order to better understand the nature of the relationships between international law and international politics concerning the threat and use of force.[2] By now, political science regime theorists have established the critical importance of international law and organizations to the areas of international trade, monetary policy, human rights, natural resources, the environment, etc. But when it comes to questions dealing with the threat and use of force, their general conclusion seems to have been that there really is not a "regime" as defined within that framework of reference. Or if there is such a regime, that it is not terribly "effective." Yet, these neo-realist political scientists were assessing the "effectiveness" of the international law and organizations "regime" when it comes to international conflict in accordance with Hobbesian criteria. But even from that perspective, a good case can be made that such an international law regime exists and works fairly effectively at the maintenance of international peace and security.

*II. Realism and Law*

Political science regime theorists have pointed out the critical importance of a Hobbesian "hegemon" for the creation of an international regime. So, with its near-total monopoly of nuclear, military, economic, and political power immediately after World War II, it was the U.S. that served as the regime theorist hegemon for the creation and preservation of an international law regime regulating the threat and use of force that still exists today in international relations. At the time, the creation of an international regime to regulate and reduce the transnational threat and use of force was deemed to be not only consistent with, but a vital part of, American national security interests. In the immediate aftermath of World War II, the classic Machiavellian dichotomy between the "is" and the "ought to be" did not hold true for American foreign policy decision-making. That which was just and that which was expedient coincided and reinforced each other to call for America to create a regime regulating the transnational threat and use of force in international relations.

By virtue of its victory, the preservation of the resulting political, economic, and military status quo was to America's enormous advantage. American national security interests were best served by the creation of an international regime for the threat and use of force applicable to both itself as well as to other states because such a regime would better preserve the status quo as well as encourage its peaceful, instead of violent, evolution. To the superlative degree that the United States enjoyed the benefits of the then existing configuration of international relations, the greater was its commitment to the creation and maintenance of an international regime of law and institutions for regulating and reducing the transnational threat or use of force.

Phenomenologically, law is the instrument *par excellence* for the peaceful preservation and peaceful transformation of any political or economic status quo, whether domestic or international. By its very nature, the creation of this post–World War II international legal regime represented an attempt by advantaged international actors such as (primarily) the United States, as well as by the other victors—the Soviet Union, Great Britain, France, and China—to legitimate (i.e., impart a moral value content to) currently existing and proposed power relationships. A fundamental transformation in the international balance of power produced by systemic warfare from 1939 resulted in the establishment of a regime of new international law and organizations regulating the threat and use of force,[3] which in turn endowed these postwar power relationships with a connotation of international and domestic moral value, legitimacy, and authentication. As Hans Morgenthau used to teach his students, power endowed with legitimacy (i.e., the so-called Rule of Law) is far more powerful, effective, and efficient than naked power alone.

Even the archrealist Machiavelli once observed in *The Prince:* "The principal foundations of all states . . . consist of good laws and good armed forces."[4] And later on: "You should know, then, that there are two ways of fighting: one with the law, the other with force."[5] A government committed to the preservation of the status quo must learn how to "fight" by means of the law.

Machiavelli knew something that the sophist Callicles did not:[6] Law was not a social convention created by the weak to protect them from the strong, but rather an instrumentality created by the strong to better keep them in power against the demands for change by the weak.[7] These same principles generally held true for the regime of international law and organizations created by the United States and its allied victors. For the leading status quo states in the post–World War II international political system, the wisdom of the fox (i.e., international law and organizations) became just as important as the strength of the lion (i.e., military force).[8]

*III. The Institutions, Rules, and Procedures of This Regime*

There is not space to discuss all the institutions, procedures, and rules of the international law regime concerning the threat and use of force that was set up by the U.S. government, *inter alia,* after 1945. Of course, its central component was the United Nations Organization as well as its affiliated organizations and institutions in numerous functionalist areas (e.g., WHO, FAO, UNESCO, IAEA, IMCO, etc.). To this list should also be added the UN affiliated international economic institutions that the United States government established contemporaneously for the express purpose of controlling the international economic order, especially the IMF, the World Bank, and the GATT. In addition, came the so-called regional organizations that were brought into affiliation with the United Nations Organization by means of Chapter 8 of the United Nations Charter (i.e., the OAS, the League of Arab States, later the OAU, perhaps someday ASEAN and the CSCE). And, of course, most importantly, were the so-called collective self-defense arrangements organized under Article 51 of the United Nations Charter that constituted such an integral part of the post–World War II U.S. foreign policy objective of "containment" of the Soviet Union: NATO, the Rio Pact, the Baghdad Pact/CENTO, SEATO, ANZUS, etc. Finally, came the numerous bilateral self-defense treaties concluded under Article 51 by the United States government with states along the periphery of the Soviet empire such as Japan, South Korea, the Philippines, Iran, Pakistan, Taiwan, etc. for the exact same purpose.

Quite obviously, it would take an entire book to discuss all the elemental institutions, procedures, and rules of the current regime of international law and organizations that regulate and reduce the threat and use of force in international relations that was created by the United States government during and immediately after the Second World War.[9] Suffice it to say, that the basic principles underlying this regime were and still are two strong preferences: (1) against the threat or use of military force in international relations, and (2) in favor of the peaceful resolution of international disputes. To be sure, sometimes these tendencies do not prove to be decisive. Nevertheless, the rules, procedures, structures, weight, and momentum of this international law regime work strongly against resort to the threat or use of military force by government decision-makers.

The United States government established these presumptions, tendencies, and procedures most forthrightly and effectively in the Charter of the UN. Under the direction of American hegemony, the only legitimate justifications and procedures for the perpetration of violence and coercion by one state against another became those set forth in the UN Charter. The Charter alone contains those rules which have been consented to by the virtual unanimity of the international community that has voluntarily joined the UN. This currently existing international legal regime concerning the threat and use of force "authenticates" what are legitimate and illegitimate threats or uses of force that are either proposed or ongoing. For this reason, in times of international crisis, there exist strong pressures upon decision-makers to act in a manner that limits the exercise of their threats or uses of transnational force in basic concordance with the conditions prescribed by the Charter.

Succinctly put, these rules include the UN Charter's Article 2(3) and Article 33(1) obligations for the peaceful settlement of international disputes; the Article 2(4) prohibition on the threat or use of force; and the Article 51 restriction of the right of individual or collective self-defense to the occurrence of an actual "armed attack" or "aggression armée." Related to this right of self-defense are its two fundamental requirements for the "proportionality" and the "necessity" of the forceful response to the threat. Furthermore, as definitively stated by Secretary of State Daniel Webster in the famous case of The Caroline, "anticipatory" self-defense might be justified when the "necessity of that self-defence is instant, overwhelming, and leaving no choice of means, and no moment for deliberation."[10] Thus, according to the French-language version of the UN Charter—which is equally authentic with the English—an "armed aggression" that is short of an actual "armed attack" could nevertheless trigger the right of a state to use force in self-defense.

Likewise, there exist several institutions and procedures that function as integral parts of this international law regime to regulate and reduce the transnational threat and use of force. To mention only the most well-known: (1) "enforcement action" by the UN Security Council as specified in Chapter 7 of the Charter; (2) "enforcement action" by the appropriate regional organizations acting with the authorization of the Security Council as required by Article 53 and specified in Chapter 8; (3) the so-called peacekeeping operations and monitoring forces organized under the jurisdiction of the Security Council pursuant to Chapter 6; (4) peacekeeping operations under the auspices of the UN General Assembly in accordance with the Uniting for Peace Resolution; and (5) peacekeeping operations and monitoring forces deployed by the relevant regional organizations acting in conformity with their proper constitutional procedures.[11]

Finally, in the event that military force is ultimately used by government decision-makers, this international law regime concerning the transnational threat and use of force also contains rules, procedures, and institutions that will nonetheless operate: (1) to limit the number of actors involved in the conflict as well as its geographical extent; (2) to limit the intensity and ferocity of the conflict; and (3) to encourage the peaceful settlement of the underlying dispute. This first task is discharged by the well-recognized customary and conventional international laws of neutrality that constitute a "nested" international sub-regime in their own right (e.g., the two 1907 Hague Neutrality Conventions on Land and Sea Warfare, respectively).

Next, limitations on the conduct of military operations have historically been considered important by government decision-makers for reasons of both military efficiency and humanitarian concerns. This dual rationale has given birth to and sustained the customary and conventional international laws of war (e.g., the 1907 Hague Regulations on Land Warfare, the 1909 Declaration of London on Sea Warfare, and the 1923 Draft Hague Rules of Air Warfare), as well as the international laws of humanitarian armed conflict (e.g., the four Geneva Conventions of 1949 and their two Additional Protocols of 1977). The International Committee of the Red Cross (ICRC) plays the multifarious roles of supervisor, intermediator, conciliator, and protector of this humanitarian subregime that is "nested" within the overall international law regime concerning the threat and use of force.

These two interconnected sub-regimes of neutrality and humanitarian law operate to keep an armed conflict within limited geographical, numerical, and psychological parameters so that the aforementioned international institutions and procedures for the peaceful settlement of international disputes can ultimately come into play: the UN Security Council, the General Assembly, and the "good offices" of the UN Secretary General; the same with respect to the regional organizations and arrangements; UN, regional, and ad hoc peacekeeping operations and monitoring forces; the International Court of Justice, as well as international arbitration, mediation, and conciliation, etc. When government decision-makers eventually conclude that their use of military force has spent its utility, they have invariably resorted to the international law regime concerning the threat and use of force in order to produce a peaceful resolution to their basic conflict—what else can they do? Witness, for example, the termination of the bitter and long-standing Iraq-Iran war when both exhausted belligerents finally turned to the UN Security Council in order to establish a ceasefire as well as to create a UN monitoring force to facilitate and guarantee it.

*IV. Hegemonic Stability?*

Moreover, the "effectiveness" of this international law regime concerning the threat and use of force is no longer dependent upon the "hegemonic stability" that had once been provided by the United States government. In this short space, the analysis can only incorporate by reference and extend by analogy many of the arguments that have already been developed by Robert Keohane in *After Hegemony* to explain in this case why there still persists a fairly effective international law regime regulating the transnational threat and use of force despite the obvious decline of U.S. hegemony over international military, political, and economic relationships between the end of World War II and today. To the same effect would be arguments found in Robert Axelrod's *The Evolution of Cooperation;* in Kenneth Oye, ed., *Cooperation under Anarchy* (1986); and in Duncan Snidal's trenchant critique of the "hegemonic stability" thesis from the perspective of collective action theory.[12] As Snidal aptly put it with respect to the dynamics of the international economic order:[13]

> Therefore the decline of [U.S.] hegemonic power will facilitate collective action by increasing its importance and changing the strategic interrelations of the actors. Further, it will lead to an outcome collectively superior to that which occurred under the dominance of the hegemonic power . . . and one that may even have preferable distributive characteristics. . . .
>
> Secondary powers will be willing to participate in collective action provided that they have incentives to avoid the collapse of the regime—which follows both from

[the] assumption that they benefit from it and from the observation that they are sufficiently powerful to have an impact on it. *This changed strategic situation may even lead to higher levels of cooperation.* [Emphasis added.]

The next section of this essay will argue that the world is currently witnessing the manifestation of Snidal's envisioned phenomena with respect to the international law regime concerning the transnational threat and use of force. The decline in U.S. "hegemony" produced (1) a major increase of support by the then Soviet Union for the international law regime concerning the threat and use of force, as well as (2) a willingness by both superpowers to collaborate in order to shore up and then strengthen this regime. This superpower collaboration in turn produced an increasing degree of collective action in support of this international law regime by the other "great power" permanent members of the UN Security Council (viz., United Kingdom, China and France). Their collective action in support of this regime as a generally perceived international "public good" proved to be sufficient to produce "higher levels of cooperation" at the United Nations Security Council, the General Assembly, and the World Court, among other institutional fora.

*V. Regime Effectiveness*

There is no way this brief essay can "prove" the "effectivenes" of this international law regime concerning the threat and use of force. Fortunately, part of that task has already been accomplished by Ernst Haas in his introductory chapter to the aforementioned UNITAR book.[14] Haas' study was a masterful survey of the actual record of the United Nations Organization when it came to the successful management of international conflict during the first forty years of its existence.

Haas' research was also a powerful antidote to the vicious attacks against the UN that had been mounted by the Reagan administration and its acolytes throughout the academic world and in the mainstream news media. Because of the general prevalence of these latter criticisms in public discourse, it would be important to reproduce Haas' summary of conclusions here.[15] Perhaps the most important lesson to be learned from analyzing Haas' meticulous study is that the UN will become even more effective at the task of maintaining international peace and security to the extent that it has the active support of the United States government.

When the Bush administration assumed power and apparently returned to the traditional American approach toward and support for international law and organizations, the world experienced the somewhat amazing situation where for the first time in forty-five years, both superpowers were actively supporting the UN and its international law regime regulating the transnational threat and use of force. Gorbachev launched a foreign policy with a central component strengthening the international law regime concerning the threat and use of force that is found in the Charter and elsewhere.[16] In significant part, Gorbachev was spurred into action by the curious spectacle of the Reagan administration striving mightily to undermine this very regime that America had created in 1945 in order to better serve and promote its own interests. Here the world witnessed the strange phenomenon of the declining hegemon seeking to devour its own children.

Once it became clear that the overall objective of the Reagan administration was to bypass or undercut this UN regime, the Soviet Union felt compelled to recognize its stake in the effectiveness of the United Nations, and thus quickly acted to shore up this regime by using all its influence and power as well as those of its allies and supporters. Under the tutelage of Gorbachev and Bush, the Soviet Union and the United States attempted to reach a formal understanding to reinforce and expand the currently existing UN regime and to shape an international political climate that would be more conducive to the creation of an actual international security "regime" between them, as that term has been traditionally defined by neo-realists. Yet that effort is still incomplete, after the demise of the Soviet Union.

The United Nations regime regulating the transnational threat and use of force is alive and well, but troubled. As confirmation, witness the problematic efflorescence of UN peacekeeping operations or proposals for their deployment around the world today: in the Middle East, Cambodia, the Persian Gulf, Namibia, Angola, Somalia, Central America, Afghanistan, Western Sahara, etc. Even from a *realpolitik* perspective, this is the only way most of these serious international conflicts possessing destabilizing tendencies can be dealt with effectively.

*VI. The American Constitutional Regime Controlling Force*

There is one more point to be made about regime theory per se, which draws upon the rich literature of the "linkage-politics" approach to understanding the relationship between American domestic politics and its conduct of international affairs, namely, the importance and complexities of the interplay among the President, Congress, the courts, and the people with respect to the formulation of American foreign policy. The unitary rational-actor model postulated by the political realists and the neo-realists completely breaks down when it comes to explaining the manner in which American foreign policy is actually made and conducted under its constitutionally mandated system of separation of powers. The United States of America speaks and acts with many voices on foreign affairs. That is all for the better—despite the hallowed teachings of the political realists to the contrary.

After all, America is supposed to be a constitutional democracy with a commitment to the Rule of Law both at home and abroad. If the executive branch of the federal government decides to embark upon a course of egregiously lawless behavior abroad, then it is a testament to the strength and resilience of American democracy that Congress, the courts, and the American people refuse to go along with it. This dynamic has not been appreciated by most of the self-styled "realist" or "neo-realist" analysts of American foreign policy decision-making precisely because of their Hobbesian perspective on the world of both domestic affairs and international relations.

It is an undeniable fact that American foreign policy decision-making has been substantially subjected to the Rule of Law by the United States Constitution. And this is true whether the realists and neo-realists like it or not. Despite their Hobbesian predilections, it is the unalterable nature of this "legalist" reality so intrinsic to the United States of America that must be understood, internalized, and effectuated by its foreign policy decision-makers.

The pernicious thesis incessantly propounded by international political "realists" that for some mysterious reason American democracy is inherently incapable of developing a coherent, consistent, and non-Hobbesian foreign policy without Hobbism simply reflects their obstinate refusal to accept the well-established primacy of law over power in the U.S. constitutional system of government. The American people have never been willing to provide sustained popular support for a foreign policy that has flagrantly violated elementary norms of international law precisely because they have habitually perceived themselves to constitute a democratic political society governed by an indispensable commitment to the Rule of Law in all sectors of their national endeavors.

Thus, the U.S. government's good faith dedication to the pursuit of international law and international organizations in foreign affairs has usually proven to be critical both for the preservation of America's internal psychic equilibrium as well as for the consequent protection of its global position.

For these very *realpolitik* considerations, then, historically it has always proven to be in the so-called "national interest" of the United States of America to subject other states to the Rule of Law as well. In other words, since the United States Constitution has severely limited the ability of the United States government to threaten or use military force abroad for a variety of reasons too numerous to list here,[17] it has therefore proven to be in America's best interest likewise to severely limit the freedom of action by other states to resort to the threat or use of force by means of first establishing and then maintaining an international law regime to that effect.[18] Here, once again, that which is just and that which is expedient have coincided and reinforced each other.

## VII. The Hobbesian Spillover Phenomenon

In any event, an American foreign affairs analyst cannot even begin to comprehend the rudiments of U.S. foreign policy decision-making processes without possessing at least a sound working knowledge of international law, and especially of the interpenetration of the international legal regime and the American constitutional regime concerning the threat and use of force. To the contrary, America's self-styled "realist" geopolitical practitioners of Hobbesian power politics such as Kissinger, Brzezinski, Haig, Kirkpatrick, and Shultz demonstrated little appreciation, knowledge, or sensitivity to the requirements of the U.S. constitutional system of government premised upon fundamental commitment to the Rule of Law, whether at home or abroad. To be sure, it was a tribute to the genius and compassion of the late Hans Morgenthau that he alone was perhaps the only archetypal political realist who had a profound appreciation of, and deep respect for, the American democratic system of constitutional government.[19]

These other self-proclaimed "realist" American foreign policy decision-makers could not realistically hope to construct a watertight compartment around their exercise of Hobbesian power politics in international relations without creating a deleterious spillover effect into the domestic affairs of the American people. The Nixon-Kissinger administration was the paradigmatic example of the validity of this proposition with its interconnected tragedies of Vietnam and Watergate. The same can be said for the Reagan administration's Iran-contra scandal.

This spillover phenomenon was produced by the fact that Hobbesian power politics violently contradict several of the most fundamental normative principles upon which the United States of America is founded: the inalienable rights of the individual, the self-determination of peoples, the sovereign equality and independence of states, noninterventionism, respect for international law and organizations, and the peaceful settlement of international disputes, etc. Painfully aware of this connection, the American people historically have stridently resisted the practice of Hobbesian power politics by their governmental leaders both at home and abroad.

For at least the past thirty years, American governmental decision-makers have repeatedly tried to base their foreign affairs and defense policies on Hobbesian power politics. The net result has been the counterproductive creation of a series of unmitigated disasters for the United States, both at home and abroad, as well as the subversion of the entire post–World War II international legal order that the United States, *inter alia*, constructed at the 1945 San Francisco Conference in order to protect its own interests and advance its own values.[20] At a minimum, the executive branch of the federal government must come to understand that the constitutionally mandated separation-of-powers system, together with its concomitant Rule of Law, must be accepted as an historical fact to be dealt with on its own terms, rather than subverted, ignored, or expressly violated. If the executive branch wishes to design and execute a coherent and consistent foreign policy, then it must take into account and cooperate with the Congress, and to a lesser extent the courts, in the formulation of American foreign policy. The much vaunted goal of developing a truly "bipartisan" approach to foreign affairs cannot be achieved unless and until the President is willing to recognize the constitutional facts of life that: (1) Congress is an independent and co-equal branch of government; and (2) the President is subject to the Rule of Law in the field of foreign policy as well as in domestic affairs.

### VIII. Using International Law to Analyze American Foreign Policy

International law and organizations are simply facts of international politics as well as of U.S. domestic constitutional and political life. Hence, U.S. government decision-makers must routinely take into account considerations of international law and organizations in their formulation of American foreign policy, whether they want to or not. Either they view the rules of international law as something they should attempt to comply with as best as possible under the unique circumstances of an historical situation (e.g., the Cuban missile crisis),[21] or else they view the rules of international law as something that they have to overcome in order to accomplish their illicit objectives (e.g., the Iran-contra scandal).[22] For both reasons the rules of international law are therefore "relevant" to the formulation and conduct of American foreign policy. For example, the Reagan administration's attempt to circumvent the prohibitions of international law found in the Boland Amendment prohibiting its paramilitary contra war against Nicaragua ultimately led to its downfall as an effective force in both international relations and domestic affairs.

Nevertheless, this section assumes that U.S. government decision-makers really pay no meaningful attention whatsoever to the rules of international law when they formulate American foreign policy, but instead only invoke those rules or pander to international organizations on an *ex post facto* basis in order to justify whatever decisions they have made for Hobbesian or Machiavellian reasons. Would this then mean that the rules of international law are indeed "irrelevant"? The answer to this question for all teachers, scholars, students, and analysts of international relations is definitely in the negative. International law and organizations still remain critically relevant for any concerned citizen living in a democracy with a constitutional commitment to the Rule of Law for the purpose of formulating his or her own opinion on whether to support or oppose their own government's foreign affairs and defense policies, especially concerning the threat or use of force.

Precisely because of the existence of an American constitutional regime severely regulating the transnational threat or use of force by the United States government, invariably it has proven to be the case that executive branch decision-makers publicly attempt to justify their foreign policies in terms of international law and organizations and, more broadly put, in terms of what is legally/morally right or wrong for the consumption of domestic, allied, and international public opinion. It may be true that the actual motivation for a decision had been considerations of power politics. But it would be extremely difficult, if not impossible, to sell pure, unadulterated *realpolitik*—whether Hobbesian or Machiavellian—to the American people and Congress as the proper basis for the conduct of United States foreign policy.

Thus, U.S. government decision-makers oftentimes resort to legalistic subterfuges by pleading principles of international law in order to disguise their *realpolitik* foreign policy decisions. This was certainly true for the better part of the Reagan administration.[23] Of course this phenomenon seems to confirm the worst suspicions held by the "realist" political scientists that international law and organizations are therefore really irrelevant to the proper conduct of American foreign policy and to international relations as a whole.[24]

But even if U.S. government decision-makers pay absolutely no meaningful attention to the rules of international law, nevertheless they will and indeed must attempt to justify their policies to domestic and international public opinion by invoking the norms of international law. Therefore, if a foreign policy analyst possesses a rudimentary knowledge of international law and organizations, it would then be possible for him or her to apply these criteria to the government's stated rationalizations in order to determine whether or not the policy can be justified in accordance with the government's own explanation. If it cannot, then obviously the analyst must realize that he or she is not being told the truth and therefore something else must be going on behind the scenes that is quite different from what government officials are saying in public.

By thus using the principles of international law as an analytical tool, the student, scholar, and concerned citizen can first identify such legalistic deceptions, and then proceed to pierce through the veil of legal and moral obfuscations put forth by government officials in order to grasp the real heart of what the policy is all about. Such analysts might not like what they find when they get there—Hobbesian or Machiavellian power politics. But at least a substantive knowledge of international law and organizations would have enabled them to reach that point.

In addition, many foreign states also try to justify their foreign and domestic policies to the United States government and to the American people by invoking the rules of international law. Therefore, American foreign policy decision-makers, academic foreign policy analysts, and even concerned American citizens must be able to evaluate those foreign claims in accordance with the standard recognized criteria of international law. If the claims of the foreign government fall within the "ballpark" of international legality, then U.S. government decision-makers, private-sector foreign policy analysts, and the American people should be willing to give these foreign claims the benefit of the doubt and do their best to accommodate them within the overall conduct of American foreign policy to whatever extent is feasible.

On the other hand, when the foreign or domestic policy of the foreign state does not even fall within the "ballpark" of international legality, then it really is entitled to no respect at all on America's part, and U.S. foreign policy decision-makers should be wary of associating the American government with it in any way, shape or form. To the extent that American foreign policy decision-makers do so associate the U.S. government with the illegal policies and practices of a foreign government, then a basic knowledge of international law will put academic and private-sector foreign policy analysts as well as concerned American citizens in a better position to intelligently criticize that policy. Conversely, the same analytical principles would hold true when the executive branch of the United States government unjustifiably adopts an adversarial stance against a foreign government whose foreign or domestic policies basically comport with the rules of international law.

Furthermore, once foreign policy analysts (scholars, students, citizens) have unmasked the true nature of U.S. foreign policy by evaluating it in accordance with the standard recognized criteria of international law, then they can proceed to construct an alternative policy that is based upon considerations of international law and organizations. Unfortunately it is the case that most international political scientists of the realist school and most international lawyers of the positivist school really have no constructive alternatives to offer anyone. The realists simply insist that all is a matter of power and interest, which means reliance upon political and economic coercion, and ultimately upon the threat and use of military force. Whereas the legalists lament the fact that international law cannot be enforced and there is thus little that can be done, except that the devil takes the hindmost. In the final analysis, both schools lead to the same Hobbesian prescriptions.

It is never satisfactory for American foreign policy analysts just to criticize the U.S. government's decisions. Rather, they owe it to their students, to the American people and Congress, to U.S. government decision-makers themselves, as well as to foreign states and peoples, to develop a constructive alternative approach toward resolving the major problems of international relations. How many times have the American people heard the refrain, especially during the tenure of the Reagan administration, that there are really only two alternative courses of conduct: Either the threat or use of U.S. military force in a particular situation; or else the "enemies" of the United States government will prevail? There is, however, a third alternative to either Hobbesian interventionism or doing nothing (i.e., isolationism). It consists of the rules of international law and the procedures of international organizations for the peaceful settlement of international disputes (i.e., internationalism).

## IX. The Case of the Reagan Doctrine against Nicaragua

The Reagan administration's covert war against Nicaragua was generally said to have been the classic exemplar of the self-styled Reagan Doctrine of supporting anti-communist guerrilla movements around the world. The Reagan administration routinely cited principles of international law in order to justify its gratuitously aggressive policies against Nicaragua.[25] A basic knowledge of the rules of international law would have helped an analyst (or concerned citizen) to unravel the true purpose of the Reagan administration's foreign policy toward that country. In addition, international law and organizations could then have been used to develop an alternative constructive foreign policy that rejected the Reagan administration's bogus alternatives of indirect and direct U.S. military intervention, or else "communist domination" of Central America.

Applying basic rules of international law to the Reagan administration's foreign policy toward Nicaragua, it would have been possible to conclude that it could not be justified in accordance with the terms of the United Nations Charter, the Charter of the Organization of American States, and the Geneva Conventions of 1949, at a minimum.[26] Therefore, a foreign policy analyst (or concerned citizen) would be forced to conclude that there was much more behind it than simply trying to interdict an alleged flow of weapons, equipment and supplies from Nicaragua through Honduras to El Salvador, which the Reagan administration maintained was the basis of its policy from the outset. Eventually, it became quite clear through the fog of legalistic lies, distortions, and obfuscations that the real purpose of the Reagan administration's policy was to overthrow the Sandinista government, which could not be justified at all under basic norms of international law. Finally, the Reagan administration was forced to publicly admit that this had been its true objective all along.

As for the constructive alternative, a rudimentary knowledge of international law and organizations would have pointed out the utility of the Organization of American States, or the United Nations Security Council, or both for settling the conflict. In particular, it would have been possible to deploy UN or OAS peacekeeping forces along the borders between Nicaragua and Honduras as well as between Nicaragua and Costa Rica, if the Reagan administration was truly concerned about Nicaragua's supposed aggression against its neighbors. But, since terminating the flow of munitions and guerrillas was never the basis of the policy in the first place, the Reagan administration quite naturally rejected any resolution involving an international peacekeeping force.

Such a force would have been quite useful to prevent the alleged flow of munitions and supplies, but it would have been completely useless for the purpose of overthrowing the Sandinista government. To the contrary, the interposition of such international peacekeeping forces on Nicaragua's border would have prevented the infiltration of contra terrorists by the Reagan administration from Honduras and Costa Rica into Nicaragua. This is precisely why the Nicaraguan government eventually came around to propose the creation of such international peacekeeping forces along its borders, and also why the Reagan administration promptly rejected such a proposal. So much for the Reagan administration's alleged commitment to obtaining a negotiated solution for the conflicts in Central America.

In 1986 the International Court of Justice (ICJ) soundly condemned the Reagan administration's covert contra war against Nicaragua as a violation of basic norms of international law, and ordered its termination.[27] But the war continued. Nevertheless, the World Court's decision in the Nicaragua case was quite effectively utilized by the anti-contra protest movement and lobbying groups in the United States to oppose renewed funding for the contras by Congress.

In this case, therefore, even though the ICJ adjudication did not produce instant compliance by the Reagan administration, it nonetheless substantially contributed to the ultimate resolution of this problem by means of further, if not completely, delegitimizing (i.e., "de-authenticating") this contra military "option." With the election of the Bush administration in 1988, both governments proceeded to rely quite extensively upon the rules of international law and the procedures of international organizations—including the deployment of an international monitoring force organized under the joint auspices of the United Nations and the Organization of American States—in order to obtain a mutually satisfactory result that restored a modicum of peace and stability to Nicaragua.

## X. Beyond Regime Theory

International law and organizations comprise a most powerful analytical instrument for professional foreign policy analysts (whether lawyers, political scientists, historians, or economists) to use for the purpose of first understanding and then evaluating the conduct of American foreign policy as well as the foreign and domestic behavior of other nation-states—whether allied, friendly, neutral, non-aligned, or overtly hostile. The rules of international law can also provide objective criteria for making predictions and value judgments as to the feasibility, the propriety, and the ultimate success or failure of interactive foreign policy behavior among nation-states. Finally, the rules of international law can be used by concerned citizens living in a popularly elected democracy with a constitutional commitment to the Rule of Law in order to serve as a check-and-balance against the natural abuses of power endemic to any form of government when it comes to the conduct of foreign affairs and defense policies.

Concerning this latter point, if U.S. government decision-makers essentially operate according to the political realist credo that the rules of international law are irrelevant, then what they will be doing is acting in a manner that indicates that the United States government does not really care about the expectations held by other states and peoples as to what they believe is the minimal degree of respect and deference that they are entitled to in their relations with the U.S. government. When this Hobbesian attitude is translated into the conduct of American foreign policy, it then quite naturally becomes a prescription for disagreement, difficulties, and conflict with other states and peoples. The U.S. government thus places itself into a position where the primary means by which it can achieve its objectives become through the brute application of political, economic and military coercion. Needless to say, these latter techniques have a very high cost to pay, both internationally and domestically, in today's interdependent world.

By contrast, if in the formulation of American foreign policy decision-making, serious attention is paid to the rules of international law, what this will mean is that in essence U.S. government decision-makers will be taking into account the reasonable expectations of other states and peoples in order to define their objectives (i.e., the ends) and then to accomplish them (i.e., the means). It seems almost intuitively obvious that if this process should transpire, then it would be far easier for the United States government to carry out its foreign policy and to achieve its ultimate goals. To be sure, U.S. objectives might have to be scaled down somewhat by taking into account the criteria of international law (e.g., the inalienable right of the self-determination of peoples); or certain means would have to be discarded in order to achieve American objectives because of the requirements of international law (e.g., the general prohibition on the unilateral threat and use of force). From this anti-Hobbesian perspective, therefore, maybe the United States government will not obtain everything it wants, but perhaps approximately 90% of the desired objective could be obtained and the countervailing costs would have been minimized.

For these reasons, then, the rules of international law provide useful criteria by which U.S. government decision-makers can and should formulate their foreign affairs and defense policies. This does not mean, however, that the rules of international law are so clear that all the U.S. government has to do is to apply them in order to achieve its objectives. Rather, the rules of international law typically tell U.S. government decision-makers what they should not do in order to avoid foreign affairs disasters. Similarly, in a more positive sense, the rules of international law and the techniques of international organizations usually provide a guiding way out of some of the basic dilemmas that confront American foreign policy decision-makers in today's interdependent world.

To be sure, international law and organizations are no panacea for the numerous problems of contemporary international relations. But they do provide one promising medium for extricating the American foreign policy decision-making establishment from the oppressive Hobbesian morass that has enmired it for at least the past three decades. By conceptualizing international law and organizations in these anti-Hobbesian terms, scholars can objectively demonstrate their relevance to the study and practice of international relations, as well as to the future conduct of American foreign policy. In the process, scholars can also point out the way for new directions in the study of international politics, law, organizations, and regimes toward the start of the third millennium of humankind's parlous existence.

# Notes

## Introduction

1 See Dean Acheson, *Present at the Creation* (1969).
2 See, e.g., Michael Zurn, *Bringing the Second Image (Back) In: About the Domestic Sources of Regime Formation*, in Regime Theory and International Relations 282–311 (Volker Rittberger ed., 1993).
3 See, generally, Francis A. Boyle, *International Law and the Use of Force: Beyond Regime Theory*, in Ideas and Ideals: Essays on Politics in Honor of Stanley Hoffmann 376–94 (Linda B. Miller & Michael Joseph Smith eds., 1993). This article is reprinted as the Appendix to this book with the permission of Westview Press.

## 1 The Legalist Approach to International Relations

1 See Francis A. Boyle, *The Irrelevance of International Law: The Schism between International Law and International Politics*, 10 Cal. W. Int'l L.J. 193 (1980) [hereinafter cited as Boyle, *Irrelevance*]. For an analysis of the relationship between international political realism and the American legal realist movement of the 1920s and 1930s, see Henry Steiner and Detlev Vagts, Transnational Legal Problems 346–52 (2d ed. 1976).
2 See, generally, Hans Morgenthau, Politics among Nations 4–15 (5th ed. 1973). But cf. James B. Scott, *Lawyer-Secretaries of Foreign Relations of the United States*, 3 Am. J. Int'l L. 942–46 (1909) (the great U.S. secretaries of state were lawyers). Hereinafter the *American Journal of International Law* will be cited as AJIL.
3 Thomas Hobbes, Leviathan 100 (Michael Oakeshott ed., 1962).
4 See H. Morgenthau, In Defense of the National Interest 144 (1951).
5 See President Wilson's State Papers and Addresses 464–72 (Albert Shaw ed., 1918).
6 See Jean-Jacques Rousseau, *Discourse on the Origin and Foundations of Inequality (Second Discourse)*, in The First and Second Discourses 77 (Roger D. Masters ed., 1964).
7 See, e.g., Edward H. Carr, The Twenty Years' Crisis, 1919–1939 at 22–40 (2d ed. 1946).
8 Treaty of Versailles, June 28, 1919, 2 Bevans 42, 225 Parry's T.S. 188, reprinted in 13 AJIL 151 (Supp. 1919).
9 See, e.g., Denna F. Fleming, The United States and the League of Nations 1918–1920,

at 57 (1932); Manley O. Hudson, Woodrow Wilson's Fourteen Points after Eight Years 9 (Woodrow Wilson Foundation: n.d.) (Dec. 28, 1925 dinner speech).

10    Kellogg-Briand Pact, Aug. 27, 1928, 46 Stat. 2343, 94 L.N.T.S. 57.

11    U.S. Department of State Press Releases 41 (Jan. 7, 1932).

12    George Santayana, 1 The Life of Reason 284 (1905).

13    See F. Boyle, *The Law of Power Politics*, 1980 U. Ill. L.F. 901, 928–29 [hereinafter cited as Boyle, *Power Politics*].

14    John Austin, *The Province of Jurisprudence Determined* 121–26, 137–44 (1954).

15    See Thomas Kuhn, *The Structure of Scientific Revolutions* (2d ed. 1970).

16    From an international legal positivist perspective, the McDougal-Lasswell jurisprudence of international law is atavistic because of its self-proclaimed value orientation. See Boyle, *Irrelevance, supra* this chapter, at 206–14. I develop a "functionalist" approach to analyzing the relationship between international law and politics in F. Boyle, *International Law in Time of Crisis: From the Entebbe Raid to the Hostages Convention*, 75 Nw. U. L. Rev. 769 (1980) [hereinafter cited as Boyle, *Entebbe*].

17    See Lassa Oppenheim, *The Science of International Law: Its Task and Method*, 2 AJIL 313 (1908). See also L. Oppenheim, *Introduction* to The Collected Papers of John Westlake on Public International Law at v (1914); J. B. Scott, *The Whewell Professorship of International Law*, 2 AJIL 862–65 (1908). But see Frederick Pollock, *The Sources of International Law*, 2 Colum. L. Rev. 511 (1902).

18    Cf. J. B. Scott, *The Papacy in International Law*, 8 AJIL 864–65 (1914); J. B. Scott, *Peace through the Development of International Law*, 8 AJIL 114–19 (1914).

19    Cf. J. B. Scott, *Louis Renault*, 2 AJIL 152, 153 (1908).

20    See authorities collected in *Power Politics, supra* this chapter, at 908 n. 17.

21    Thus international legal positivists have traditionally favored the "dualist" over the "monist" argument in favor of a nonhierarchical relationship between international law and municipal law. International law is not superior to municipal law or vice versa; the two coexist as interdependent and interpenetrated systems. Cf. *The Paquete Habana: The Lola*, 175 U.S. 677, 700 (1900); Quincy Wright, *Conflicts of International Law with National Laws and Ordinances*, 11 AJIL 1 (1917). But see J. G. Starke, *Monism and Dualism in the Theory of International Law*, 17 Brit. Y. B. Int'l L. 66 (1936).

22    See Elihu Root, *The Sanction of International Law*, 2 AJIL 451 (1908); J. Scott, *The Legal Nature of International Law*, 1 AJIL 831 (1907). See also Ernest Nys, *The Development and Formation of International Law*, 6 AJIL 1, 4, 20 (1912); Jesse S. Reeves, *The Influence of the Law of Nature upon International Law in the United States*, 3 AJIL 547 (1909) (no great influence). But see Robert Lansing, *Notes on Sovereignty in a State*, 1 AJIL 105 (1907) (Austinian position); W. W. Willoughby, *The Legal Nature of International Law*, 2 AJIL 357 (1908) (critique of Scott).

23    See, e.g., Ellery C. Stowell, *Plans for World Organization*, 18 Colum. U. Q. 226 (1916).

24    See Paul S. Reinsch, *International Administrative Law and National Sovereignty*, 3 AJIL 1 (1909). See also Simeon E. Baldwin, *The International Congresses and Conferences of the Last Century as Forces Working toward the Solidarity of the World*, 1 AJIL 565 (1907).

25    Cf. William I. Hull, The Two Hague Conferences and Their Contributions to Interna-

tional Law 496–500 (1908) [hereinafter cited as Hull, Two Hague Conferences]. See, generally, Valerie H. Ziegler, The Advocates of Peace in Antebellum America (1992).

26  See, e.g., R. Lansing, *Notes on World Sovereignty*, 15 AJIL 13 (1921) (written for publication in 1906); John B. Moore, *International Law: Its Present and Future*, 1 AJIL 11 (1907); Amos J. Peaslee, *The Sanction of International Law*, 10 AJIL 328 (1916); Alpheus H. Snow, *International Law and Political Science*, 7 AJIL 315 (1913); A. Snow, *The Law of Nations*, 6 AJIL 890 (1912).

27  See Boyle, *Irrelevance, supra* this chapter, at 196–98.

28  See F. Boyle, *International Law and the Use of Force: Beyond Regime Theory*, in Ideas and Ideals: Essays on Politics in Honor of Stanley Hoffmann 376 (Linda Miller & Michael J. Smith eds., 1993), reprinted as the Appendix.

29  See *Power Politics, supra* this chapter, at 931–56.

30  Niccolò Machiavelli, The Prince 127 (Mark Musa trans., 1964).

31  Id. at 99 (need for good laws); id. at 145 (fighting by means of law).

32  See Albert B. Hart, *American Ideals of International Relations*, 1 AJIL 624, 635 (1907).

33  Elbert J. Benton, International Law and Diplomacy of the Spanish-American War 108 (1908): "In the opinion of nearly all writers on international law the particular form of intervention in 1898 was unfortunate, irregular, precipitate and unjust to Spain."

34  See William L. Leuchtenburg, *Progressivism and Imperialism: The Progressive Movement and American Foreign Policy, 1898–1916*, 39 Miss. Valley Hist. Rev. 483, 498 (1952) (Progressives had negative attitude toward the American Negro). Compare generally with Joseph M. Siracusa, *Progressivism, Imperialism, and the Leuchtenburg Thesis, 1952–1974: An Historiographical Appraisal*, 20 Austl. J. Pol. & Hist. 312 (1974) (Progressives were anti-imperialists).

35  See David S. Patterson, *The United States and the Origins of the World Court*, 91 Pol. Sci. Q. 279, 283 (1976).

36  See Philip C. Jessup, 1 Elihu Root 215 (1938).

37  See J. B. Scott, *Editorial Comment*, 1 AJIL 129 (1907); Scott, *Societies of International Law*, 1 AJIL 135 (1907). The nucleus for the Society came from those members of the Lake Mohonk Conference on International Arbitration who wished to found an organization devoted exclusively to international law. See also George A. Finch, *The American Society of International Law 1906-1956*, 50 AJIL 293, 295–98 (1956); John M. Raymond & Barbara J. Frischholz, *Lawyers Who Established International Law in the United States, 1776–1914*, 76 AJIL 802, 823 (1982). See, generally, Frederick L. Kirgis, *The Formative Years of the American Society of International Law*, 90 AJIL 559 (1996).

38  Cf. J. B. Scott, *The Revista de Derecho Internacional*, 16 AJIL 437–38 (1922). The first issue of the *American Political Science Review* had been published in November 1906.

39  See Arthur E. Sutherland, The Law at Harvard: A History of Ideas and Men, 1817–1967, at 209 (1967); J. B. Scott, *Editorial Comment*, 1 AJIL 129, 130, 134 (1907).

40  See James Richardson, 1 A Compilation of the Messages and Papers of the President 205 (1911) (Farewell Address) [hereinafter cited as Richardson]; id. at 776 (Monroe Doctrine).

41  See, e.g., Robert W. Tucker & David C. Hendrickson, Empire of Liberty 204–56 (1990);

Mlada Bukovansky, *American Indentity and Neutral Rights from Independence to the War of 1812*, 51 Int'l Organization 209 (1997).

42　Cf. Scott, *Tripoli*, 6 AJIL 149, 155 (1912) (Mexican-American War was unjust and unjustifiable); Henry B. Brown, *International Courts*, 20 Yale L.J. 1, 13 (1911) (the Mexican War was a war of conquest in the interests of slavery).

43　See Pitman B. Potter, *The Nature of American Territorial Expansion*, 15 AJIL 189 (1921). See also P. Potter, *The Nature of American Foreign Policy*, 21 AJIL 53 (1927).

44　Treaty of Peace, Dec. 10, 1898, U.S.-Spain, 30 Stat. 1754. See C. G. Fenwick, *The Scope of Domestic Questions in International Law*, 19 AJIL 143–47 (1925) (the United States was entitled to abate the international nuisance in Cuba in 1898). See, generally, Carl R. Fish, The Path of Empire (1919); Frank Freidel, The Splendid Little War (1958); Parker T. Moon, Imperialism and World Politics 407–56 (1928); Julins W. Pratt, Expansionists of 1898: The Acquisition of Hawaii and the Spanish Islands (1936); William A. Williams, The Roots of the Modern American Empire 408–53 (1969).

45　See Abram Chayes, Thomas Ehrlich, & Andreas F. Lowenfeld, 2 International Legal Process: Materials for an Introductory Course 920–26 (1969).

46　See 9 Richardson, *supra* this chapter, at 7,024, 7,053.

47　Army Appropriation Act, ch. 803, art. III, 56th Cong., 2d Sess., 31 Stat. 895, 897 (1901).

48　See William L. Langer, The Diplomacy of Imperialism 1890–1902, at 167–94, 385–414B, 445–83, 677–786 (2d ed. 1950).

49　See Cyrus F. Wicker, *Some Effects of Neutralization*, 5 AJIL 639, 652 (1911); Erving Winslow, *Neutralization*, 2 AJIL 366 (1908).

50　See, e.g., A. Snow, *Neutralization versus Imperialism*, 2 AJIL 562 (1908).

51　See A. Hart, *American Ideals of International Relations*, 1 AJIL 624 (1907); A. Snow, *The American Philosophy of Government and Its Effect on International Relations*, 8 AJIL 191 (1914).

52　See, e.g., J. B. Scott, *The Baltic and the North Seas*, 2 AJIL 646–48 (1908); Scott, *The Dissolution of the Union of Norway and Sweden*, 1 AJIL 440–44 (1907); Scott, *The Integrity of Norway Guaranteed*, 2 AJIL 176–78 (1908) (purpose is to keep Russia out of Western Europe). See also Editorial Comment, *The Fortification of the Aland Islands*, 2 AJIL 397–98 (1908).

53　See Fenwick, *Mediation in the Turko-Italian War*, 6 AJIL 463–67 (1912) (favors mediation by great powers); Fenwick, *The Basis of Mediation in the War between Italy and Turkey*, 6 AJIL 719–22 (1912) (mediation undertaken by great powers); Scott, *Peace between Italy and Turkey*, 7 AJIL 155–58 (1913) (Italy unjustified and lawless); Scott, *The Closing and Reopening of the Dardanelles*, 6 AJIL 706–09 (1912); Scott, *Tripoli*, 6 AJIL 149–55 (1912) (Italy violated international law by declaring war on Turkey). See also Editorial Comment, *The Use of Balloons in the War between Italy and Turkey*, 6 AJIL 485–87 (1912).

54　See, e.g., Scott, *Anglo-French-Italian Agreement Regarding Abyssinia*, 1 AJIL 484–85 (1907).

55　See, e.g., Editorial Comment, *England and Russia in Central Asia*, 3 AJIL 170–75 (1909); Scott, *Russia and Persia*, 6 AJIL 155–59 (1912) (joint protectorate over Persia); Editorial Comment, *The Persian Revolution and the Anglo-Russian Entente*, 3 AJIL 969–75 (1909) (downfall of the shah and intervention by British and Russian troops); Editorial Comment, *The Recent Anglo-Russian Convention*, 1 AJIL 979–84 (1907) (establishing spheres of influence in Persia; assigning Afghanistan to Britain, and Tibet to China).

56   For the history of the establishment of the French protectorate in Morocco, see Editorial Comment, *An Antecedent Algeciras*, 8 AJIL 867–73 (1914); Editorial Comment, *Recent Disturbances in Morocco*, 1 AJIL 975–78 (1907); Norman D. Harris, *The New Moroccan Protectorate*, 7 AJIL 245 (1913); Scott, *A New Sultan in Morocco*, 3 AJIL 446–48 (1909); Scott, *French Protectorate Established in Morocco*, 6 AJIL 699–702 (1912); Scott, *Morocco*, 6 AJIL 159–67 (1912); Scott, *The Algeciras Conference*, 1 AJIL 138–40 (1907); Scott, *The Treaty of November 27, 1912, between France and Spain Concerning Morocco*, 7 AJIL 357–59 (1913). See also Scott, *Anglo-French Convention Respecting the New Hebrides*, 1 AJIL 482–83 (1907); Scott, *Egypt a British Protectorate*, 9 AJIL 202–04 (1915).

57   See Editorial Comment, *Macedonian Railways and the Concert of Europe*, 2 AJIL 644–46 (1908) (end of Austro-Hungarian/Russian entente); Theodore P. Ion, *The Cretan Question*, 4 AJIL 276 (1910); G. Schelle, *Studies on the Eastern Question* (pt. 1), 5 AJIL 144, 174 (1911) (violation of Treaty of Berlin by Austria and Bulgaria was flagrant breach of international law); id. (pts. 2 & 3) at 394, 680; Scott, *The Balkan Situation*, 2 AJIL 864–65 (1908) (violation of Treaty of Berlin); Scott, *The Balkan Situation*, 3 AJIL 448–51 (1909) (satisfactory settlement of violation); Scott, *The Balkan Situation*, 3 AJIL 688–90 (1909) (Austrian annexation of Bosnia-Herzegovina will be countered by renewed Russian support for southern Slavs). See also Scott, *Edward VII*, 4 AJIL 662, 664 (1910) (fear of Anglo-German war).

58   See, e.g., J. Scott, *America and the New Diplomacy*, Int'l Conciliation, March 1909, at 4–5.

59   See, generally, Alfred Vagts & Detlev F. Vagts, *The Balance of Power in International Law: A History of an Idea*, 73 AJIL 555 (1979).

60   See, e.g., Dennis, *The Fourteenth Lake Mohonk Conference*, 2 AJIL 615–21 (1908); M. Jarousse de Sillac, *Periodical Peace Conferences*, 5 AJIL 968 (1911); Amos Hershey, *Convention for the Peaceful Adjustment of International Differences*, 2 AJIL 29 (1908); Scott, *Joint Resolution to Authorize the Appointment of a Commission in Relation to Universal Peace*, 5 AJIL 433–38 (1911); Scott, *Lake Mohonk Conference on International Arbitration*, 1 AJIL 140–41 (1907); Scott, *Mr. Roosevelt's Nobel Address on International Peace*, 4 AJIL 700 (1910); Scott, *President Taft on International Peace*, 5 AJIL 718–25 (1911); Scott, *The Fifteenth Lake Mohonk Conference on International Arbitration*, 3 AJIL 683–88 (1909); Scott, *The Eighteenth Lake Mohonk Conference on International Arbitration*, 6 AJIL 725–29 (1912); Editorial Comment, *The Pennsylvania Arbitration and Peace Conference*, 2 AJIL 611–15 (1908).

61   See, e.g., J. Scott, 1 The Hague Peace Conferences of 1899 and 1907, at 465–66 (1909) [hereinafter cited as Scott, Hague Peace Conferences]; Editorial Note, *The Congress of Nations*, Advocate of Peace, July 1906, at 144.

62   See, e.g., S. Baldwin, *The Membership of a World Tribunal for Promoting Permanent Peace*, 12 AJIL 453 (1918); Philip M. Brown, *The Theory of the Independence and Equality of States*, 9 AJIL 305 (1915); Arthur W. Spencer, *The Organization of International Force*, 9 AJIL 45 (1915).

63  See, e.g., Warren F. Kuehl, Seeking World Order 91–95 (1969) (Walter J. Bartnett, Justice David J. Brewer, John Bassett Moore, Joseph C. Clayton).

64  See, e.g., id., at 134–37, 144–45, 161.

65  Cf. Stanley Hoffmann, *International Systems and International Law*, in The State of War 88–122 (1965).

66  See, e.g., Editorial Comment, *Secretary Knox and International Unity*, 4 AJIL 180–84 (1910); A. Snow, *The Law of Nations*, 6 AJIL 890 (1912).

67  The great powers of Europe formally admitted Turkey to the European public international law system by the Treaty of Paris of 1856. See Lawrence B. Evans, *The Primary Sources of International Obligations*, 5 Proc. Am. Soc. Int'l L. 257, 265–67 (1911).

68  Although not formally admitted like Turkey, Japan was generally considered "one of the Great Powers that lead the Family of Nations" by virtue of its military victory over China in 1895. See L. Oppenheim, 1 International Law, A Treatise: Peace 34 (Ronald F. Roxburgh ed., 3d ed. 1920).

## 2   The Obligatory Arbitration of International Disputes

1  See, e.g., William L. Penfield, *International Arbitration*, 1 AJIL 330 (1907). But cf. F. E. Chadwick, *The Anglo-German Tension and a Solution*, 6 AJIL 601 (1912).

2  See Jacques Dumas, *Sanctions of International Arbitration*, 5 AJIL 934 (1911).

3  For a detailed history of arbitration from the founding of the Republic, see *Arbitration and the United States*, 9 World Peace Foundation Pamphlets 453 (1926).

4  See 1 Encyclopedia of Public International Law 108 (Rudolf Bernhardt ed., 1981) [hereinafter Encyclopedia of Public International Law]; Mark W. Janis, *Protestants, Progress and Peace: Enthusiasm for an International Court in Early Nineteenth-Century America*, in The Influence of Religion on the Development of International Law 223–42 (M. Janis ed., 1991).

5  See Daniel G. Lang, Foreign Policy in the Early Republic 160–61 (1985).

6  See F. Pollock, *Methods of International Arbitration*, 35 Law Q. Rev. 320 (1919); Jens I. Westengard, *American Influence on International Law*, 18 J. Comp. Legis. & Int'l L. 2, 7–8 (1918); Quincy Wright, *The American Civil War (1861–65)*, in The International Law of Civil War 30–109 (Richard A. Falk ed., 1971); Peter Seidel, *The Alabama*, 1 Encyclopedia of Public International Law 97 (1992).

7  See Irwin Abrams, *The Emergence of the International Law Societies*, 19 Rev. Pol. 361 (1957).

8  Arbitration Treaty, Jan. 11, 1897, U.S.-Gr. Brit., in 3 Unperfected Treaties of the United States of America 253 (Christian L. Wiktor ed., 1976) [hereinafter cited as Unperfected Treaties].

9  See Nelson M. Blake, *The Olney-Pauncefote Treaty of 1897*, 50 Am. Hist. Rev. 228 (1945).

10  See, generally, F. Boyle, Defending Civil Resistance under International Law 283–316 (1987).

11  Correspondence from Ethan Hitchcock to William Day (Aug. 25, 1898), reprinted in U.S. Dep't of State, 1898 Papers Relating to the Foreign Relations of the United States

540 (1901). Hereinafter this series of documents will be cited as FRUS. See Calvin D. Davis, The United States and the First Hague Peace Conference 36–53 (1962) [hereinafter cited as Davis, Hague I].

12   See Basis for Establishment of Peace, Aug. 12, 1898, U.S.-Spain, 30 Stat. 1742.

13   Telegram from Ethan Hitchcock to William Day (Sept. 3, 1898), 1898 FRUS 542–43.

14   Correspondence from Ethan Hitchcock to John Hay (Jan. 14, 1899), 1898 FRUS 551, 553.

15   See analysis *supra* this chapter.

16   Address by John Hay to Hague Delegation (Apr. 18, 1899), 1899 FRUS 511, 513.

17   See Scott, 2 Hague Peace Conferences, *supra* chapter 1, at 15.

18   See Davis, Hague I, *supra* this chapter, at 137–38.

19   See The Proceedings of the Hague Peace Conferences: The Conference of 1899, at 833, Annex 7 (J. Scott ed., 1920) [hereinafter cited as Hague I Proceedings].

20   Id. at 813, Annex 2, B.

21   See *Report of Mr. White, Mr. Low, and Mr. Holls, to the American Commission to the International Conference at The Hague, Regarding the Work of the Third Committee of the Conference* (July 31, 1899), in Scott, 2 Hague Peace Conferences, *supra* chapter 1, at 52.

22   See *General Report of the Commission of the United States of America to the International Conference at The Hague* (July 31, 1899), in Scott, 2 Hague Peace Conferences, *supra* chapter 1, at 17, 24.

23   See Hague I Proceedings, *supra* this chapter, at 767–72; Davis, Hague I, *supra* this chapter, at 158–64; Hull, Two Hague Conferences, *supra* chapter 1, at 297–311; Scott, 1 Hague Peace Conferences, *supra* chapter 1, at 321.

24   See Hague I Proceedings, *supra* this chapter, at 799, Annex 1, A, art. 10.

25   International Conference at The Hague: Report of the Commission of the United States of America (July 31, 1899), 1899 FRUS 513, 518.

26   See Andrew D. White, The First Hague Conference 19 (1912).

27   See generally Barbara W. Tuchman, The Guns of August (1962).

28   Convention for the Pacific Settlement of International Disputes, July 29, 1899, Title IV, 32 Stat. 1779 (Pt. 2), 1788 (Pt. 2), T.S. No. 392. See Denys P. Myers, *The Origin of the Hague Arbitral Courts*, 8 AJIL 769 (1914).

29   The PCA's rules of procedure were revised and expanded in 1907. See *Report of the Delegates of the United States to the Second International Peace Conference at The Hague from June 15 to October 18, 1907*, in Scott, 2 Hague Peace Conferences, *supra* chapter 1, at 198, 210–12.

30   See, generally, Jackson H. Ralston, *Some Suggestions as to the Permanent Court of Arbitration*, 1 AJIL 321 (1907).

31   This provision was carried over into article 45 of the 1907 Convention for the Pacific Settlement of International Disputes, and amended to provide that only one of these appointed arbitrators could be a national of the party or chosen from among the persons selected by the party as members of the PCA. See Hull, Two Hague Conferences, *supra* chapter 1, at 387–89.

32   This provision was carried forward into article 45 of the 1907 Convention, which in addition provided that if within two months' time these two powers could not come to an agreement, each of them would present two candidates taken from the list of

PCA members, exclusive of members selected by the parties and not being nationals of either of them. The umpire would be determined by the drawing of lots among the candidates. Thus, under the procedure of article 45, the umpire would probably, though not necessarily, be from a third state. So under the 1907 convention, it was probable that three out of five members of the arbitration panel would be nonnationals of the parties in dispute, which was not the case under the 1899 convention. This development was said to represent a distinct advance because such a composition would guarantee impartiality in the rendering of the award. See Hull, Two Hague Conferences, *supra* chapter 1, at 389–90; Scott, 1 Hague Peace Conferences, *supra* chapter 1, at 282–84.

33    See Scott, 1 Hague Peace Conferences, *supra* chapter 1, at 298.

34    Scott, 1 Hague Peace Conferences, *supra* chapter 1, at 300–301 & n. 1.

35    See Hull, Two Hague Conferences, *supra* chapter 1, at 304–11.

36    The Hague Court Reports, at civ (J. Scott ed., 1916) [hereinafter cited as Hague Ct. Rep.]. See also Dexter Perkins, A History of the Monroe Doctrine 204 (1963).

37    Compare Convention for the Pacific Settlement of International Disputes, July 29, 1899, art. 27, 32 (Pt. 2) Stat. 1779, 1791, T.S. No. 392 with Convention for the Pacific Settlement of International Disputes, Oct. 18, 1907, art. 48, 36 Stat. 2199, 2224, T.S. No. 536. See Hull, Two Hague Conferences, *supra* chapter 1, at 320–26.

38    See The Hague Ct. Rep., *supra* this chapter, at cvi.

39    See Scott, 1 Hague Peace Conferences, *supra* chapter 1, at 286 n. 1.

40    See J. B. Scott, *Treaties of Arbitration since the First Hague Conference*, 2 AJIL 823–30 (1908).

41    See Hans Wehberg, *Restrictive Clauses in International Arbitration Treaties*, 7 AJIL 301 (1913). But see Amaro Cavalcanti, *Restrictive Clauses in Arbitration Treaties*, 8 AJIL 723 (1914).

42    See Scott, *Treaties of Arbitration since the First Hague Conference*, 2 AJIL 823, 827 (1908).

43    See, e.g., Arbitration Convention, Nov. 23, 1904, U.S.-Port., art. 1, in 3 Unperfected Treaties, *supra* this chapter, at 487, 488.

44    See C. Davis, The United States and the Second Hague Peace Conference 97–103 (1975) [hereinafter cited as Davis, Hague II]; John B. Moore, 7 A Digest of International Law 99–103 (1906) [hereinafter cited as Moore, Digest].

45    See, e.g., Arbitration Convention, Nov. 23, 1904, U.S.-Port., art. 2, in 3 Unperfected Treaties, *supra* this chapter, at 489.

46    See Scott, *A New General Arbitration Treaty with Great Britain*, 5 AJIL 451, 455–56 (1911). See also Scott, *The American Theory of International Arbitration*, 2 AJIL 387–91 (1908).

47    See 3 Unperfected Treaties, *supra* this chapter, at 487–89.

48    See Davis, Hague II, *supra* this chapter, at 116–18.

49    Id.

50    See Editorial Comment, *The Second Peace Conference of The Hague*, 1 AJIL 944, 951 (1907); Scott, *A New General Arbitration Treaty with Great Britain*, 5 AJIL 451, 457 (1911). For Root's instructions to the U.S. delegates, see Scott, 2 Hague Peace Conferences, *supra* chapter 1, at 181, 189–90.

51    See 2 The Proceedings of the Hague Peace Conferences: Conference of 1907, at 47–54

(J. Scott ed., 1921) [hereinafter cited as Hague II Proceedings]; Davis, Hague II, *supra* this chapter, at 256, 258, 277–84; Hull, Two Hague Conferences, *supra* chapter 1, at 311–26; Scott, 1 Hague Peace Conferences, *supra* chapter 1, at 330–79; Hull, *Obligatory Arbitration and the Hague Conferences*, 2 AJIL 731 (1908).

52   See Scott, 1 Hague Peace Conferences, *supra* chapter 1, at 352–74.

53   Final Act and Conventions of the Second Hague Peace Conference, Oct. 18, 1907, reprinted in 2 AJIL 1, 25–26 (Supp. 1908).

54   See *Report of the Delegates of the United States to the Second International Peace Conference at The Hague from June 15 to October 18, 1907*, in Scott, 2 Hague Peace Conferences, *supra* chapter 1, at 198, 205–06.

55   See Heinrich Lammasch, *Compulsory Arbitration at the Second Hague Conference*, 4 AJIL 83, 94, & n. 3 (1910).

56   See, e.g., Arbitration Convention, Feb. 10, 1908, U.S.-Fr., art. 2, 35 (Pt. 2) Stat. 1925, 1926.

57   See List of Arbitration Treaties and Conventions Submitted to and Acted upon by the Senate, S. Doc. No. 373, 62d Cong., 2d Sess. (1912). See also William C. Dennis, *The Arbitration Treaties and the Senate Amendments*, 6 AJIL 614 (1912); Scott, *Arbitration Treaty with Austria-Hungary*, 3 AJIL 696–97 (1909); Scott, *Recent Arbitration Treaties Concluded by the United States*, 2 AJIL 624 (1908); Scott, *Senator Root and the Nobel Peace Prize*, 8 AJIL 133–37 (1914); Scott, *The Pending Treaty of Arbitration between the United States and Great Britain*, 6 AJIL 167–77 (1912); Scott, *The Treaties of Arbitration with Great Britain and France*, 6 AJIL 460–63 (1912).

58   3 Unperfected Treaties, *supra* this chapter, at 487.

59   See P. Jessup, 2 Elihu Root, *supra* chapter 1, at 79–82; Richard W. Leopold, Elihu Root and the Conservative Tradition 56–59 (1954).

60   Cf. Scott, *A New General Arbitration Treaty with Great Britain*, 5 AJIL 451–57 (1911) (comment on Hay conventions).

61   Compare Restatement (Second) of Foreign Relations Law of the United States § 124 cmt. c with § 147 cmt. d(e) (1965).

62   See 2 Hague II Proceedings, *supra* this chapter, at 47, 52–53.

63   See Hague Ct. Rep., *supra* this chapter, at cvii.

64   See M. Hudson, The Permanent Court of International Justice 1920–1942, at 11 (1943) [hereinafter cited as Hudson, PCIJ].

65   See Hague Ct. Rep., *supra* this chapter, at 1 (Perm. Ct. Arb. 1902). The U.S. government thus bore the distinction of bringing the first case before the Hague tribunal. See Davis, Hague II, *supra* this chapter, at 51–61.

66   Hague Ct. Rep., *supra* this chapter, at 55 (Perm. Ct. Arb. 1904).

67   Hague Ct. Rep., *supra* this chapter, at 110 (Perm. Ct. Arb. 1909). See Scott, *The Casablanca Arbitration*, 3 AJIL 946 (1909); Scott, *The Casablanca Arbitration Award*, 3 AJIL 698–701 (1909); Scott, *The Casablanca Incident and Its Reference to Arbitration at The Hague*, 3 AJIL 176–78 (1909); Robert A. Friedlander, *Who Put Out the Lamps? Thoughts on International Law and the Coming of World War I*, 20 Duq. L. Rev. 569, 575–76 (1982).

68   Hague Ct. Rep., *supra* this chapter, at 121 (Perm. Ct. Arb. 1909). See Editorial Comment, *The Norway-Sweden Boundary Arbitration*, 4 AJIL 186–87 (1910).

69   North Atlantic Fisheries Case (Gr. Brit. v. U.S.), Hague Ct. Rep. (Scott) 141 (Perm. Ct.

Arb. 1910). See Anderson, *Boundary Waters between the United States and Canada,* 4 AJIL 668–73 (1910); Anderson, *Settlement of the Canadian Questions,* 2 AJIL 630–34 (1908); Anderson, *The Boundary-Fisheries Treaty,* 2 AJIL 637–40 (1908); Anderson, *The Final Outcome of the Fisheries Arbitration,* 7 AJIL 1 (1913); Anderson, *The Northeastern Fisheries Question,* 1 AJIL 963–64 (1907); Editorial Comment, *Was the Award in the North Atlantic Fisheries Case a Compromise?,* 6 AJIL 178–80 (1912); Lansing, *The Newfoundland Fisheries Question,* 3 AJIL 461–64 (1909); Lansing, *The North Atlantic Coast Fisheries Arbitration,* 5 AJIL 1 (1911); Lansing, *The North Atlantic Coast Fisheries,* 4 AJIL 903–08 (1910); Scott, *Anglo-American Relations,* 1 AJIL 480–82 (1907); Scott, *Renewal of Modus Vivendi Concerning Newfoundland Fisheries,* 3 AJIL 953–54 (1909); Scott, *Statement by the President of the Tribunal That the North Atlantic Fisheries Award Was a Compromise,* 5 AJIL 725–26 (1911); Scott, *The Final Settlement of the North Atlantic Coast Fisheries Controversy,* 7 AJIL 140–44 (1913); Scott, *The United States at the Hague Court of Arbitration,* 4 AJIL 675–77 (1910). See also Anderson, *Our Northern Boundary,* 2 AJIL 634–37 (1908) (U.S.-Canada arbitral tribunal).

70  Hague Ct. Rep., *supra* this chapter, at 226 (Perm. Ct. Arb. 1910). See W. Dennis, *The Orinoco Steamship Company Case before the Hague Tribunal,* 5 AJIL 35 (1911); H. Lammasch, *Address of Dr. H. Lammasch on Opening the Arbitration between the United States and Venezuela in the Matter of the Orinoco Steamship Company's Claim, September 28, 1910,* 5 AJIL 32 (1911); H. Lammasch, *Address of Dr. H. Lammasch on Closing the Arbitration between the United States and Venezuela in the Matter of the Orinoco Steamship Company's Claim, October 25, 1910,* 5 AJIL 65 (1911).

71  Hague Ct. Rep., *supra* this chapter, at 275 (Perm. Ct. Arb. 1911). See Scott, *The Savarkar Case,* 5 AJIL 208–10 (1911).

72  See Anthony Giustini, *Compulsory Adjudication in International Law: The Past, the Present, and Prospects for the Future,* 9 Fordham Int'l L.J. 213, 220 (1985–86).

73  See Davis, Hague II, *supra* this chapter, at 73–90.

74  See 2 Encyclopedia of Public International Law 234 (1981); D. Patterson, Toward a Warless World: The Travail of the American Peace Movement: 1887–1914, at 155 (1976) [hereinafter cited as Patterson, Toward a Warless World]; D. Perkins, History of the Monroe Doctrine, *supra* chapter 2, at 234–38.

75  See chapter 5 *infra.*

76  See Karl Doehring, *Casablanca Arbitration,* 2 Encyclopedia of Public International Law 45 (1981).

77  See Walther Schücking, The International Union of the Hague Conferences 28 (C. Fenwick trans., 1918) (comment by Wehberg); Scott, *The Casablanca Arbitration Award,* 3 AJIL 698, 701 (1909).

78  For a succinct recapitulation of the history of the Triple Alliance and Triple Entente, see New Columbia Encyclopedia, at 2787, cols. 1–3 (William H. Harris & Judith S. Levey eds., 1975).

79  See also Scott, *The Arbitral Award in the Peru-Bolivia Boundary Controversy,* 3 AJIL 949–53 (1909) (Argentina as sole arbitrator). But see Dennis, *The Dispute between the Argentine Republic and Uruguay As to Their Jurisdiction in the Rio de la Plata,* 1 AJIL 984–88 (1907) (Argentina opposed arbitration); Dennis, *The Jurisdiction of the Rio de la Plata,* 4 AJIL 430–31 (1910).

80   See, e.g., Christine Gray & Benedict Kingsbury, *Inter-State Arbitration since 1945: Overview and Evaluation,* in International Courts for the Twenty-first Century 55 (M. Janis ed., 1992).

3   *The Foundation of an International Court of Justice*

1   See Scott, *The Casablanca Arbitration Award,* 3 AJIL 698, 701 (1909); Scott, *Statement by the President of the Tribunal That the North Atlantic Fisheries Award Was a Compromise,* 5 AJIL 725–26 (1911); Editorial Comment, *Was the Award in the North Atlantic Fisheries Case a Compromise?,* 6 AJIL 178–80 (1912).

2   See, e.g., Scott, *The Annual Meeting of the Society of International Law,* 3 AJIL 191 (1909); Scott, *The Evolution of a Permanent International Judiciary,* 6 AJIL 316 (1912).

3   See, e.g., Scott, *Fourth Annual Meeting of the American Society for Judicial Settlement of International Disputes,* 8 AJIL 129–33 (1914); Scott, *The American Society for the Judicial Settlement of International Disputes,* 4 AJIL 930–32 (1910); Scott, *The Meeting of the American Society for the Judicial Settlement of International Disputes,* 5 AJIL 193–95 (1911).

4   U.S. Const. art. III, § 2. See Scott, 2 Hague Peace Conferences, *supra* chapter 1, at 181, 191.

5   Articles of Confederation art. 9. See Scott, 1 Hague Peace Conferences, *supra* chapter 1, at 460–64; Scott, *The Proposed Court of Arbitral Justice,* 2 AJIL 772 (1908).

6   U.S. Const. art. III, § 2.

7   See, e.g., Anderson, *The Growth of International Law under a Permanent Court of Arbitration,* 1 AJIL 730–34 (1907). See also Scott, *The Judicial Settlement of Disputes between States of the American Union,* 17 AJIL 326–28 (1923).

8   Cf. Thomas C. Schelling, The Strategy of Conflict 48–49 (1960) (minimax theory).

9   See, e.g., Scott, *The Gradual and Progressive Codification of International Law,* 21 AJIL 417 (1927); Jesse S. Reeves, *The Hague Conference on the Codification of International Law,* 24 AJIL 52 (1930).

10   See 2 Hague II Proceedings, *supra* chapter 2, at 1,016, Annex 76, art. VI.

11   Final Act and Conventions of the Second Peace Conference, Oct. 18, 1907, Annex to the First Recommendation Uttered by the Second Peace Conference, Draft of a Convention Relative to the Institution of a Court of Arbitral Justice, reprinted in 2 AJIL 1, 29 (Supp. 1908). See Denys P. Myers, *The Origin of the Hague Arbitral Courts,* 10 AJIL 270 (1916).

12   See Davis, Hague II, *supra* chapter 2, at 264–70.

13   See Protocol of Signature Relating to the Permanent Court of International Justice (Dec. 16, 1920), 2 League of Nations Official J. 14 (1921), reprinted in 17 AJIL 55 (Supp. 1923).

14   See 2 Hague II Proceedings, *supra* chapter 2, at 641. "But the competence of the court or its delegation to frame the *compromis,* upon the request of one litigant when a treaty of arbitration exists between the litigants binding them to arbitrate, seems to be a long step toward introducing into the law of nations the procedure of a common-law court by which a defendant may be brought into court at the instance of a plaintiff" (Scott, 1 Hague Peace Conferences, *supra* chapter 1, at 453).

15  See Statute for the Permanent Court of International Justice Provided for by Article
14 of the Covenant of the League of Nations, 2 League of Nations Official J. 14 (1921),
reprinted in 17 AJIL 57 (Supp. 1923).

16  See Paul S. Reinsch, *The Concept of Legality in International Arbitration*, 5 AJIL 604
(1911).

17  See P. Jessup, 2 Elihu Root, *supra* chapter 1, at 75–76.

18  Scott, *The Election of Judges for the Permanent Court of International Justice*, 15 AJIL
556 (1921).

19  See David J. Hill, The Problem of a World Court 24–25 (1927).

20  See P. Jessup, 2 Elihu Root, *supra* chapter 1, at 419–20.

21  See Hudson, PCIJ, *supra* chapter 2, at 117.

22  J. Scott, *Elihu Root's Services to International Law*, 207 Int'l Conciliation 25, 66
(1925).

23  See Frederick C. Hicks, *The Equality of States and the Hague Conferences*, 2 AJIL
530, 538–39 (1908).

24  See *infra* chapter 4 and accompanying notes.

25  See 2 Hague II Proceedings, *supra* chapter 2, at 1031, Annex 84.

26  See A. G. de Lapradelle & Ellery C. Stowell, *Latin America at the Hague Conference*,
17 Yale L.J. 270 (1908). See also Amos S. Hershey, *The Calvo and Drago Doctrines*, 1
AJIL 26 (1907).

27  See Hull, Two Hague Conferences, *supra* chapter 1, at 419–20 (Mexico, Serbia, Haiti,
Venezuela, Brazil, Bulgaria, Portugal, Romania, and Uruguay). See also 2 Hague II
Proceedings, *supra* chapter 2, at 1027, 1029 (Annex 83 was a Brazilian proposal for
absolute equality in appointments to the court).

28  See Scott, 1 Hague Peace Conferences, *supra* chapter 1, at 95–101.

29  Final Act and Conventions of the Second Peace Conference, Oct. 18, 1907, reprinted
in 2 AJIL 1, 27 (Supp. 1908).

30  See Scott, 2 Hague Peace Conferences, *supra* chapter 1, at 198, 244–45.

31  See J. Scott, An International Court of Justice 69–70 (1916) [hereinafter cited as Scott,
International Court of Justice].

32  Identic Circular Note of the Secretary of State of the United States Proposing Alternative Procedure for the International Prize Court and the Investment of the International Prize Court with the Functions of a Court of Arbitral Justice (Oct. 18, 1909),
1910 FRUS 597, 603, reprinted in 4 AJIL 102, 109 (Supp. 1910) [hereinafter cited as Identic Circular Note]. See D. Patterson, Toward a Warless World, *supra* chapter 2, at 162.
See also Editorial Comment, *Proposal to Modify the International Prize Court and to
Invest It As Modified with the Jurisdiction and Functions of a Court of Arbitral Justice*, 4 AJIL 163–66 (1910); Editorial Comment, *The Sixteenth Annual Lake Mohonk
Conference on International Arbitration*, 4 AJIL 689–92 (1910).

33  "[I]t is not too much to hope that some day, either by the appointment of the same
judges for both courts or by a reorganization, there may be one great international
court of justice with a twofold division into civil and prize chambers" (Scott, 1 Hague
Peace Conferences, *supra* chapter 1, at 451).

34  Identic Circular Note (Oct. 18, 1909), *supra* this chapter, 1910 FRUS 597, 604, reprinted
in 4 AJIL 102, 111 (Supp. 1910).

35  Scott, International Court of Justice, *supra* this chapter, at 70.

36 Id. at 70–74.

37 Id. at 74.

38 Id. at 91.

39 Id. at 92–94.

40 See D. Patterson, Toward a Warless World, *supra* chapter 2, at 163.

41 Scott, International Court of Justice, *supra* this chapter, at 1, 6, 18.

42 Id.

43 See *infra* chapter 5 and accompanying notes.

44 D. Fleming, The United States and the World Court 1920–1966, at 36 (1968); D. Patterson, *The United States and the Origins of the World Court*, 91 Pol. Sci. Q. 279, 290 (1976).

45 D. Patterson, *The United States and the Origins of the World Court*, 91 Pol. Sci. Q. 279, 280, 293–94 (1976); D. Patterson, Toward a Warless World, *supra* chapter 2, at 254–55.

46 George A. Finch, *James Brown Scott: 1866–1943*, 38 AJIL 183, 202 (1944). See, generally, Frederic R. Coudert, *An Appreciation of James Brown Scott*, 37 AJIL 559 (1943).

47 See, e.g., D. Hill, The Problem of a World Court, *supra* this chapter, at 21–25.

48 See Scott, *A Permanent Court of International Justice*, 14 AJIL 581–82 (1920).

49 See id. at 583.

50 See G. Finch, *James Brown Scott, supra* this chapter, at 202–03.

51 See E. Root, *The Constitution of an International Court of Justice*, 15 AJIL 1 (1921) (remarks made in June 1920).

52 D. Fleming, The United States and the World Court 1920–1966, *supra* this chapter, at 43.

53 Simeon E. Baldwin, *The Evolution of a World Court*, 1 B.U. L. Rev. 6, 11 (1921).

54 John B. Moore, *The Organization of the Permanent Court of International Justice*, 22 Colum. L. Rev. 497, 500 (1922).

55 For the British origins of this particular language found in article 13(2) of the Covenant, see Martin D. Dubin, *Toward the Concept of Collective Security: The Bryce Group's "Proposals for the Avoidance of War," 1914–1917*, 24 Int'l Organization 288, 291–92 (1970).

56 See League of Nations, The Records of the First Assembly, 1 Meetings of the Committees 472–73 (1920); Hudson, PCIJ, *supra* chapter 2, at 118–20; Scott, *The Institute of International Law*, 16 AJIL 243, 247–48 (1922).

57 A. Giustini, *Compulsory Adjudication in International Law: The Past, the Present, and Prospects for the Future*, 9 Fordham Int'l L.J. 213, 227 (1986).

58 See J. Moore, *The Organization of the Permanent Court of International Justice*, 22 Colum. L. Rev. 497, 500–501 (1922).

59 See Scott, *The Permanent Court of International Justice*, 15 AJIL 260–66 (1921).

60 A. Giustini, *Compulsory Adjudication in International Law: The Past, the Present, and Prospects for the Future*, 9 Fordham Int'l L.J. 213, 227 (1986).

61 Id.

62 Id. at 227–28.

63 For the text of the PCIJ Protocol of Signature, see Hudson, PCIJ, *supra* chapter 2, at 665.

64 Id. at 677.

65  J. Moore, *The Organization of the International Court of Justice*, 22 Colum. L. Rev. 497, 501 (1922).

66  See A. Giustini, *Compulsory Adjudication in International Law: The Past, the Present, and Prospects for the Future*, 9 Fordham Int'l L.J. 213, 232–35 (1986).

67  2 League of Nations Official J. 14 (1921); 3 id. at 306 (1922). See G. Finch, James Brown Scott: 1866–1943, *supra* this chapter, at 203.

68  See Scott, *The Election of Judges for the Permanent Court of International Justice*, 15 AJIL 556–58 (1921).

69  See also Charles C. Hyde, *The Election of Mr. Hughes to the World Court*, 22 AJIL 822–23 (1928).

70  Scott, *The Election of Judges for the Permanent Court of International Justice*, 15 AJIL 556, 557 (1921).

71  For the subsequent history of unsuccessful U.S. efforts to join the PCIJ, see Warren G. Harding, *Message of the President of the United States to the Senate Recommending Participation of the United States in the Permanent Court of International Justice at The Hague*, reprinted in 17 AJIL 331–32 (1923); Charles E. Hughes, *Letter of the Secretary of State to the President of the United States Recommending the Participation of the United States in the Permanent Court of International Justice at The Hague*, reprinted in 17 AJIL 332–38 (1923); Eugène Borel, *The United States and the Permanent Court of International Justice*, 17 AJIL 429 (1923); Philip M. Brown, *The Rule of Unanimity and the Fifth Reservation to American Adherence to the Permanent Court*, 22 AJIL 599–603 (1928); G. Finch, *The United States and the Permanent Court of International Justice*, 17 AJIL 521–26 (1923); M. Hudson, *The United States Senate and the Permanent Court of International Justice*, 20 AJIL 330–35 (1926); M. Hudson, *The American Reservations and the Permanent Court of International Justice*, 22 AJIL 776 (1928); M. Hudson, *The World Court Protocols before the United States Senate*, 26 AJIL 569–72 (1932); P. Jessup, *The New Protocol for American Accession to the Permanent Court of International Justice*, 24 AJIL 105–10 (1930); P. Jessup, *Revising the Statute of the Permanent Court of International Justice*, 24 AJIL 353–56 (1930); P. Jessup, *The Protocol for American Adherence to the Permanent Court*, 25 AJIL 308–12 (1931); Quincy Wright, *The United States and the Permanent Court of International Justice*, 21 AJIL 1 (1927); Current Note, *The Permanent Court of International Justice*, 20 AJIL 150–51 (1926); Current Note, *Adherence of the United States to the Permanent Court of International Justice*, 20 AJIL 552–55 (1926). See also Hudson, PCIJ, *supra* chapter 2, at 216–38.

72  See Michael Dunne, The United States and the World Court 1920–1935, at 44 (1988).

73  See, e.g., D. Hill, *The Permanent Court of International Justice*, 14 AJIL 387–92 (1920). See generally Scott, *Interpretation of Article X of the Covenant of the League of Nations*, 18 AJIL 108–13 (1924).

74  But cf. Hill, *The Relation of the United States to the Permanent Court of International Justice*, 20 AJIL 326 (1926).

75  See Davis, Hague II, *supra* chapter 2, at 363.

76  See, e.g., D. Hill, The Problem of a World Court, *supra* this chapter.

77  See Hudson, PCIJ, *supra* chapter 2, at 669, for the Revised PCIJ Statute.

78  See Shabtai Rosenne, The World Court: What It Is and How It Works 27 (4th rev. ed. 1989).

4   *The Codification of Customary International Law*

1   See, e.g., Davis, Hague I, *supra* chapter 2; Davis, Hague II, *supra* chapter 2.

2   See, e.g., F. Boyle, World Politics and International Law 136–54 (1985) (drafting the International Convention against the Taking of Hostages at the United Nations).

3   For a good comparative analysis of the actual texts of these respective sets of Regulations, see The Laws of Armed Conflicts: A Collection of Conventions, Resolutions and Other Documents 63–98 (Dietrich Schindler & Jiří Toman eds., 3d ed. 1988) [hereinafter cited as The Laws of Armed Conflicts].

4   See id. at 3. See, generally, Burrus M. Carnahan, *Lincoln, Lieber and the Laws of War*, 92 AJIL 213 (1998); Adam Roberts, *Land Warfare*, in The Laws of War 116 (Michael Howard, George J. Andreopoulos, & Mark Shulman eds., 1994) [hereinafter cited as The Laws of War].

5   J. Westengard, *American Influence upon International Law*, 18 J. Comp. Legis. & Int'l L. 2, 13 (1918).

6   See James Wilford Garner, 1 International Law and the World War 17–18 (1920) [hereinafter cited as Garner].

7   See id. at 18.

8   Id. at 20.

9   See The Laws of Armed Conflicts, *supra* this chapter, at 367–599.

10  Id. at 605–734. See, generally, F. Boyle, *Preserving the Rule of Law in the War against International Terrorism*, in The Future of International Law and American Foreign Policy 79–109 (1989).

11  See, e.g., 1 Garner, *supra* this chapter, at 18–20.

12  See E. Nys, *The Codification of International Law*, 5 AJIL 871 (1911); E. Root, *The Function of Private Codification in International Law*, 5 AJIL 577 (1911); Scott, *The Third Annual Meeting of the American Society of International Law*, 3 AJIL 674–83 (1909).

13  See J. Choate, The Two Hague Conferences 65–74 (1913) [hereinafter cited as Choate, Two Hague Conferences]; Davis, Hague II, *supra* chapter 2, at 190, 220–27; Hudson, PCIJ, *supra* chapter 2, at 71–72.

14  Convention Relative to the Creation of an International Prize Court, Oct. 18, 1907, in 4 Unperfected Treaties, *supra* chapter 2, at 57, reprinted in 2 AJIL 174 (Supp. 1908). See Scott, *The Work of the Second Hague Peace Conference*, 2 AJIL 1, 21–22 (1908).

15  See E. Root, *The Real Significance of the Declaration of London*, 6 AJIL 583 (1912).

16  Convention Relative to the Creation of an International Prize Court, Oct. 18, 1907, arts. IV & V, in 4 Unperfected Treaties, *supra* chapter 2, at 57.

17  See Hull, Two Hague Conferences, *supra* chapter 1, at 430–31.

18  See Scott, 1 Hague Peace Conferences, *supra* chapter 1, at 487–88.

19  See P. Brown, *The Individual and International Law*, 18 AJIL 532, 533 (1924). See also Edwin M. Borchard, *Limitations on Coercive Protection*, 21 AJIL 303 (1927).

20  See H. Brown, *The Proposed International Prize Court*, 2 AJIL 476 (1908) (unconstitutional); Scott, *The International Court of Prize*, 5 AJIL 302 (1911) (constitutional); Thos. Roeburn White, *Constitutionality of the Proposed International Prize Court—Considered from the Standpoint of the United States*, 2 AJIL 490 (1908) (constitutional). See also E. Root, *The Relations between International Tribunals of Arbitration and the Jurisdiction of National Courts*, 3 AJIL 529 (1909).

21   See Scott, 1 Hague Peace Conferences, *supra* chapter 1, at 473–84.

22   Additional Protocol to the Convention Relative to the Establishment of an International Court of Prize, Sept. 19, 1910, in 4 Unperfected Treaties, *supra* chapter 2, at 177, reprinted in 5 AJIL 95 (Supp. 1911). See George C. Butte, *The "Protocole Additionnel" to the International Prize Court Convention*, 6 AJIL 799 (1912).

23   See John W. Coogan, The End of Neutrality: The United States, Britain, and Maritime Rights 1899–1915, at 94–100 (1981) [hereinafter cited as Coogan, End of Neutrality]; Charles N. Gregory, *The Proposed International Prize Court and Some of Its Difficulties*, 2 AJIL 458 (1908).

24   See Scott, *Proposed Conference for the Settlement of Certain Questions of Maritime Law*, 2 AJIL 830–35 (1908); James L. Tryon, *The International Prize Court and Code*, 20 Yale L.J. 604 (1911).

25   Declaration of London, Feb. 26, 1909, in 4 Unperfected Treaties, *supra* chapter 2, at 129. See C. H. Stockton, *The International Naval Conference of London, 1908–1909*, 3 AJIL 596 (1909).

26   See Coogan, End of Neutrality, *supra* this chapter, at 114–17; Scott, 1 Hague Peace Conferences, *supra* chapter 1, at 698–730; Ellery C. Stowell, *The International Naval Conference and the Declaration of London*, 3 Am. Pol. Sci. Rev. 489 (1909). See also John B. Hattendorf, *Maritime Conflict*, in The Laws of War, *supra* this chapter, at 98.

27   See Scott, *Approval of the Declaration of London by the United States Senate on April 24, 1912*, 6 AJIL 723–25 (1912).

28   See Scott, *Elihu Root's Services to International Law*, 207 Int'l Conciliation 25, 47 (1925).

29   See Fenwick, *Naval Prize Bill and the Declaration of London*, 6 AJIL 180–86 (1912); Arthur Cohen, *The Declaration of London*, 27 Law Q. Rev. 9 (1911).

30   Convention Relative to the Conversion of Merchant Ships into War Ships, Oct. 18, 1907, in 4 Unperfected Treaties, *supra* chapter 2, at 51, reprinted in 2 AJIL 133 (Supp. 1908). See Report of the British Delegates (March 1, 1909), in The Declaration of London, February 26, 1909: A Collection of Official Papers and Documents Relating to the International Naval Conference Held in London December, 1908–February, 1909, Official Documents 235, 251–52 (J. Scott ed., 1919) [hereinafter cited as Declaration of London Documents]; George G. Wilson, *Conversion of Merchant Ships into War Ships*, 2 AJIL 271 (1908).

31   See Instructions Addressed to the British Delegates by Sir Edward Grey (Dec. 1, 1908), in Declaration of London Documents, *supra* this chapter, at 210, 230–31.

32   See Coogan, End of Neutrality, *supra* this chapter, at 128–36.

33   Naval Prize Bill, 1911, 1 & 2 Geo. 5, 7 Sessional Papers, H.L. 643. See J. Scott, *The Declaration of London of February 26, 1909*, 8 AJIL 274 (1914).

34   Declaration of London, Feb. 26, 1909, in 4 Unperfected Treaties, *supra* chapter 2, at 129. See also D. Myers, *The Legal Basis of the Rules of Blockade in the Declaration of London*, 4 AJIL 571, 572 (1910).

35   See Scott, *The Declaration of London of February 26, 1909 Part II*, 8 AJIL 520, 553 (1914).

36   See Coogan, End of Neutrality, *supra* this chapter, at 126 & n. 7.

37   Id. at 145.

38  See Scott, *Prefatory Note* to Declaration of London Documents, *supra* this chapter, at v; 1 Garner, *supra* this chapter, at 34; 2 Garner, *supra* this chapter, at 268. See also Scott, *The Declaration of London of February 26, 1909*, 8 AJIL 274 (1914). See, generally, L. Oppenheim, 2 International Law, A Treatise: War and Neutrality 546–52 (2d ed. 1912).

39  Telegram from William Jennings Bryan to Walter Hines Page (Aug. 6, 1914), 1914 FRUS 216 (Supp.), reprinted in 9 AJIL 1 (Spec. Supp. 1915).

40  See Telegram from Ambassador Penfield to Secretary of State Bryan (Aug. 13, 1914), 1914 FRUS 217 (Supp.), reprinted in 9 AJIL 1 (Spec. Supp. 1915) (Austria-Hungary); Telegram from Ambassador Gerard to Secretary of State Bryan (Aug. 22, 1914), 1914 FRUS 218 (Supp.), reprinted in 9 AJIL 2 (Spec. Supp. 1915) (Germany).

41  Richard W. Van Alstyne, *The Policy of the United States Regarding the Declaration of London, at the Outbreak of the Great War*, 7 J. Mod. Hist. 434, 436 (1935).

42  Telegram from Ambassador Page to Secretary of State Bryan (Aug. 26, 1914), 1914 FRUS 218, 219 (Supp.) (Great Britain); Telegram from Chargé Wilson to Secretary of State Bryan (Aug. 27, 1914), 1914 FRUS 220 (Supp.), reprinted in 9 AJIL 5 (Spec. Supp. 1915) (Russia); Telegram from Ambassador Herrick to Secretary of State Bryan (Sept. 3, 1914), 1914 FRUS 222 (Supp.), reprinted in 9 AJIL 6 (Spec. Supp. 1915) (France).

43  Telegram from Acting Secretary of State Lansing to Ambassador Page (Oct. 22, 1914), 1914 FRUS 257 (Supp.), reprinted in 9 AJIL 7 (Spec. Supp. 1915). See James W. Garner, *Some Questions of International Law in the European War*, 9 AJIL 372 (1915); R. Van Alstyne, *The Policy of the United States Regarding the Declaration of London, at the Outbreak of the Great War*, 7 J. Mod. Hist. 434 (1935).

44  See, e.g., 2 Garner, *supra* this chapter, at 296.

45  See Coogan, End of Neutrality, *supra* this chapter, at 154–68.

46  See, e.g., The Declaration of London Order in Council (Oct. 29, 1914), 1914 FRUS 263 (Supp.), reprinted in 9 AJIL 14 (Spec. Supp. 1915). See also Simeon E. Baldwin, *An Anglo-American Prize Tribunal*, 9 AJIL 297 (1915).

47  See, e.g., Finch, *Seizure and Detention of Neutral Cargoes—Visit and Search—Continuous Voyage*, 9 AJIL 456–61 (1915); Finch, *The Use of Neutral Flags on Merchant Vessels of Belligerents*, 9 AJIL 471–73 (1915); Louis Renault, *War and the Law of Nations in the Twentieth Century*, 9 AJIL 1 (1915); Scott, *The Questions in Dispute between the United States and Great Britain with Reference to Interference with Neutral Trade*, 9 AJIL 680–87 (1915); Scott, *The Seizure of Enemy Subjects upon Neutral Vessels upon the High Seas*, 10 AJIL 117–18 (1916).

48  See, e.g., Correspondence from Ambassador Page to Secretary of State Bryan (July 10, 1916), 1916 FRUS 413 (Supp.), reprinted in 10 AJIL 5 (Spec. Supp. 1916) (1916 Maritime Rights Order in Council); Correspondence from Ambassador Sharp to Secretary of State Bryan (July 11, 1916), 1916 FRUS 416 (Supp.), reprinted in 10 AJIL 9 (Spec. Supp. 1916) (French decree). See also G. Wilson, *The Withdrawal of the Declaration of London Orders in Council*, 10 AJIL 843 (1916).

49  Scott, *Status of the Declaration of London*, 9 AJIL 199, 202 (1915).

50  For a fuller explanation of the role international law plays in defining the contours of international crises for governmental decision makers, see Boyle, *Entebbe*, *supra* chapter 1, at 778–79.

51   See Ernest R. May, The World War and American Isolation 1914–1917, at 335–36 (1966) [hereinafter cited as May, World War and American Isolation]; A. Hershey, Some Popular Misconceptions of Neutrality, 10 AJIL 118–21 (1916); 2 Garner, supra this chapter, at 281. See also A. Hershey, The So-Called Inviolability of the Mails, 10 AJIL 580–84 (1916).

52   See E. May, World War and American Isolation, supra this chapter, at 113–301, 387–437.

53   Telegram from Ambassador Gerard to Secretary of State Bryan (Feb. 6, 1915), 1915 FRUS 94 (Supp.), reprinted in 9 AJIL 83 (Spec. Supp. 1915). See also Finch, Mines, Submarines and War Zones — The Absence of Blockade, 9 AJIL 461–71 (1915).

54   Telegram from Ambassador Bernstorff to Secretary of State Lansing (Jan. 31, 1917), 1917 FRUS 97, 100, 101 (1 Supp. 1917).

55   See, e.g., Declaration of London, Feb. 26, 1909, in 4 Unperfected Treaties, supra chapter 2, at 142, arts. 48, 49, 50.

56   See James W. Garner, Some Questions of International Law in the European War (pts. 3, 8, & 9), 9 AJIL 594, 612 (1915), 9 AJIL 818, 825 (1915), 10 AJIL 12 (1916).

57   See generally Scott, Armed Merchant Ships, 10 AJIL 113–16 (1916); Finch, The Status of Armed Merchant Vessels, 9 AJIL 188–89 (1915).

58   See Finch, The Use of Neutral Flags on Merchant Vessels of Belligerents, 9 AJIL 471–73 (1915).

59   See Telegram from Ambassador Bernstorff to Secretary of State Bryan (Feb. 7, 1915), 1915 FRUS 95 (Supp.).

60   Id. at 96.

61   See T. Baty, Naval Warfare: Law and License, 10 AJIL 42 (1916); Scott, The Controversy between the United States and Germany over the Use of Submarines against Merchant Vessels, 9 AJIL 666–80 (1915); Scott, The Secretary of State on the Violations of International Law in the European War As They Affect Neutrals, 10 AJIL 572–75 (1916).

62   See Scott, The United States at War with the Imperial German Government, 11 AJIL 617–27 (1917).

63   See Scott, War between Austria-Hungary and the United States, 12 AJIL 165–72 (1918).

64   Act of April 6, 1917, ch. 1, 65th Cong., 1st Sess., 40 Stat. 1 (Pt. 1) (declaration of war between the United States and Germany).

65   Address of the President of the United States Delivered at a Joint Session of the Two Houses of Congress, April 2, 1917, reprinted in 11 AJIL 143, 144 (Supp. 1917). See, generally, Daniel M. Smith, National Interest and American Intervention, 1917: An Historiographical Appraisal, 52 J. Am. Hist. 5 (1965).

66   See, e.g., P. Brown, War and Law, 12 AJIL 162, 164 (1918): "This is truly a war in defense of law." See also P. Brown, Economic Warfare, 11 AJIL 847–50 (1917) (the war demonstrates the futility of a system of international law based on the balance of power, suppression of nationality, and denial of self-government).

67   See United States, President's Transmittal of the United Nations Convention on the Law of the Sea and the Agreement Relating to the Implementation of Part XI to the U.S. Senate with Commentary [October 7, 1994], 34 Int'l L. Mats. 1393 (1995).

68   See, e.g., Fact Sheet: U.S. Oceans Policy and the Law of the Sea Convention, U.S. Department of State Dispatch, Mar. 11, 1996, Vol. 7, No. 11, at 108–09.

69   See, e.g., Paul Kennedy, The Rise and Fall of the Great Powers: Economic Change and Military Conflict from 1500 to 2000 (1987).

5   *Creating a New Regime for the Peaceful Settlement of International Disputes*

1   Translation of Document from Count Mouravieff to Ethan Hitchcock (Aug. 12 (24), 1898), 1898 FRUS 541, 541.

2   See R. Floyd Clarke, *A Permanent Tribunal of International Arbitration: Its Necessity and Value*, 1 AJIL 342 (1907). See also Thomas K. Ford, *The Genesis of the First Hague Conference*, 51 Pol. Sci. Q. 354 (1936); Dan L. Morrill, *Nicholas II and the Call for the First Hague Conference*, 46 J. Mod. Hist. 296 (1974).

3   Telegram from Moore to Ethan Hitchcock (Sept. 6, 1898), 1898 FRUS 543.

4   Address by John Hay to Hague Delegation (Apr. 18, 1899), 1899 FRUS 511, 512.

5   See Davis, Hague 1, *supra* chapter 2, at 110–24; Report of Captain Crozier to the Commission of the United States of America to the International Conference at The Hague Regarding the Work of the First Committee of the Conference and Its Sub-Committee (July 31, 1899), in Scott, 2 Hague Peace Conferences, *supra* chapter 1, at 29; Report of Captain Mahan to the United States Commission to the International Conference at the Hague, on Disarmament, Etc., with Reference to Navies (July 31, 1899), in Scott, 2 Hague Peace Conferences, *supra* chapter 1, at 36.

6   See Davis, Hague I, *supra* chapter 2, at 110–24.

7   See B. Tuchman, The Proud Tower 302 (1966).

8   Final Act of the International Peace Conference, July 29, 1899, reprinted in 1 AJIL 103, 105 (Supp. 1907) [hereinafter cited as Final Act of the International Peace Conference].

9   Id. at 106.

10   Id.

11   See, e.g., Scott, 1 Hague Peace Conferences, *supra* chapter 1, at 61: "The means of warfare and the preparation for war will exist until a substitute for war be proposed which is not only reasonable in itself, but which is so reasonable that its non-acceptance would be unreasonable. It may be that the inter-relation and interdependence of States must be accepted in theory and practice, and that the judicial organization of the world be realized before armies and navies will cease to be used in foreign affairs, and will be confined to protecting commerce and policing the seas." See also General Report of the Commission of the United States of America to the International Conference at The Hague (July 31, 1899), in Scott, 2 Hague Peace Conferences, *supra* chapter 1, at 17, 21; Richmond P. Hobson, *Disarmament*, 2 AJIL 743 (1908). But see Benjamin F. Trueblood, *The Case for Limitation of Armaments*, 2 AJIL 758 (1908).

12   Declaration Prohibiting Discharge of Projectiles and Explosives from Balloons, July 29, 1899, 32 Stat. 1839 (Pt. 2), 1 Bevans 270. See George B. Davis, *The Launching of Projectiles from Balloons*, 2 AJIL 528 (1908). A U.S. military delegate successfully opposed the imposition of a permanent ban on this practice. See Hull, Two Hague Conferences, *supra* chapter 1, at 76–79. He argued that at the end of five years, states would have a better idea of the military capabilities of airships. See B. Tuchman, The Proud Tower, *supra* this chapter, at 306. See generally Tami Davis Biddle, *Air Power, in The Laws of War, supra* chapter 4, at 140.

13   Declaration Respecting the Prohibition of the Use of Expanding Bullets, July 29,

1899, 187 Parry's Consol. T.S. 459, and in 1 AJIL 155 (Supp. 1907). Only Britain and the United States opposed prohibiting the use of so-called dum-dum bullets. See B. Tuchman, The Proud Tower, *supra* this chapter, at 306. The U.S. delegation did not sign this Declaration. See Hull, Two Hague Conferences, *supra* chapter 1, at 181–87.

14   Declaration Respecting the Prohibition of the Use of Projectiles Diffusing Asphyxiating Gases, July 29, 1899, 187 Parry's Consol. T.S. 453, and in 1 AJIL 157 (Supp. 1907). The proposed ban on the use of asphyxiating gas failed of unanimity by one vote— Captain Mahan of the United States. See B. Tuchman, The Proud Tower, *supra* this chapter, at 307; A. White, The First Hague Conference, at 40, 82 (1912). The U.S. delegation did not sign this Declaration. Hull, Two Hague Conferences, *supra* chapter 1, at 87–90.

15   Declaration renouncing the Use in Time of War of Explosive Projectiles under 400 Grammes Weight, Dec. 11, 1868, 138 Parry's Consol. T.S. 297, and in 1 AJIL 95, 96 (Supp. 1907).

16   Id. at 96.

17   See Hull, Two Hague Conferences, *supra* chapter 1, at 69–75; Scott, 1 Hague Peace Conferences, *supra* chapter 1, at 101–06.

18   See Davis, Hague II, *supra* chapter 2, at 140–61, 215–19.

19   Final Act and Conventions of the Second Peace Conference, Oct. 18, 1907, reprinted in 2 AJIL 1, 26–27 (Supp. 1908). See Hull, Two Hague Conferences, *supra* chapter 1, at 69–75.

20   Convention Relative to the Laying of Submarine Mines, Oct. 18, 1907, 36 Stat. 2332 (Pt. 2), reprinted in 2 AJIL 138 (Supp. 1908).

21   Declaration Prohibiting the Discharge of Projectiles and Explosives from Balloons, Oct. 18, 1907, 36 Stat. 2439 (Pt. 2), reprinted in 2 AJIL 216 (Supp. 1908). By its own terms this declaration applied "for a period extending to the close of the Third Peace Conference." See Hull, Two Hague Conferences, *supra* chapter 1, at 79–82; 1 Garner, *supra* chapter 4, at 466.

22   See Report of the American Delegation to the Conference on the Limitation of Armament, S. Doc. No. 125, 67th Cong., 2d Sess. (1922), reprinted in 16 AJIL 159 (1922). See also the analysis in chapter 8 *infra.*

23   See Scott, *The Use of Poisonous Gases in War,* 9 AJIL 697–98 (1915); 1 Garner, *supra* chapter 4, at 277, 286–87. See, generally, Finch, *Some Technical Points Regarding the Hague Conventions,* 9 AJIL 191–95 (1915).

24   Protocol for the Prohibition of the Use in War of Asphyxiating, Poisonous or Other Gases, and of Bacteriological Materials of Warfare, *opened for signing* June 17, 1925, 94 L.N.T.S. 65, *entered into force for the United States* Apr. 10, 1975, 26 U.S.T. 571 (Pt. 2).

25   More recent allegations that the former Soviet Union violated the Geneva Protocol by using chemical weapons in Afghanistan, even if established to be factually and legally correct, should properly be interpreted as a setback for the humanitarian laws of armed conflict, not for the negotiation of arms control and reduction agreements between the two nuclear superpowers. See F. Boyle, The Future of International Law and American Foreign Policy, *supra* chapter 4, at 277–97.

26   Convention for the Pacific Settlement of International Disputes, July 29, 1899, tit. II, art. II, 32 Stat. 1779, 1785 (Pt. 2), 1 Bevans 230, 234.

27   "The convention draws no distinction between 'good offices' and 'mediation.' They are considered as identical expressions, denoting, it may be, a greater degree of intensity" (Scott, 1 Hague Peace Conferences, *supra* chapter 1, at 259).

28   See Davis, Hague I, *supra* chapter 2, at 141–45.

29   More recently, in December 1990, this author tried to convince the government of Iraq to invoke article 8 against the United States in order to buy more time for diplomacy and thus prevent the Gulf War of January 1991. But in the confusion and pressure during the run-up to war, Baghdad never issued instructions to that effect to its ambassador to the United Nations. Then, former U.S. attorney general Ramsey Clark and this author tried to convince the member states of the United Nations to invoke Hague article 8 against both Iraq and the United States to prevent the Gulf War. Regrettably for all concerned, we could not find one state with the courage or willingness to do so.

30   See D. Hill, *The Second Peace Conference at The Hague*, 1 AJIL 671, 681 (1907).

31   Treaty of Peace, Sept. 5, 1905, Japan-Russia, I Jap. Tr. 585, 199 Parry's Consol. T.S. 144.

32   See Scott, *Mr. Roosevelt's Nobel Address on International Peace*, 4 AJIL 700–03 (1910). See, generally, Scott, *The Nobel Peace Prize*, 12 AJIL 383–86 (1918).

33   Convention for the Pacific Settlement of International Disputes, July 29, 1899, tit. III, 32 Stat. 1779, 1787 (Pt. 2), 1 Bevans 230, 236. See Hull, Two Hague Conferences, *supra* chapter 1, at 277–88.

34   Hague Ct. Rep., *supra* chapter 2, at 403. See Davis, Hague II, *supra* chapter 2, at 114; J. Scott, *The Work of the Second Hague Peace Conference*, 2 AJIL 1, 9 (1908); Peter Schneider, *Dogger Bank Incident*, 10 Encyclopedia of Public International Law 131 (1987).

35   See Hudson, PCIJ, *supra* chapter 2, at 38–39, 40.

36   See Hull, Two Hague Conferences, *supra* chapter 1, at 474.

37   Convention for the Pacific Settlement of International Disputes, Oct. 18, 1907, arts. 15–36, 36 Stat.-2199, 2,215–20 (Pt. 2), reprinted in 2 AJIL 43, 50–57 (Supp. 1908). See Hull, Two Hague Conferences, *supra* chapter 1, at 288–97; Edward G. Elliott, *The Development of International Law by the Second Hague Conference*, 8 Colum. L. Rev. 96, 101–02 (1908). Revised article 12 of the 1907 convention provided that in the absence of a special agreement to the contrary, international commissioners of inquiry shall be chosen in accordance with articles 45 and 57 of the 1907 convention, which pertained to the appointment of arbitrators and the selection of an umpire for the Permanent Court of Arbitration. According to article 45 of the 1907 convention, only one of the appointed arbitrators could be the party's national or chosen from among the persons selected by it as members of the PCA. In regard to international commissions of inquiry, the net result of this incorporation was that after the 1907 revision a commission would consist of five members, at least two of whom must be strangers to the controversy. See Report of the Delegates of the United States to the Second International Peace Conference at The Hague from June 15 to October 18, 1907, in Scott, 2 Hague Peace Conferences, *supra* chapter 1, at 198, 208–10.

38   See Hudson, PCIJ, *supra* chapter 2, at 40.

39   Convention Relative to the Opening of Hostilities, Oct. 18, 1907, 36 Stat. 2259 (Pt. 2), reprinted in 2 AJIL 85 (Supp. 1908).

40   Hull, Two Hague Conferences, *supra* chapter 1, at 263.

41   G. Davis, *The Amelioration of the Rules of War on Land*, 2 AJIL 63, 64 (1908).

42   See Editorial Comment, *Historical Extracts Showing When Hostilities Began without Declarations of War*, 2 AJIL 57 (1908).

43   See E. Stowell, *Convention Relative to the Opening of Hostilities*, 2 AJIL 50, 53 (1908).

44   Davis, Hague II, *supra* chapter 2, at 341–42.

45   See Memorandum of a Conversation between the Japanese Ambassador and the Secretary of State (Dec. 7, 1941), 2 FRUS: Japan 1931–1941, at 786; Memorandum Handed by the Japanese Ambassador (Nomura) to the Secretary of State at 2:20 P.M. on December 7, 1941, id. at 787.

46   See Robert J. C. Butow, Tojo and the Coming of the War 371–87 (1961).

47   Potsdam Proclamation, July 26, 1945, 3 Bevans 1,204.

48   See F. Boyle, The Future of International Law and American Foreign Policy 317–68 (1989) (the lessons of Hiroshima and Nagasaki).

49   See Robert F. Kennedy, Thirteen Days: A Memoir of the Cuban Missile Crisis 9 (1971).

50   Id. at 17.

51   Id. at 9.

52   Id. at 15–17.

53   Id. at 17. "We struggled and fought with one another and with our consciences, for it was a question that deeply troubled us all." Id.

54   Id. at 12, 14, 15.

55   Id. at 23.

56   Id. at 26–27, 35.

57   Id. at 27.

58   Convention Respecting the Limitation of the Employment of Force for the Recovery of Contract Debts, Oct. 18, 1907, 36 Stat. 2241 (Pt. 2), reprinted in 2 AJIL 81 (Supp. 1908).

59   See Davis, Hague II, *supra* chapter 2, at 255–58, 284–85; Hull, Two Hague Conferences, *supra* chapter 1, at 349–70.

60   This term was purposefully left undefined (see Scott, 1 Hague Peace Conferences, *supra* chapter 1, at 416–18), yet it was considered to include public debts. See Hull, Two Hague Conferences, *supra* chapter 1, at 360–63. See, generally, J. Scott, *Hague Convention Restricting the Use of Force to Recover on Contract Claims*, 2 AJIL 78 (1908).

61   See Convention Respecting the Limitation of the Employment of Force for the Recovery of Contract Debts, Oct. 18, 1907, 36 Stat. 2241 (Pt. 2), 1 Bevans 607.

62   See G. Finch, *The Legality of the Occupation of the Ruhr Valley*, 17 AJIL 724–33 (1923). But see Ernest J. Schuster, *The Question As to the Legality of the Ruhr Occupation*, 18 AJIL 407 (1924).

63   See Davis, Hague II, *supra* chapter 2, at 73–90; Seward W. Livermore, *Theodore Roosevelt, the American Navy, and the Venezuelan Crisis of 1902–1903*, 51 Am. Hist. Rev. 452 (1946); Edward B. Parsons, *The German-American Crisis of 1902–1903*, 33 Historian 436 (1971). But cf. Platt, *The Allied Coercion of Venezuela, 1902–03: A Reassessment*, Inter-American Econ. Aff., Spring 1962, at 3 (Britain did not intervene to protect bondholders).

64   Instructions of the Minister of Foreign Relations of the Argentine Republic to the

Minister of the Argentine Republic to the United States (Dec. 29, 1902), reprinted in 1 AJIL 1 (Supp. 1907). See A. Hershey, *The Calvo and Drago Doctrines*, 1 AJIL 26 (1907); T. S. Woolsey, *Drago and the Drago Doctrine*, 15 AJIL 558–59 (1921).

65 Paul S. Reinsch, *Failures and Successes at the Second Hague Peace Conference*, 2 Am. Pol. Sci. Rev. 204, 207 (1908).

66 See Davis, Hague II, *supra* chapter 2, at 73–90. The Hague tribunal upheld the demand by the blockading powers for priority of payment on their claims over those of creditor states that had not resorted to the use of force. The Venezuelan Preferential Case (Germany, Gr. Brit. and Italy v. Venez.), Hague Ct. Rep., *supra* chapter 2, at 55 (Perm. Ct. Arb. 1904). See Scott, 1 Hague Peace Conferences, *supra* chapter 1, at 316: "This decision awarding a preference to the blockading powers in the customs of Venezuela has been criticised as a premium on force and war; but if war is legal, and if Venezuela consented to the preferential treatment although under pressure of war, the decision seems good in law, however questionable it may be in morals."

67 "Through Dr. Drago, the Monroe Doctrine has made its formal entry into public law as distinct from national policy" (Scott, 1 Hague Peace Conferences, *supra* chapter 1, at 421). See also J. Scott, *The Work of the Second Hague Peace Conference*, 2 AJIL 1, 15 (1908).

68 J. Scott, *Recommendation for a Third Peace Conference at The Hague*, 2 AJIL 815, 817–18 (1908); Scott, *William Randal Cremer*, 2 AJIL 858, 861 (1908).

69 See Proposal for a Second Hague Conference (Oct. 21, 1904), 1904 FRUS 10, reprinted in 1 AJIL 432 (1907).

70 See Scott, *The Second Peace Conference of the Hague*, 1 AJIL 431–40 (1907).

71 Final Act and Conventions of the Second Peace Conference, Oct. 18, 1907, reprinted in 2 AJIL 1, 28 (Supp. 1908).

72 Id. at 28–29.

73 See Hill, *The Fifteenth Conference of the Interparliamentary Union*, 3 AJIL 180–85 (1909).

74 See Davis, Hague II, *supra* chapter 2, at 286–88; Kuehl, Seeking World Order, *supra* chapter 1, at 104.

75 See Scott, *Sixth Annual Meeting of the American Society of International Law*, 6 AJIL 197–202 (1912); Scott, *The Sixth Annual Meeting of the Society*, 6 AJIL 729–33 (1912).

76 See also William C. Dennis, *The Necessity for an International Code of Arbitral Procedure*, 7 AJIL 285 (1913); Richard Olney, *General Arbitration Treaties*, 6 AJIL 595 (1912).

77 D. Patterson, Toward a Warless World, *supra* chapter 2, at 214.

78 See Editorial Comment, *The Nineteenth Lake Mohonk Conference on International Arbitration*, 7 AJIL 584–87 (1913). See also Scott, *The Lake Mohonk Conference on International Arbitration*, 8 AJIL 608–13 (1914).

79 Circular Note from William Jennings Bryan to U.S. Diplomatic Officers (Jan. 31, 1914), 1914 FRUS 4. See Scott, *Mr. Bryan and the Third Hague Peace Conference*, 8 AJIL 330–35 (1914).

80 Circular Note from William Jennings Bryan to U.S. Diplomatic Officers (June 22, 1914), 1914 FRUS 10.

81 Kathryn Sellers, *Chronicle of International Events*, 8 AJIL 890, 891 (1914). See also Edi-

torial Comment, *Germany and International Peace*, 8 AJIL 881–86 (1914) (Germany favors Third Hague Peace Conference too).

82   K. Sellers, *Chronicle of International Events, supra* this chapter, at 890, 892.

83   D. Patterson, Toward a Warless World, *supra* chapter 2, at 230.

84   See, generally, B. Tuchman, The Guns of August, *supra* chapter 2.

85   See, generally, Harold Nicholson, Peacemaking 1,919 (1965).

*6   U.S. Legalist Imperial Policy toward Latin America,*
*the Caribbean, and the Far East*

1    See P. Jessup, 1 Elihu Root, *supra* chapter 1, at 470.

2    See, e.g., Lindley M. Keasbey, *The Nicaragua Canal and the Monroe Doctrine*, 7 Annals Am. Acad. Pol. & Soc. Sci. 1, 9–10 (1896).

3    See 1 Richardson, *supra* chapter 1, at 776.

4    See E. McCormac, James K. Polk: A Political Biography 690, 698 (1965).

5    Cf. Oppenheim, *The Science of International Law: Its Task and Method*, 2 AJIL 313, 353–54 (1908).

6    See Editorial Comment, *The Monroe Doctrine Again*, 5 AJIL 729–35 (1911).

7    For example, in regard to the Monroe Doctrine the United States made identical reservations to both the 1899 and the 1907 Conventions for the Pacific Settlement of International Disputes as follows: "nor shall anything contained in the said Convention be construed to imply a relinquishment by the United States of America of its traditional attitude toward purely American questions." Hague Ct. Rep., *supra* chapter 2, at civ, cvi.

8    See Luis M. Drago, *State Loans in Their Relation to International Policy*, 1 AJIL 692, 719 (1907). See also C. L. Chandler, *The Pan American Origin of the Monroe Doctrine*, 8 AJIL 515 (1914); William S. Robertson, *Hispanic American Appreciations of the Monroe Doctrine*, 3 Hispanic Am. Hist. Rev. 1 (1920).

9    See 9 Richardson, *supra* chapter 1, at 7,024, 7,053.

10   See L. Drago, *State Loans in Their Relation to International Policy*, 1 AJIL 692, 721–22 (1907).

11   See Richard Olney, *The Development of International Law*, 1 AJIL 418, 423 (1907); Root, *The Real Monroe Doctrine*, 8 AJIL 427, 433–37 (1914). See also Whitelaw Reid, *The Monroe Doctrine; The Polk Doctrine; Anarchism*, 13 Yale L.J. 16 (1903).

12   See Alejandro Alvarez, *Latin America and International Law*, 3 AJIL 269 (1909); L. Drago, *State Loans in Their Relation to International Policy*, 1 AJIL 692, 714–16 (1907).

13   See, e.g., Robert D. Armstrong, *Should the Monroe Policy Be Modified or Abandoned?*, 10 AJIL 77 (1916); Charles L. Chandler, *The Pan American Origin of the Monroe Doctrine*, 8 AJIL 515, 518 (1914); Scott, *President Wilson and Latin America*, 7 AJIL 329–33 (1913); Scott, *Secretary Knox's Visit to Central America*, 6 AJIL 493–98 (1912); Scott, *The Development of the Monroe Doctrine* 6 AJIL 712–13 (1912). See also Hughes, *Observations on the Monroe Doctrine*, 17 AJIL 611 (1923).

14   See, e.g., Germanicus, *The Central American Question from a European Point of View*, 8 AJIL 213 (1914); Root, *The Real Monroe Doctrine*, 8 AJIL 427, 440 (1914).

15  See, e.g., David McCullough, The Path between the Seas 376 (1977).

16  Hay–Bunau Varilla Treaty, Nov. 18, 1903, U.S.-Pan., art. III, 33 Stat. 2234, 2235. The Clayton-Bulwer Treaty of 1850 between the United States and Great Britain had prohibited either party from ever obtaining or maintaining for itself any exclusive control over an interoceanic ship canal across the Central American isthmus. Clayton-Bulwer Treaty, Apr. 19, 1850, U.S.-Gr. Brit., 9 Stat. 995. The Hay-Pauncefote Treaty of 1901 between the United States and the United Kingdom on an interoceanic canal "superseded" the Clayton-Bulwer Treaty without, however, impairing the "general principle" of "neutralization" for any canal across the Central American isthmus established by article VIII of the latter convention. Hay-Pauncefote Treaty, Nov. 18, 1901, U.S.-Gr. Brit., 32 Stat. 1903.

17  See, e.g., Note from Secretary of State for Foreign Affairs of Great Britain to United States Ambassador Bryce (Nov. 14, 1912), reprinted in 7 AJIL 48, 53 (Supp. 1913) (the British recognized that the United States had become "practical sovereign" of the canal by virtue of the Hay–Bunau Varilla Treaty).

18  See Frederick C. Hicks, The Equality of States and the Hague Conferences, 2 AJIL 530, 535, 560 (1908).

19  See R. Olney, The Development of International Law, 1 AJIL 418, 426 (1907); Treaty for the Settlement of Differences, Apr. 6, 1914, U.S.-Colom., 42 Stat. 2122.

20  See e.g., A. Hershey, The Calvo and Drago Doctrines, 1 AJIL 26, 42 (1907). See also E. Root, The Real Monroe Doctrine, 8 AJIL 427, 440 (1914).

21  For a description of the role played by John Bassett Moore—one of the foremost international lawyers of his era—in support of U.S. intervention in Panama, see S. F. Bemis, A Diplomatic History of the United States 514–15 (rev. ed. 1942) [hereinafter cited as Bemis, Diplomatic History]. See also H. Reid, International Servitudes in Law and Practice 241–45 (1932) (text of Moore memorandum in favor of intervention). Elihu Root also supported the intervention in Panama on dubious legal grounds. See D. A. Graber, Crisis Diplomacy 138 (1959); P. Jessup, 1 Elihu Root, supra chapter 1, at 401–07.

22  But cf. Friedlander, A Reassessment of Roosevelt's Role in the Panamanian Revolution of 1903, 14 W. Pol. Q. 535 (1961) (intervention was lawful).

23  See Alfred L. Dennis, Adventures in American Diplomacy 1896–1906, at 312–13 (1928).

24  See, generally, D. Patterson, Toward a Warless World, supra chapter 2, at 123–25.

25  See, e.g., Edwin M. Borchard, Basic Elements of Diplomatic Protection of Citizens Abroad, 7 AJIL 497, 515–20 (1913); Julius Goebel Jr., The International Responsibility of States for Injuries Sustained by Aliens on Account of Mob Violence, Insurrections and Civil Wars, 8 AJIL 802 (1914). But see Harmodio Arias, The Non-liability of States for Damages Suffered by Foreigners in the Course of a Riot, an Insurrection, or a Civil War, 7 AJIL 724 (1913) (Latin American perspective).

26  See Dana G. Munro, Intervention and Dollar Diplomacy in the Caribbean 78–125 (1964) [hereinafter cited as Munro, Intervention and Dollar Diplomacy].

27  Convention Concerning Customs Revenues, Feb. 8, 1907, U.S.-Dom. Rep., 35 Stat. 1880. See Hollander, The Convention of 1907 between the United States and the Dominican Republic, 1 AJIL 287 (1907). An earlier 1905 convention had failed to gain

Senate support because in it the United States undertook the duty of determining the validity of claims against the Dominican Republic. See Message to the Senate by President Theodore Roosevelt (Mar. 6, 1905), in 9 Richardson, *supra* chapter 1, at 7,080; Annual Message to Congress by President Theodore Roosevelt (Dec. 5, 1905), id. at 7,353, 7,375–79. Undaunted, Roosevelt brought a customs agreement into effect on his own accord by the conclusion of a *modus vivendi* pending the Senate's ratification of some treaty. See D. Perkins, The Monroe Doctrine 1867–1907, at 435 (1966).

28    See James F. Rippy, *The Initiation of the Customs Receivership in the Dominican Republic*, 17 Hispanic Am. Hist. Rev. 419, 448 (1937). See also Act of Dominican Congress Authorizing Executive to Issue and Sell $20,000,000 Bonds, Sept. 18, 1907, reprinted in 1 AJIL 408 (Supp. 1907); Editorial Comment, *The San Dominican "Enabling Act,"* 1 AJIL 978 (1907).

29    Convention Concerning Customs Revenues, Feb. 8, 1907, U.S.–Dom. Rep., art. II., 35 Stat. 1880, 1883.

30    See P. Brown, *The Armed Occupation of Santo Domingo*, 11 AJIL 394, 395 (1917).

31    Convention Respecting Customs Revenues, Sept. 24, 1940, U.S.–Dom. Rep., art. I, 55 Stat. 1104, 1105.

32    Convention Concerning a Loan, Jan. 10, 1911, U.S.-Hond., in 4 Unperfected Treaties, *supra* chapter 2, at 195, reprinted in 5 AJIL 274 (Supp. 1911). See Editorial Comment, *The Proposed Loan Conventions between the United States and Honduras and the United States and Nicaragua*, 5 AJIL 1,044–51 (1911). See also George W. Baker, *Ideals and Realities in the Wilson Administration's Relations with Honduras*, 21 Americas 3 (1964).

33    Convention Concerning a Loan, June 6, 1911, U.S.-Nicar., in 4 Unperfected Treaties, *supra* chapter 2, at 213, reprinted in 5 AJIL 291 (Supp. 1911).

34    Convention Regarding a Canal Route and Naval Base, Aug. 5, 1914, U.S.-Nicar., 39 Stat. 1661. See Harold E. Davis, John J. Finan, & F. Taylor Peck, Latin American Diplomatic History 160–62 (1977) [hereinafter cited as Davis et al., Latin American Diplomatic History].

35    Treaty Regarding Finances, Economic Development and Tranquility, Sept. 16, 1915, U.S.-Haiti, 39 Stat. 1654, reprinted in 10 AJIL 234 (Supp. 1916).

36    See Lester D. Langley, The United States and the Caribbean 1900–1970, at 53–58, 116–25, 149–50 (1980); D. Munro, The United States and the Caribbean Republics 1921–1933, at 277, 309 (1974) [hereinafter cited as Munro, United States and Caribbean Republics]; D. Munro, *Dollar Diplomacy in Nicaragua, 1909–1913*, 38 Hispanic Am. Hist. Rev. 209 (1958).

37    Munro, United States and Caribbean Republics, *supra* this chapter, at 72, 309–41.

38    Id. at 139–43. See also George W. Baker Jr., *The Woodrow Wilson Administration and Guatemalan Relations*, 27 Historian 155, 165–66 (1965) (U.S. troops landed in 1920 to protect legation); Theodore P. Wright Jr., *Honduras: A Case Study of United States Support of Free Elections in Central America*, 40 Hispanic Am. Hist. Rev. 212 (1960) (dismal!).

39    See, generally, Selig Adler, *Bryan and Wilsonian Caribbean Penetration*, 20 Hispanic Am. Hist. Rev. 198 (1940).

40   Carman F. Randolph, *Some Observations on the Status of Cuba*, 9 Yale L.J. 353, 356 (1900).

41   Army Appropriation Act, ch. 803, art. III, 56th Cong., 2d Sess., 31 Stat. 895, 897 (1901). See also Scott, *The Restoration of Cuban Self-Government*, 3 AJIL 431–34 (1909).

42   Constitution of the Republic of Cuba, Feb. 21, 1901, reprinted in 94 British and Foreign State Papers 554, 577 (1900–01).

43   Treaty Defining Future Relations, May 22, 1903, U.S.-Cuba, 33 Stat. 2248, 2251.

44   See Lejeune Cummins, *The Formulation of the "Platt Amendment*," 23 Americas 370 (1967); Scott, *The Origin and Purpose of the Platt Amendment*, 8 AJIL 585–91 (1914); P. Jessup, 1 Elihu Root, *supra* chapter 1, at 308–28.

45   See Munro, Intervention and Dollar Diplomacy, *supra* this chapter, at 125–40, 469–529; Munro, United States and Caribbean Republics, *supra* this chapter, at 16–17; Pedro Capo-Rodríquez, *The Platt Amendment*, 17 AJIL 761 (1923).

46   Treaty Defining Relations, May 29, 1934, U.S.-Cuba, art. I, 48 Stat. 1682, 1683.

47   See G. Baker, *The Wilson Administration and Cuba, 1913–1921*, 46 Mid-America 48 (1964).

48   See Scott, *A Caribbean Policy for the United States*, 8 AJIL 886–89 (1914); Robert F. Smith, *Cuba: Laboratory for Dollar Diplomacy, 1898–1917*, 28 Historian 586, 597–98 (1966).

49   See P. Brown, *The Armed Occupation of Santo Domingo*, 11 AJIL 394–99 (1917).

50   See P. Brown, *American Intervention in Haiti*, 16 AJIL 607 (1922); P. Brown, *International Responsibility in Haiti and Santo Domingo*, 16 AJIL 433 (1922); Charles E. Hughes, *Observations on the Monroe Doctrine*, 17 AJIL 611 (1923) (speech by U.S. secretary of state).

51   Hughes, *Observations on the Monroe Doctrine*, 17 AJIL 611 (1923).

52   The U.S. Congress purportedly annexed Hawaii on July 7, 1898. Pub. Res. 55, 55th Cong., 2d Sess., 30 Stat. 750 (1898). Today a movement by Native Hawaiians to reestablish their independent nation-state is quickly gaining momentum. See F. Boyle, *Restoration of the Independent Nation State of Hawaii under International Law*, 7 St. Thomas L. Rev. 723 (1995).

53   See, e.g., Editorial Comment, *The Emperor of Japan*, 6 AJIL 944, 948–49 (1912); Scott, *The Annexation of Korea to Japan*, 4 AJIL 923–25 (1910). See also Scott, *The International Status of Korea*, 1 AJIL 444–49 (1907).

54   See also Bemis, Diplomatic History, *supra* this chapter, at 493 (Taft-Katsura memorandum).

55   See P. Jessup, 2 Elihu Root, *supra* chapter 1, at 5–7; John A. S. Grenville & George B. Young, Politics, Strategy and American Diplomacy 315 (1966); D. Graber, Crisis Diplomacy, *supra* this chapter, at 180–81; J. Cooper, Pivotal Decades: The United States, 1900–1920, at 103 (1990); A. Dennis, Adventures in American Diplomacy, *supra* this chapter, at 416–17.

56   See Albert B. Hart, *Pacific and Asiatic Doctrines Akin to the Monroe Doctrine*, 9 AJIL 802, 816 (1915).

57   See Scott, *Arbitration Treaty with China*, 3 AJIL 166–68 (1909).

58   See, e.g., J. Grenville & G. Young, Politics, Strategy, and American Diplomacy, *supra* this chapter, at 308–09.

59 Letter from John Hay to Joseph Choate (Sept. 6, 1899), 1899 FRUS 131, 132.

60 Circular Note to the Powers Cooperating in China, Defining the Purposes and Policy of the United States (July 3, 1900), reprinted in 1 AJIL 386 (Supp. 1907). See Editorial Comment, *The Integrity of China and the "Open Door,"* 1 AJIL 954 (1907); William R. Manning, *China and the Powers since the Boxer Movement*, 4 AJIL 848 (1910).

61 Circular Note to the Powers Cooperating in China, Defining the Purposes and Policy of the United States (July 3, 1900), reprinted in 1 AJIL 386, 387 (Supp. 1907).

62 Agreement Concerning Maintenance of Interests in China, Oct. 16, 1900, Gr. Brit.-Germany, 92 Brit. For. 31, 189 Parry's Consol. T.S. 95.

63 Agreement Concerning Relations with the East, Jan. 30, 1902, Gr. Brit.-Japan, Mac-Murray 324, 190 Parry's Consol. T.S. 457.

64 Agreement Concerning Relations in the East, Aug. 12, 1905, U.K.-Japan, 98 Brit. For. 136, 199 Parry's Consol. T.S. 90.

65 Agreement of Alliance, July 13, 1911, U.K.-Japan, 104 Brit. For. 173, 214 Parry's Consol. T.S. 107.

66 Peace of Portsmouth, Sept. 5, 1905, Russia-Japan, 98 Brit. For. 735, 199 Parry's Consol. T.S. 144.

67 St. Petersburg Convention, July 17 (30), 1907, Russia-Japan, I Jap. Tr. 606, 204 Parry's Consol. T.S. 339.

68 Agreement Concerning Policies in China, June 10, 1907, Fr.-Japan, 3 Basdevant 1, 204 Parry's Consol. T.S. 227. See Editorial Comment, *The Recent Agreements Concluded between Japan and France*, 1 AJIL 748–49 (1907).

69 Root-Takahira Agreement on Pacific Possessions, Nov. 30, 1908, U.S.-Japan, T.S. 511 1/2. See Scott, *United States and Japan in the Far East*, 3 AJIL 168–70 (1909).

70 See Scott, *The Revised Anglo-Japanese Alliance*, 5 AJIL 1,054, 1,055 (1911).

71 Treaty of Guadalupe-Hidalgo, Feb. 2, 1848, U.S.-Mex., 9 Stat. 922. See Scott, *Tripoli*, 6 AJIL 149, 155 (1912) (Mexican war was unjust and unjustifiable).

72 See Editorial Comment, *Secretary Root's Visit to Mexico*, 1 AJIL 964, 965 (1907).

73 See Scott, *Diaz and Mexico*, 5 AJIL 714–16 (1911); Scott, *Mexico*, 6 AJIL 475–78 (1912).

74 See Edward J. Berbusse, *Neutrality-Diplomacy of the United States and Mexico, 1910-1911*, 12 Americas 265 (1956).

75 S.J. Res. 89, 62d Cong., 2d Sess., 37 Stat. 630 (1912), reprinted in 1912 FRUS 745.

76 Presidential Proclamation No. 1185, 37 Stat. 1733 (1912). See Scott, *Mexico*, 6 AJIL 475 (1912).

77 Davis et al., Latin American Diplomatic History, *supra* this chapter, at 174.

78 See Lowell L. Blaisdell, *Henry Lane Wilson and the Overthrow of Madero*, 43 Sw. Soc. Sci. Q. 126 (1962); Lloyd C. Gardner, *Woodrow Wilson and the Mexican Revolution*, in Woodrow Wilson and a Revolutionary World, 1913-1921, at 3, 8–10 (Arthur S. Link ed., 1982).

79 See Editorial Comment, *Mexico*, 7 AJIL 832–36 (1913).

80 Letter from Thomas Jefferson to Gouverneur Morris (Nov. 7, 1792), in 8 The Writings of Thomas Jefferson 436 (Library ed. 1903).

81 Letter from Thomas Jefferson to Gouverneur Morris (Mar. 12, 1793), in 9 id. at 36.

82 See Scott, *President Wilson and Latin America*, 7 AJIL 329–33 (1913).

83 Presidential Proclamation No. 1263, 38 Stat. 1992, reprinted in 1914 FRUS 447. See Scott, *Mediation in Mexico*, 8 AJIL 579, 580 (1914).

84   See Davis et al., Latin American Diplomatic History, *supra* this chapter, at 174–75; Ted C. Hinckley, *Wilson, Huerta and the Twenty-One Gun Salute*, 22 Historian 197 (1960); Scott, *Mediation in Mexico*, 8 AJIL 579, 581–82 (1914).

85   See World Peace Foundation, Arbitration and the United States, in 9 World Peace Foundation Pamphlets 453, 486–87 (1926).

86   Pub. Res. 22, 63d Cong., 2d Sess., 38 Stat. 770 (1914).

87   Amendment Offered by Senator Lodge to H.R.J. Res. 251, 63d Cong., 2d Sess., 51 Cong. Rec. 7005 (1914). See Scott, *Mediation in Mexico*, 8 AJIL 579, 582 (1914).

88   See Scott, *Mediation in Mexico*, 8 AJIL 579, 582 (1914); *Chronicle of International Events*, 8 AJIL 615, 620 (1914).

89   See Finch, *The Eighth Annual Meeting of the Society*, 8 AJIL 597, 608 (1914).

90   See Letter from Secretary Dodge to the Secretary of State and Text of Mediation Protocol No. 4 (June 25, 1914), 1914 FRUS 547, 548–49.

91   Id. at 547, 548.

92   See A. Hershey, *The Calvo and Drago Doctrines*, *supra* chapter 3, at 31.

93   See Green H. Hackworth, 5 Digest of International Law 672–73 (1927) [hereinafter cited as Hackworth].

94   See Finch, *Mexico*, 8 AJIL 860, 863 (1914).

95   See Finch, *The Recognition of the De Facto Government in Mexico*, 10 AJIL 357–67 (1916).

96   See Gardner, *Woodrow Wilson and the Mexican Revolution*, in Woodrow Wilson and a Revolutionary World, 1913–1921, at 3, 28–29 (A. Link ed., 1982).

97   See *Chronicle of International Events*, 10 AJIL 379, 386 (1916).

98   Telegram from the Secretary of State to All American Consular Officers in Mexico (Mar. 10, 1916), 1916 FRUS 484.

99   Telegram from Special Agent Silliman to the Secretary of State (Mar. 10, 1916), 1916 FRUS 485.

100  Note from the Secretary of State to Special Agent Silliman (Mar. 13, 1916), 1916 FRUS 487; Note from Mr. Arredondo to the Secretary of State (Mar. 18, 1916), 1916 FRUS 493.

101  Note from the Secretary of Foreign Relations of the De Facto Government of Mexico to the Secretary of State (May 22, 1916), 1916 FRUS 552.

102  Note from the Secretary of State to the Secretary of Foreign Relations of the De Facto Government in Mexico (June 20, 1916), 1916 FRUS 581, 588–91.

103  Id. at 581, 591–92.

104  See *Chronicle of International Events*, 10 AJIL 610, 621 (1916).

105  Letter from Mr. Arredondo to the Secretary of State (July 4, 1916), 1916 FRUS 599.

106  Letter from Mr. Arredondo to the Secretary of State (July 12, 1916), 1916 FRUS 601.

107  Letter from the Acting Secretary of State to Mr. Arredondo (July 28, 1916), 1916 FRUS 604.

108  See *Chronicle of International Events*, 10 AJIL 898, 900–901 (1916).

109  Treaty of Guadalupe-Hidalgo, Feb. 2, 1848, U.S.-Mex., art. 21, 9 Stat. 922, 938. See Scott, *Mexico and the United States and Arbitration*, 10 AJIL 577–80 (1916); Scott, *The American-Mexican Joint Commission of 1916*, 10 AJIL 890–96 (1916).

110  Letter from American Commissioners to Secretary of State and Report on the Proceedings of the Commission (Apr. 26, 1917), 1917 FRUS 916, 920.

111  Id. at 925.

112  Id. at 927–28.

113  Id. at 932.

114  Id. at 937.

115  G. Finch, *Mexico and the United States*, 11 AJIL 399, 406 (1917).

116  See Louis G. Kahle, *Robert Lansing and the Recognition of Venustiano Carranza*, 38 Hispanic Am. Hist. Rev. 353 (1958).

117  See, e.g., G. Finch, *Mexico and the United States*, 11 AJIL 399, 404–05 (1917).

118  See Scott, *The American Punitive Expedition into Mexico*, 10 AJIL 337, 338 (1916).

119  See, e.g., N. Chomsky, Turning the Tide (1985); Jack Nelson-Pallmeyer, War against the Poor (1989); F. Boyle, World Politics and International Law, *supra* chapter 4, at 266–90; F. Boyle, Defending Civil Resistance under International Law 155–210 (1987); F. Boyle, *The U.S. Invasion of Panama: Implications for International Law and Politics*, 1 East African J. Peace & Human Rights 80 (Uganda, 1993).

120  Cf. Lars Schoultz, Beneath the United States (1998) (U.S. policies toward Latin America and the Caribbean have always been based on racist assumptions).

7  *The Foundation of the Inter-American System of International Relations and Its Central American Subsystem*

1  See, e.g., Kuehl, Seeking World Order, *supra* chapter 1, at 118; Alejandro Alvarez, *Latin America and International Law*, 3 AJIL 269 (1909); Robert D. Armstrong, *Should the Monroe Policy Be Modified or Abandoned?*, 10 AJIL 77, 99 (1909); Charles E. Hughes, *Observations on the Monroe Doctrine*, 17 AJIL 611 (1923); Richard Olney, *The Development of International Law*, 1 AJIL 418, 425 (1907); Theodore S. Woolsey, *An American Concert of the Powers*, 45 Scribners Mag. 364 (1909).

2  Here I am using the terms *system* and *subsystem* in the manner described by the self-styled "systems analysis" school of international political science that was in vogue during the 1960s. The foremost exemplar of this approach is Morton A. Kaplan, System and Process in International Politics 4 (1957): "A system of action is a set of variables so related, in contradistinction to its environment, that describable behavioral regularities characterize the internal relationships of the variables to each other and the external relationships of the set of individual variables to combinations of external variables." See, generally, L. von Bertalanffy, General System Theory (1968); and the authorities collected in F. Boyle, World Politics and International Law, *supra* chapter 4, at 299–300 n. 41. In international politics, a system or subsystem can contain within itself regimes and subregimes dealing with the various functional aspects of international relations within the system or subsystem itself.

3  See, e.g., Mark T. Gilderhus, *Pan-American Initiatives: The Wilson Presidency and "Regional Integration," 1914–17*, 4 Dipl. Hist. 409 (1980).

4  See C. Fenwick, The Organization of American States 14–19 (1963). See also Alonso M. Aguilar, Pan-Americanism from Monroe to the Present (1968).

5  Note from Mr. Blaine to Mr. Osborn (Nov. 29, 1881), 1881–82 FRUS 13. See Scott, *The Fourth Pan-American Conference*, 3 AJIL 963–69 (1909). See also Russell H. Bastert, *Diplomatic Reversal: Frelinghuysen's Opposition to Blaine's Pan-American Policy in*

*1882*, 42 Miss. Valley Hist. Rev. 653 (1956); J. Grenville & G. Young, Politics, Strategy and American Diplomacy, *supra* chapter 6, at 90–92.

6   See, generally, A. Aguilar, Pan-Americanism from Monroe to the Present, *supra* this chapter, at 36–40.

7   See Alva C. Wilgus, *James G. Blaine and the Pan American Movement*, 5 Hispanic Am. Hist. Rev. 662 (1922).

8   See Inter-American Institute of International Legal Studies, The Inter-American System: Its Development and Strengthening, at xv–xxxiii (1966) [hereinafter cited as Inter-American System].

9   See 6 Moore, *supra* chapter 2, § 969, at 599–602.

10  See International American Conference, 2 Reports of Committees and Discussions Thereon 1,078 (Eng. ed. 1890) (presenting the text of the model treaty) [hereinafter cited as International American Conference].

11  See The International Conferences of American States 1889–1928, at 40 n. 4 (J. Scott ed., 1931) (texts available) [hereinafter cited as Inter-American Conferences].

12  See 1 Moore, *supra* chapter 2, § 87, at 292.

13  2 International American Conference, *supra* this chapter, at 1,123–24.

14  Id. at 1147–48. See 7 Moore, *supra* chapter 2, § 1084, at 71.

15  Kellogg-Briand Pact, Aug. 27, 1928, 46 Stat. 2343, 2345–46 (Pt. 2).

16  See Philip Q. Wright, *Stimson Note of January 7, 1932*, 26 AJIL 342 (1932).

17  See League of Nations Official Journal: Records of the Thirteenth Ordinary Session of the Assembly, Mar. 11, 1932, at 87–88.

18  See, e.g., Burns H. Weston, Richard A. Falk, & Anthony D'Amato, International Law and World Order 158 (2d ed. 1990).

19  1 International American Conference, *supra* this chapter, at 404–08.

20  See Inter-American Conferences, *supra* this chapter, at 36 n. 2.

21  6 Moore, *supra* chapter 2, § 969, at 601.

22  See Inter-American Conferences, *supra* this chapter, at 44.

23  See id. at 11–45.

24  See A. C. Wilgus, *James G. Blaine and the Pan American Movement*, 5 Hispanic Am. Hist. Rev. 662, 707 (1922).

25  See, generally, F. V. García-Amador, *Calvo Doctrine, Calvo Clause*, in 1 Encyclopedia of Public International Law 521 (1992).

26  6 Moore, *supra* chapter 2, § 969, at 602; A. C. Wilgus, *The Second International American Conference at Mexico City*, 11 Hispanic Am. Hist. Rev. 27 (1931).

27  See 7 Moore, *supra* chapter 2, § 1087, at 94.

28  See Convention for the Pacific Settlement of International Disputes, *supra* chapter 2; Convention with Respect to the Laws and Customs of War on Land, July 29, 1899, 32 Stat. 1803; and Convention for the Adaptation to Maritime Warfare of the Principles of the Geneva Convention, Aug. 22, 1899, 32 Stat. 1827.

29  See General Secretary of the Second International Conference, Second International American Conference, Mexico: 1901–1902, at 336–37 (Eng. ed. 1902) [hereinafter cited as Second Inter-American Conference].

30  Protocol of Adhesion to the Convention for the Pacific Settlement of International Disputes, June 14, 1907, in Reports to the Hague Conferences of 1899 and 1907, at

193–94 (J. Scott ed., 1917), reprinted in Scott, 2 Hague Peace Conferences, *supra* chapter 1, at 252.

31   *Procès-verbal* of Adhesion to the Treaty on the Pacific Settlement of International Disputes, June 25, 1907, in Reports to the Hague Conferences of 1899 and 1907, at 254 (J. Scott ed., 1917), reprinted in Scott, 2 Hague Peace Conferences, *supra* chapter 1, at 254.

32   See Inter-American Conferences, *supra* this chapter, at 62 n. 1.

33   Id. at 62.

34   Treaty of Obligatory Arbitration, Jan. 29, 1902, XCV Brit. For. 1009, 190 Parry's Consol. T.S. 432, and in 1 AJIL 299 (Supp. 1907).

35   See Inter-American Conferences, *supra* this chapter, at 100 n. 1.

36   Treaty for the Arbitration of Pecuniary Claims, Jan. 30, 1902, 34 Stat. 2845, reprinted in 1 AJIL 303 (Supp. 1907).

37   7 Moore, *supra* chapter 2, § 1087, at 95.

38   See Inter-American Conferences, *supra* this chapter, at 104 n.2.

39   Id. at 132.

40   Arbitration of Pecuniary Claims: Extending Convention of January 30, 1902, Aug. 13, 1906, 37 Stat. 1648. See Inter-American Conferences, *supra* this chapter, at 132 n. 1.

41   See Inter-American Conferences, *supra* this chapter, at 183.

42   Arbitration of Pecuniary Claims, Aug. 11, 1910, 38 Stat. 1799. See Inter-American Conferences, *supra* this chapter, at 183 n. 1.

43   See Inter-American System, *supra* this chapter, at xxii.

44   See Second Inter-American Conference, *supra* this chapter, at 248–52.

45   See Inter-American Conferences, *supra* this chapter, at 63–109.

46   Second Inter-American Conference, *supra* this chapter, at 272–91. See Harmodio Arias, *The Non-liability of States for Damages Suffered by Foreigners in the Course of a Riot, an Insurrection, or a Civil War*, 7 AJIL 724, 757 (1913).

47   See Inter-American Conferences, *supra* this chapter, at 96–97.

48   Letter from the Brazilian Ambassador to the Secretary of State (Apr. 25, 1906), 1906 FRUS 1565. See A. C. Wilgus, *The Third International American Conference at Rio de Janeiro, 1906*, 12 Hispanic Am. Hist. Rev. 420 (1932).

49   See Inter-American Conferences, *supra* this chapter, at 124.

50   Id. at 135. See Scott, 1 Hague Peace Conferences, *supra* chapter 1, at 397–400; A. Hershey, *Calvo and Drago Doctrines*, 1 AJIL 26 (1907); Wolfgang Benedek, *Drago-Porter Convention (1907)*, 8 Encyclopedia of Public International Law 141–43 (1985).

51   Convention Respecting the Limitation of the Employment of Force for the Recovery of Contract Debts, Oct. 18, 1907, 36 Stat. 2241, reprinted in 2 AJIL 81 (Supp. 1908).

52   Inter-American Conferences, *supra* this chapter, at 135 n. 2.

53   Id. at 125.

54   Id. at 129. See Scott, *Dedication of the Pan-American Building*, 4 AJIL 679–87 (1910); Scott, *The New Building of the International Bureau of American Republics*, 2 AJIL 621–24 (1908).

55   Convention Establishing an International Commission of Jurists, Aug. 23, 1906, 37 Stat. 1554, reprinted in 6 AJIL 173 (Supp. 1912).

56   See Editorial Comment, *Congress of Jurists at Rio de Janeiro*, 6 AJIL 931–35 (1912).

57   See Inter-American Conferences, *supra* this chapter, at 144 n. 1.

58   See Editorial Comment, *International Law at the First Pan-American Scientific Congress*, 3 AJIL 429–31 (1909); Scott, *The Pan-American Scientific Congress*, 9 AJIL 919–23 (1915).

59   See J. Scott, *The Second Pan-American Scientific Congress*, 10 AJIL 130 (1916). For the subsequent history of these congresses, see Inter-American Conferences, *supra* this chapter, at 185 n. 1.

60   See Finch, *Postponement of the Annual Meeting of the Society*, 9 AJIL 473–74 (1915); Finch, *The Ninth Annual Meeting of the American Society of International Law*, 9 AJIL 915–19 (1915); G. Finch, *The Annual Meeting of the Society*, 10 AJIL 133–37 (1916).

61   See Editorial Comment, *Project for the Creation of an American Institute of International Law*, 6 AJIL 952–54 (1912); Scott, *The American Institute of International Law*, 6 AJIL 949–51 (1912); Scott, *The American Institute of International Law*, 9 AJIL 923–27 (1915).

62   See A. Hershey, *Projects Submitted to the American Institute of International Law*, 11 AJIL 390 (1917); E. Root, *The Declaration of the Rights and Duties of Nations Adopted by the American Institute of International Law*, 10 AJIL 211 (1916); Scott, *The American Institute of International Law*, 10 AJIL 121–26 (1916).

63   See Scott, *International Cooperation and the Equality of States*, 18 AJIL 116, 118 (1924).

64   See Inter-American Conferences, *supra* this chapter, at 146.

65   Inter-American System, *supra* this chapter, at xxiii–xxiv.

66   Copyright Convention, Aug. 11, 1910, 38 Stat. 1785.

67   Convention on the Arbitration of Pecuniary Claims, Aug. 11, 1910, 38 Stat. 1799.

68   Convention for the Protection of Industrial Property, Aug. 20, 1910, 38 Stat. 1811.

69   Trade Mark Convention, Aug. 20, 1910, 39 Stat. 1675.

70   Inter-American Conferences, *supra* this chapter, at 172.

71   Id. at 176.

72   See C. Fenwick, The Organization of American States, *supra* this chapter.

73   Inter-American System, *supra* this chapter, at xxxii.

74   Paul S. Reinsch, *The Fourth International Conference of American Republics*, 4 AJIL 777 (1910) (emphasis added). See also A. Hershey, *Projects Submitted to the American Institute of International Law*, 11 AJIL 390 (1917).

75   Hay–Bunau Varilla Treaty, Nov. 18, 1903, U.S.-Pan., 33 Stat. 2234.

76   See Munro, Intervention and Dollar Diplomacy, *supra* chapter 6, at 143–46.

77   Treaty of Peace, July 20, 1906, Guat.-Hond.–El Sal., 1906 Descamps 742, 202 Parry's Consol. T.S. 217. See Scott, *The Peace of the Marblehead*, 1 AJIL 142 (1907).

78   See Davis et al., Latin American Diplomatic History, *supra* chapter 6, at 158–59.

79   Protocol Respecting the Meeting of a Conference at Washington for the Maintenance of Peace in Central America, Sept. 17, 1907, 204 Parry's Consol. T.S. 418, and in 1 AJIL 406 (Supp. 1907). See Munro, Intervention and Dollar Diplomacy, *supra* chapter 6, at 146–55.

80   General Treaty of Peace and Amity, Dec. 20, 1907, 206 Parry's Consol. T.S. 63.

81   Additional Convention, General Treaty of Peace and Amity, Dec. 20, 1907, 206 Parry's Consol. T.S. 70.

82  Convention for the Establishment of a Central American Court of Justice, Dec. 20, 1907, 206 Parry's Consol. T.S. 78, and in 2 AJIL 231 (Supp. 1908).

83  Extradition Convention, Dec. 20, 1907, 206 Parry's Consol. T.S. 126, and in 2 AJIL 243 (Supp. 1908).

84  Convention on Communications, Dec. 20, 1907, 206 Parry's Consol. T.S. 104, and in 2 AJIL 262 (Supp. 1908).

85  Convention for the Establishment of an International Central American Bureau, Dec. 20, 1907, 206 Parry's Consol. T.S. 111, and in 2 AJIL 251 (Supp. 1908).

86  Convention for the Establishment of a Central American Pedagogical Institute, Dec. 20, 1907, 206 Parry's Consol. T.S. 119, and in 2 AJIL 256 (Supp. 1908).

87  Convention Concerning Future Central American Conferences, Dec. 20, 1907, 206 Parry's Consol. T.S. 97, and in 2 AJIL 259 (Supp. 1908). See J. Scott, *The Central American Peace Conference of 1907*, 2 AJIL 121 (1908).

88  See Munro, Intervention and Dollar Diplomacy, *supra* chapter 6, at 154; Luis Anderson, *The Peace Conference of Central America*, 2 AJIL 144 (1908); D. Patterson, *The United States and the Origins of the World Court*, 91 Pol. Sci. Q. 279, 284 (1976).

89  Convention for the Establishment of a Central American Court of Justice, Dec. 20, 1907, art. I, 206 Parry's Consol. T.S. 78, 80.

90  See Editorial Comment, *The First Case before the Central American Court of Justice*, 2 AJIL 835–45 (1908).

91  Convention for the Establishment of a Central American Court of Justice, Dec. 20, 1907, arts. II & III, 206 Parry's Consol. T.S. 78, 80.

92  See M. Hudson, *The Central American Court of Justice*, 26 AJIL 759 (1932).

93  Honduras v. Guatemala (1908), reprinted in 3 AJIL 434 (Eng. trans. 1909).

94  See Munro, Intervention and Dollar Diplomacy, *supra* chapter 6, at 155–58; Scott, *The First Decision of the Central American Court of Justice*, 3 AJIL 434, 436 (1909).

95  Convention Regarding a Canal Route and Naval Base, Aug. 5, 1914, U.S.-Nicar., 39 Stat. 1661. See Thomas A. Bailey, *Interest in a Nicaraguan Canal, 1903-1931*, 16 Hispanic Am. Hist. Rev. 2 (1936); G. Finch, *The Treaty with Nicaragua Granting Canal and Other Rights to the United States*, 10 AJIL 344 (1916); D. Hill, *The Nicaraguan Canal Idea to 1913*, 28 Hispanic Am. Hist. Rev. 197 (1948); L. Keasbey, *The Nicaragua Canal and the Monroe Doctrine*, 7 Annals Am. Acad. Pol. & Soc. Sci. 1 (1896).

96  See George W. Baker, *The Woodrow Wilson Administration and El Salvador Relations 1913-1921*, 56 Soc. Stud. 97 (1965).

97  See D. Hill, *Central American Court of Justice*, in 1 Encyclopedia of Public International Law 41–45 (1981).

98  See Editorial Comment, *The Second Central American Peace Conference*, 4 AJIL 416–17 (1910).

99  See Conventions Adopted by the Fourth Central American Conference, Managua, Jan. 1-11, 1912, reprinted in 7 AJIL 34–41 (Supp. 1913).

100  See W. S. Pennfield, *The Central American Union*, 7 AJIL 829, 831 (1913).

101  Pact of Union of Central America, Jan. 19, 1921, 5 L.N.T.S. 10, reprinted in 15 AJIL 328 (Supp. 1921). See Brown, *The Federation of Central America*, 15 AJIL 255–59 (1921).

102  See Lester Langley, The United States and the Caribbean 1900-1970, *supra* chapter 6, at 106–07.

103  See L. Langley, The Banana Wars 177 (1983); Scott, *The Central American Conference,* 17 AJIL 313–19 (1923) [hereinafter cited as Scott, *Central American Conference*].

104  See M. Hudson, 2 International Legislation 901–92 (1931), for the texts.

105  See Scott, *Central American Conference, supra* this chapter, at 315–16 (quoting from the official *Bulletin of the Pan American Union*).

106  Id. at 316.

107  Id. at 318.

108  Id. at 318.

109  Id. at 316.

110  Id. at 316.

111  See United States Department of State, 1977 Digest of United States Practice in International Law 575.

112  See F. Boyle, *The U.S. Invasion of Panama: Implications for International Law and Politics,* 1 East African J. Peace & Human Rights 80 (Uganda, 1993).

113  Pan American Union, Charter of the Organization of American States, at 8 (1962).


8    *U.S. Neutrality toward the First World War*

1  See Scott, *Mr. Bryan's Proposed Commissions of Inquiry,* 7 AJIL 566–70 (1913).

2  General Arbitration Treaty, Aug. 3, 1911 U.S.-Fra., in 4 Unperfected Treaties, *supra* chapter 2, at 217, reprinted in 5 AJIL 249 (Supp. 1911); General Arbitration Treaty, Aug. 3, 1911, U.S.-Gr. Brit., in 4 Unperfected Treaties, *supra* chapter 2, at 225, reprinted in 5 AJIL 253 (Supp. 1911). See Davis, Hague II, *supra* chapter 2, at 321–25; Scott, *Admiral Togo— "The Peaceful Man of the East,"* 5 AJIL 1,051, 1,052 (1911).

3  Davis, Hague II, *supra* chapter 2, at 323.

4  Id. at 323.

5  James Brown Scott called the treaties "about the mushiest and most inconsequential, and therefore the most dangerous things, that have come across our diplomatic horizon for many moons." See John P. Campbell, *Taft, Roosevelt, and the Arbitration Treaties of 1911,* 53 J. Am. Hist. 279, 293 (1966). See also P. Jessup, 2 Elihu Root, *supra* chapter 1, at 270–76.

6  See D. Patterson, Toward a Warless World, *supra* chapter 2, at 207.

7  See, e.g., Treaty for the Advancement of General Peace, Sept. 15, 1914, U.S.-Fra., 38 Stat. 1887.

8  See Scott, *Secretary Bryan's Peace Plan,* 8 AJIL 565, 570 (1914). See, generally, Finch, *The Bryan Peace Treaties,* 10 AJIL 882–90 (1916); Scott, *The Bryan Peace Treaties,* 7 AJIL 823–29 (1913).

9  See Scott, *Arbitration and Peace Treaties,* 8 AJIL 330, 341–43 (1914).

10  See 4 Unperfected Treaties, *supra* chapter 2, at 263.

11  See Treaty for the Advancement of General Peace, Sept. 20, 1913, U.S.-Guat., 38 Stat. 1840 (advice and consent given Aug. 13, 1914); Treaty for the Advancement of General Peace, Nov. 3, 1913, U.S.-Hond., 39 Stat. 1672 (advice and consent given Aug. 13, 1914); Treaty for the Advancement of General Peace, Jan. 22, 1914, U.S.-Bol., 38 Stat. 1868 (advice and consent given Aug. 13, 1914); Treaty for the Advancement of General Peace, Feb. 4, 1914, U.S.-Port., 38 Stat. 1847 (advice and consent given Aug. 13, 1914);

Treaty for the Advancement of General Peace, Feb. 13, 1914, U.S.–Costa Rica, 38 Stat. 1856 (advice and consent given Aug. 13, 1914); Treaty for the Advancement of General Peace, May 5, 1914, U.S.-Italy, 39 Stat. 1618 (advice and consent given Aug. 13, 1914); Treaty for the Advancement of General Peace, June 24, 1914, U.S.-Nor., 38 Stat. 1843 (advice and consent given Aug. 13, 1914); Treaty for the Advancement of General Peace, July 14, 1914, U.S.-Peru, 39 Stat. 1611 (advice and consent given Aug. 20, 1914); Treaty for the Advancement of General Peace, July 20, 1914, U.S.-Uru., 38 Stat. 1908 (advice and consent given Aug. 13, 1914); Treaty for the Advancement of General Peace, July 24, 1914, U.S.-Braz., 39 Stat. 1698 (advice and consent given Aug. 13, 1914); Treaty for the Advancement of General Peace, July 24, 1914, U.S.-Chile, 39 Stat. 1645 (advice and consent given Aug. 20, 1914). Interestingly enough, the Bryan peace treaty with Chile was recently invoked by the U.S. government in an effort to resolve the dispute over the 1976 assassination of Orlando Letelier and Ronni Moffitt in Washington, D.C. See *Peaceful Settlement of Disputes*, 83 AJIL 352 (1988). The two countries entered into an agreement to establish such a commission on June 11, 1990, and the commission rendered its award on January 11, 1992. See *Claims for Wrongful Death*, 86 AJIL 347 (1992).

12   Scott, *The Bryan Peace Treaties*, 8 AJIL 876, 877 (1914). See Treaty for the Advancement of General Peace, Sept. 15, 1914, U.S.-China, 39 Stat. 1642 (advice and consent given Oct. 12, 1914); Treaty for the Advancement of General Peace, Sept. 15, 1914, U.S.-Spain, 38 Stat. 1862 (advice and consent given Sept. 25, 1914); Treaty for the Advancement of General Peace, Sept. 15, 1914, U.S.-Fra., 38 Stat. 1887 (advice and consent given Sept. 25, 1914); Treaty for the Advancement of General Peace, Sept. 15, 1914, U.S.–Gr. Brit., 38 Stat. 1853 (advice and consent given Sept. 25, 1914). See also Treaty for the Advancement of General Peace, Apr. 17, 1914, U.S.-Den., 38 Stat. 1883 (advice and consent given Sept. 30, 1914); Treaty for the Advancement of General Peace, Aug. 29, 1914, U.S.-Para., 39 Stat. 1615 (advice and consent given Oct. 22, 1914); Treaty for the Advancement of General Peace, Oct. 1, 1914, U.S.-Russia, 39 Stat. 1622 (advice and consent given Oct. 13, 1914); Treaty for the Advancement of General Peace, Oct. 13, 1914, U.S.-Ecuador, 39 Stat. 1650 (advice and consent given Oct. 20, 1914); Treaty for the Advancement of General Peace, Oct. 13, 1914, U.S.-Swed., 38 Stat. 1872 (advice and consent given Oct. 22, 1914).

13   See Scott, *Secretary Bryan's Peace Plan*, 9 AJIL 175–77 (1915). See, generally, Scott, *The Effect of Mr. Bryan's Peace Treaties upon the Relations of the United States with the Nations at War*, 9 AJIL 494–96 (1915).

14   See D. Perkins, History of the Monroe Doctrine, *supra* chapter 2, at 283.

15   See Martin D. Dubin, *Toward the Concept of Collective Security: The Bryce Group's "Proposals for the Avoidance of War," 1914-1917*, 24 Int'l Organizations 288, 291–92 (1970).

16   Scott, *The Resignation of Mr. Bryan as Secretary of State*, 9 AJIL 659–66 (1915).

17   Scott, *The Appointment of Mr. Robert Lansing as Secretary of State*, 9 AJIL 694–97 (1915).

18   See Telegram from William Jennings Bryan to Ambassador Gerard (May 13, 1915), 1915 FRUS 393 (Supp.); Telegram from Secretary Lansing to Ambassador Gerard (June 9, 1915), id. at 436.

19  Final Act of the International Peace Conference, *supra* chapter 5, at 1 AJIL 103, 106. See Hull, Two Hague Conferences, *supra* chapter 1, at 146-47.

20  Convention Respecting the Rights and Duties of Neutral Powers and Persons in Case of War on Land, Oct. 18, 1907, 36 Stat. 2310, reprinted in 2 AJIL 117 (Supp. 1908). See Hull, Two Hague Conferences, *supra* chapter 1, at 199-213; Antonia S. de Bustamante, *The Hague Convention Concerning the Rights and Duties of Neutral Powers and Persons in Land Warfare,* 2 AJIL 95 (1908).

21  Convention Respecting the Rights and Duties of Neutral Powers in Naval War, Oct. 18, 1907, 36 Stat. 2415, reprinted in 2 AJIL 202 (Supp. 1908). See Hull, Two Hague Conferences, *supra* chapter 1, at 148-66; C. Hyde, *The Hague Convention Respecting the Rights and Duties of Neutral Powers in Naval War,* 2 AJIL 507 (1908). See also G. Finch, *The Purchase of Vessels of War in Neutral Countries by Belligerents,* 9 AJIL 177-87 (1915) (violates neutrality).

22  Convention Relative to the Laying of Submarine Mines, Oct. 18, 1907, 36 Stat. 2332, reprinted in 2 AJIL 138 (Supp. 1908). See C. H. Stockton, *The Use of Submarine Mines and Torpedoes in Time of War,* 2 AJIL 276 (1908).

23  Convention Relative to Certain Restrictions on the Exercise of the Right of Capture in Maritime War, Oct. 18, 1907, 36 Stat. 2396, reprinted in 2 AJIL 167 (Supp. 1908). See S. Baldwin, *The Eleventh Convention Proposed by the Hague Conference of 1907,* 2 AJIL 307 (1908).

24  Act of June 5, 1794, ch. 50, 3d Cong., 1st Sess., 1 Stat. 381.

25  Act of March 2, 1797, ch. 5, 4th Cong., 2d Sess., 1 Stat. 497.

26  Act of April 20, 1818, ch. 88, 15th Cong., 1st Sess., 3 Stat. 447 (reissued as 18 U.S.C.A. § 967 (1969)).

27  See Charles S. Hyneman, *Neutrality during the European Wars of 1792-1815,* 24 AJIL 279 (1930); Raymond & Frischholz, *Lawyers Who Established International Law in the United States, supra* chapter 1, at 802, 805-07, 812-13, 819-20.

28  Treaty of Washington, May 8, 1871, U.S.-Gr. Brit., 17 Stat. 863. See also Report of the Delegates of the United States to the Second International Peace Conference at The Hague from June 15 to October 18, 1907, in Scott, 2 Hague Peace Conferences, *supra* chapter 1, at 198, 238-39, 241.

29  See Peter Seidel, *The Alabama,* in 2 Encyclopedia of Public International Law 11, 13 (1981).

30  Pub. Res. 72, 63d Cong., 3d Sess., 38 Stat. 1226 (1915).

31  See Scott, *The Joint Resolution of Congress to Empower the President to Better Enforce and Maintain the Neutrality of the United States,* 9 AJIL 490-93 (1915).

32  J. Scott, *Proposed Amendments to the Neutrality Laws of the United States,* 10 AJIL 602 (1916).

33  Espionage Act, ch. 30, 65th Cong., 1st Sess., 40 Stat. 217 (1917). See C. Hyde, *The Espionage Act,* 12 AJIL 142 (1918).

34  "Neutrals have the right to continue during war to trade with the belligerents, subject to the law relating to contraband and blockade. The existence of this right is universally admitted, although on certain occasions it has been in practice denied" (7 Moore, *supra* chapter 2, § 179, at 382).

35  See, e.g., 2 Garner, *supra* chapter 4, at 314.

36 See, e.g., id. at 376–77.

37 See, generally, Power Politics, *supra* chapter 1, at 936–37.

38 Convention with Respect to the Laws and Customs of War on Land, July 29, 1899, Annex, art. 46, 32 Stat. 1803, 1822; Convention with Respect to the Laws and Customs of War on Land, Oct. 18, 1907, Annex, art. 46, 36 Stat. 2277, 2306.

39 See J. Choate, Two Hague Conferences, *supra* chapter 4, at 74–77; Davis, Hague I, *supra* chapter 2, at 127–28, 133–35, 175–76; Davis, Hague II, *supra* chapter 2, at 138–40, 171–72, 227–33; Hull, Two Hague Conferences, *supra* chapter 1, at 126–41; C. H. Stockton, *Would Immunity from Capture, during War, of Non-offending Private Property upon the High Seas Be in the Interest of Civilization?*, 1 AJIL 930 (1907) (no!).

40 See J. Raymond & B. Frischholz, *Lawyers Who Established International Law in the United States, supra* chapter 1, at 806–07.

41 See Charles N. Gregory, *Neutrality and the Sale of Arms*, 10 AJIL 543 (1916); Scott, *The Sale of Munitions of War*, 9 AJIL 927–35 (1915).

42 See C. H. Stockton, *The International Naval Conference of London, 1908–1909*, 3 AJIL 596, 614 (1909). See also H. Lammasch, *Unjustifiable War and the Means to Avoid It*, 10 AJIL 689, 692, 702 (1916); Stewart M. Robinson, *Autonomous Neutralization*, 11 AJIL 607 (1917).

43 See, e.g., Ethel C. Phillips, *American Participation in Belligerent Commercial Controls 1914–1917*, 27 AJIL 675 (1933).

44 See, e.g., Scott, *The United States at War with the Imperial German Government*, 11 AJIL 617–27 (1917); Scott, *War between Austria-Hungary and the United States*, 12 AJIL 165–74 (1918).

45 But see E. Borchard & W. Lage, Neutrality for the United States (1937) (revisionist critique of Wilson's so-called neutrality policies).

46 Cf. Scott, *The Attitude of Journals of International Law in Time of War*, 9 AJIL 924–27 (1915).

47 See William C. Dennis, *The Diplomatic Correspondence Leading up to the War*, 9 AJIL 402 (1915).

48 See Scott, *Germany and the Neutrality of Belgium*, 8 AJIL 877–81 (1914). But cf. Scott, *The Neutrality of Belgium*, 9 AJIL 707–20 (1915) (including letter in defense of invasion by Prof. Karl Neumeyer of Germany).

49 See Scott, *The Binding Effect upon the German Empire of the Treaty of London of 1867 Neutralizing Luxemburg*, 9 AJIL 948–58 (1915).

50 See, e.g., Scott, *The Hague Conventions and the Neutrality of Belgium and Luxemburg*, 9 AJIL 959–62 (1915). See also D. Patterson, *The United States and the Origins of the World Court*, 91 Pol. Sci. Q. 279, 287 (1976); D. Patterson, Toward a Warless World, *supra* chapter 2, at 248–49.

51 See Scott, *Germany and the Neutrality of Belgium*, 8 AJIL 877, 880 (1914).

52 See B. Tuchman, The Guns of August, *supra* chapter 2, at 153. See also 2 Garner, *supra* chapter 4, at 215–37.

53 See, e.g., G. Finch, *The War in Europe*, 8 AJIL 853, 857 (1914); Scott, *The Right of Neutrals to Protest against Violations of International Law*, 10 AJIL 341–43 (1916). Cf. Coogan, End of Neutrality, *supra* chapter 4, at 193.

54 See Daniel M. Smith, *Robert Lansing and the Formulation of American Neutrality Policies, 1914–1915*, 43 Miss. Valley Hist. Rev. 59, 60 (1956).

55  See P. Devlin, Too Proud to Fight 156 (1975).

56  See Alexander L. George & Juliette L. George, Woodrow Wilson and Colonel House: A Personality Study 28 (1956).

57  Ross Gregory, The Origins of American Intervention in the First World War 138 (1971).

58  See Scott, The Black List of Great Britain and Her Allies, 10 AJIL 832–43 (1916); Scott, Economic Conference of the Allied Powers, 10 AJIL 845–52 (1916). See also P. Brown, Economic Warfare, 11 AJIL 847–50 (1917); John B. Clark, Shall There Be War after the War?, 11 AJIL 790 (1917).

59  See Charles N. Gregory, Neutrality and the Sale of Arms, 10 AJIL 543 (1916); William C. Morey, The Sale of Munitions of War, 10 AJIL 467 (1916); Scott, The Sale of Arms and Ammunition by American Merchants to Belligerents, 9 AJIL 687–94 (1915); Scott, The Sale of Munitions of War, 9 AJIL 927–35 (1915). See also Scott, American Neutrality, 9 AJIL 443–56 (1915).

60  W. Morey, The Sale of Munitions of War, 10 AJIL 467 (1916).

61  R. Gregory, The Origins of American Intervention in the First World War, supra this chapter, at 29, 41.

62  See, e.g., 2 Garner, supra chapter 4, at 408.

63  See, e.g., D. Smith, Robert Lansing and the Formulation of American Neutrality Policies, 1914–1915, 43 Miss. Valley Hist. Rev. 59 (1956).

64  See, generally, D. Smith, National Interest and American Intervention, 1917: An Historiographical Appraisal, 52 J. Am. Hist. 5 (1965).

65  See R. Gregory, The Origins of American Intervention in the First World War, supra this chapter, at 138–39.

66  See also A. Morrissey, The United States and the Rights of Neutrals, 1917–1918, 31 AJIL 17 (1937) (the United States generally did not recant its positions on laws of neutrality after it entered the war).

67  See J. Scott, The Dawn in Germany? The Lichnowsky and Other Disclosures, 12 AJIL 386 (1918); W. Willoughby, The Prussian Theory of Government, 12 AJIL 266 (1918); W. Willoughby, The Prussian Theory of the State, 12 AJIL 251 (1918); American Bar Association, Resolution of Sept. 4, 1917, in 3 A.B.A.J. 576–77 (1917) (submitted by Elihu Root; adopted unanimously), reprinted and approved in C. Gregory, The Annual Meeting of the American Bar Association, 11 AJIL 851 (1917). See also S. Baldwin, The Share of the President of the United States in a Declaration of War, 12 AJIL 1 (1918) (there might exist constitutional authority to wage war in order to secure the liberty of foreign peoples).

68  Address of the President of the United States Delivered at a Joint Session of the Two Houses of Congress, April 2, 1917, reprinted in 11 AJIL 350, 356 (Spec. Supp. 1917).

69  See also C. Fenwick, Germany and the Crime of the World War, 23 AJIL 812 (1929) (article 231 of the Treaty of Versailles should not be interpreted as imputing moral guilt and criminal responsibility for the war to Germany, for in 1914 there was no clear basis on which moral responsibility for a particular war could be judged); D. Myers, The Control of Foreign Relations, 11 Am. Pol. Sci. Rev. 24 (1917) (strong legal realist position); T. Woolsey, Reconstruction and International Law, 13 AJIL 187 (1919) (irrespective of idealistic motives, the war was fundamentally one of self-defense); T. Woolsey, The Relations between the United States and the Central Powers, 11 AJIL

628 (1917) (after declaration of war on Germany the United States should await the development of events before ipso facto declaring war on Austria and Turkey).

70  See also Lloyd C. Gardner, *American Foreign Policy 1900-1921: A Second Look at the Realist Critique of American Diplomacy*, in Towards a New Past: Dissenting Essays in American History 202-31 (Barton J. Bernstein ed., 1968).

71  See, e.g., P. Brown, *The Theory of the Independence and Equality of States*, 9 AJIL 305 (1915); Finch, *The Effect of the War on International Law*, 9 AJIL 475 (1915); Malbone W. Graham, *Neutrality and the World War*, 17 AJIL 704 (1923); M. Graham, *Neutralization as a Movement in International Law*, 21 AJIL 79 (1927); A. Hershey, *Projects Submitted to the American Institute of International Law*, 11 AJIL 390 (1917); E. Root, *The Outlook for International Law*, 10 AJIL 1 (1916); A. W. Spencer, *The Organization of International Force*, 9 AJIL 45 (1915); George G. Wilson, *Sanction for International Agreements*, 11 AJIL 387 (1917).

72  See, e.g., Ruhl J. Bartlett, The League to Enforce Peace 215-18 (1944); Sondra R. Herman, Eleven against War: Studies in American Internationalist Thought, 1898-1921, at 57 (1969).

73  See, e.g. Dimitri D. Lazo, *A Question of Loyalty: Robert Lansing and the Treaty of Versailles*, 9 Dipl. Hist. 35 (1985) (Secretary of State Lansing privately opposed the Treaty of Versailles and particularly article 10).

74  See Martin D. Dubin, *Elihu Root and the Advocacy of a League of Nations, 1914-1917*, 19 W. Pol. Q. 439, 453-54 (1966); E. Root, *Amending the Covenant*, Advoc. of Peace, July 1919, at 211.

75  See Kurt Wimer, *Woodrow Wilson and World Order*, in Woodrow Wilson and a Revolutionary World 1913-1921, at 146-73 (A. Link ed., 1982).

76  See Lloyd E. Ambrosius, Woodrow Wilson and the American Diplomatic Tradition: The Treaty Fight in Perspective 84-101 (1987).

77  See, generally, id. at 107-35.

78  See D. Fleming, The United States and the League of Nations 1918-1920, *supra* chapter 1, at 311.

79  See P. Jessup, 2 Elihu Root, *supra* chapter 1, at 391-400; Ronald E. Powaski, Toward an Entangling Alliance 21-22 (1991).

80  See, e.g., Kent G. Redmond, *Henry L. Stimson and the Question of League Membership*, 25 Historian 200, 201 (1963) (Stimson supported the League).

81  See Arthur M. Schlesinger Jr., The Imperial Presidency 96-109 (1973).

82  See, e.g., F. Boyle, *International Crisis and Neutrality: U.S. Foreign Policy toward the Iraq-Iran War*, in Neutrality: Changing Concepts and Practices 59 (A. Leonhard ed., 1988).

83  See, generally, Robert F. Smith, *American Foreign Relations, 1920-1942*, in Towards a New Past: Dissenting Essays in American History 232-62 (B. Bernstein ed., 1968).

84  See, generally, id. at 232-62.

85  See P. Jessup, 2 Elihu Root, *supra* chapter 1, at 457; 2 Hackworth, *supra* chapter 6, at 690-91; 6 Hackworth, *supra* chapter 6, at 466-67.

86  See R. Powaski, Toward an Entangling Alliance, *supra* this chapter, at 35ff.

87  See P. Jessup, 2 Elihu Root, *supra* chapter 1, at 461.

88  See, e.g., The Laws of Armed Conflicts, *supra* chapter 4, at 121, 126.

*Conclusion*

1   See A. Schvan, *A Practical Peace Policy*, 8 AJIL 51, 59 (1914).

2   See, e.g., Hajo Holborn, The Political Collapse of Europe (1951).

3   See Thomas J. Biersteker, *Constructing Historical Counterfactuals to Assess the Consequences of International Regimes*, in Regime Theory and International Relations 315–38 (Volker Rittberger ed., 1993).

4   See Lord Hankey, Diplomacy by Conference: Studies in Public Affairs 1920–1946, at 39 (1946): "If the habit of meetings between responsible Ministers of different nations, the moment friction arose, through some organized machinery such as the League of Nations had become the established practice before 1914, when the Archduke was assassinated at Sarajevo, it is possible that the war would not have occurred."

5   See Robert A. Friedlander, *Who Put Out the Lamps? Thoughts on International Law and the Coming of World War I*, 20 Duquesne L. Rev. 569, 581 (1982).

6   Cf. Alice M. Morrissey, The American Defense of Neutral Rights 1914–1917, at 128 (1939).

7   See David Mervin, *Henry Cabot Lodge and the League of Nations*, 4 J. Am. Stud. 201 (1971).

8   See, generally, D. Fleming, The United States and the League of Nations 1918–1920, *supra* chapter 1.

9   See E. H. Carr, The Twenty Years' Crisis 1919–1939 (1939).

10  Manley O. Hudson, *A Design for a Charter of the General International Organization*, 38 AJIL 711 (1944).

11  See *Senate Approval of Charter of the United Nations*, 13 Dept. State Bull. 138 (1945).

12  See Charles C. Hyde, *The United States Accepts the Optional Clause*, 40 AJIL 778–81 (1946); P. Jessup, *Acceptance by the United States of the Optional Clause of the International Court of Justice*, 39 AJIL 745–51 (1945); Pitman B. Potter, *"As Determined by the United States,"* 40 AJIL 792–94 (1946); Lawrence Preuss, *The International Court of Justice, the Senate, and Matters of Domestic Jurisdiction*, 40 AJIL 720 (1946); Francis O. Wilcox, *The United States Accepts Compulsory Jurisdiction*, 40 AJIL 699 (1946); Quincy Wright, *The International Court of Justice and the Interpretation of Multilateral Treaties*, 41 AJIL 445–52 (1947).

13  See Abraham D. Sofaer, *The United States and the World Court*, U.S. Dept. of State, Bureau of Public Affairs, Current Pol. No. 769 (address before Senate Foreign Relations Committee, Dec. 4, 1985).

14  See, generally, Louis B. Sohn, Cases on United Nations Law (2d ed. 1967).

15  See also Daniel P. Moynihan, On the Law of Nations (1990), reviewed by F. Boyle, *International Law vs. Military Might*, Philadelphia Inquirer, Sept. 16, 1990, Sect. H, at 1.

*Appendix*

1   See Stanley Hoffmann, "Ethics and Rules of the Game between the Superpowers," in *Right v. Might: International Law and the Use of Force* (2d ed. 1991).

2   A regime has been defined as "sets of implicit or explicit principles, norms, rules,

and decision-making procedures around which actors' expectations converge in a given area of international relations." See S. Krasner, "Structural Causes and Regime Consequences: Regimes as Intervening Variables," in *International Regimes* 2 (1982). See also R. Keohane & J. Nye, *Power and Interdependence* (1977); R. Keohane, *After Hegemony* (1984); R. Keohane, *International Institutions and State Power* (1989); Haggard & Simmons, "Theories of International Regimes," 41 *Int'l Org.* 491 (1987). But cf. *Neorealism and Its Critics* (R. Keohane ed. 1986).

3   See, e.g., R. Gilpin, *War and Change in World Politics* (1981).

4   N. Machiavelli, *The Prince*, 99 (M. Musa trans. & ed. 1964).

5   Id. at 145.

6   See Plato, *Gorgias* 78 (Penguin ed. 1960).

7   As a former corporate/tax lawyer, I can attest that Machiavelli was right.

8   See N. Machiavelli, *The Prince*, 145–149 (M. Musa trans. & ed. 1964).

9   See, e.g., L. Sohn, *Cases on United Nations Law* (2d ed. 1967).

10   See "The Caroline," in W. Bishop, *International Law* 916–919 (3rd ed. 1971).

11   See Wiseman, "The United Nations and International Peacekeeping: A Comparative Analysis," in *The United Nations and the Maintenance of International Peace and Security* 263 (1987).

12   See Snidal, "The Limits of Hegemonic Stability Theory," 39 *Int'l Org.* 573 (1985).

13   Id. at 611–612. See also Grunberg, "Exploring the 'Myth' of Hegemonic Stability," 44 *Int'l Org.* 431 (1990).

14   See Haas, "The Collective Management of International Conflict, 1945–1984," in *The United Nations and the Maintenance of International Peace and Security* 3 (1987).

15   Id. at 17–18:

1. The most intense disputes are the most likely to be successfully managed. Insignificant and very low intensity disputes can be marginally influenced. Disputes in the intermediate range are the most resistant to management.

2. Success comes most readily when the fighting is very limited. The most contagious disputes are the ones most frequently influenced, very often with great success. Disputes that the neighbours of the contending parties are about to enter actively are the most difficult to manage, whereas it seems relatively simple to score minimal impacts on purely bilateral disputes.

3. Disputes free of decolonization and Cold War complications are the most successfully managed, provided that no civil war is involved. On the other hand, such disputes arising out of an internal conflict are the most intractable. Decolonization issues are the next most amenable to United Nations management. Cold War disputes score lowest, though 37 per cent of them were influenced by United Nations action.

4. Success is easier to achieve if the contending parties are members of the same Cold War bloc or if both are non-aligned. Cold War alliances complicate conflict management.

5. Conflicts involving middle powers (such as Argentina, Mexico, Egypt, Pakistan, The Netherlands) are most easily managed, particularly when the opposing party is smaller. Conflicts involving the superpowers as a party are the most intractable.

6. Strong United Nations decisions bring results. However, the failure to make a

strong decision does not necessarily imply inability to influence the outcome of a dispute.

7. United Nations operations of a military nature are almost always successful. Field operations involving only the Secretariat are also successful over half of the time. The failure to launch any operations results in failure of management two-thirds of the time.

8. Successful action is associated most strongly with the joint leadership of the superpowers and the active intervention of the Secretary-General. But even the leadership of a single superpower brought success in 53 per cent of the cases in which it occurred. When leadership is exercised by large and middle powers the rate of success declines sharply. Small powers make the poorest leaders. Successful United Nations intervention requires a wide or very wide consensus of the membership.

16  See Weiss & Kessler, "Moscow's U.N. Policy," *Foreign Policy*, No. 79, at 97 (Summer 1990).

17  See, e.g., L. Henkin, *Foreign Affairs and the Constitution* (1975); M. Glennon, *Constitutional Diplomacy* (1990).

18  See F. Boyle, *The Foundations of World Order* (1991).

19  See H. Morgenthau, *The Purpose of American Politics* (1960).

20  See F. Boyle, *World Politics and International Law* (1985).

21  See, e.g., A. Chayes, *The Cuban Missile Crisis* (1974).

22  See, e.g., *The Tower Commission Report* (N.Y. Times ed. 1987).

23  See F. Boyle, *The Future of International Law and American Foreign Policy* (1989).

24  See, generally, *The Relevance of International Law* (K. Deutsch & S. Hoffmann eds. 1971).

25  See, e.g., Kirkpatrick & Gerson, "The Reagan Doctrine, Human Rights, and International Law," in *Right v. Might: International Law and the Use of Force* 19 (1989).

26  See F. Boyle, *Defending Civil Resistance under International Law* 155–210 (1987).

27  "Military and Paramilitary Activities in and against Nicaragua (Nica. v. U.S.)," 1986 *I.C.J.* 14 (Judgment of June 27).

.

# Index

ABC offer, 99

Acheson, Dean, 3

Adjudication, 37–38; and Advisory Committee of Jurists, 48–52; compared to international arbitration, 38–39, 58–59

Africa, 20

*Alabama* claims, 25, 128–29

Alvarez, Alejandro, 89, 113

American Academy of Political and Social Science, 114

American Institute of International Law, 113–14

American Journal of International Law, 11, 18, 47, 113

American Society of International Law, 18, 84, 98, 113, 126

Arbitration: American policy of non-entanglement, 30; and bilateral arbitration treaties, 31–34; compared to international adjudication, 38–39, 58–59; golden age of, 34–36, 38–39; and Inter-American System, 105–6, 110–11; political dimension of, 37–38; and sanction behind, 25, 80; and successes of, 34–36; utility of, 38–39. *See also* Bryan Peace Plan; Court of Arbitral Justice; Hague Peace Conferences; Knox Treaties; Permanent Court of Arbitration; Root Arbitration Conventions

Argentina, 106; adherence to the 1899 Convention for the Pacific Settlement of

International Disputes, 110; and contract debts, 112

Arms limitation: Convention for the Pacific Settlement of Disputes (1899), 71–72; and Declaration of St. Petersburg, 72; and First Hague Peace Conference, 71–72; and poison gas, 73–74; and Second Hague Peace Conference, 72–73; and Tsar Nicholas II, 71; U.S. role in, 71–73

Articles of Confederation, 37

Austin, John, 11, 13

Austria-Hungary, 21, 68, 133

Bacon, Robert, 45

Balance of power system, 135, 137, 147–48; American legalist rejection of, 20–22; compared to U.S. imperialism in Latin America, 89–90, 103

Bayard, T. F., 105

Belgium, 20, 81, 133

Bethmann-Hollweg, German Chancellor, 134

Blaine, James, 104

Bolívar, Simon, 104, 122

Bolivia, 106; adherence to the 1899 Convention for the Pacific Settlement of International Disputes, 110; and contract debts, 112

Boxer Rebellion, 95–96

Brazil, 106, 108; adherence to the 1899 Convention for the Pacific Settlement of

Francis Anthony Boyle is Professor of International Law
at the University of Illinois College of Law in Champaign.

Library of Congress Cataloging-in-Publication Data
Boyle, Francis Anthony.
Foundations of world order : the legalist approach to
international relations (1898–1922) / Francis Anthony
Boyle.
Includes index.
ISBN 0-8223-2327-3 (alk. paper).
ISBN 0-8223-2364-8 (alk. paper)
1. International law–History.   2. United States–Foreign
relations–Law and legislation–History.   I. Title.
KZ1242.B69   1999
341'.09–dc21   98-32014CIP